To Ji
Best

(signature)

GW01071968

VILLAGE BOYS STILL

*Thirty-one men from the Parish of Tillington
who gave their lives in the Great War*

Trevor Purnell

VILLAGE BOYS STILL
Thirty-one men from the Parish of Tillington
who gave their lives in the Great War

Design ©131 Design Ltd
www.131design.org
Text © Trevor Purnell

ISBN 978-1-909660-69-4

A CIP catalogue record for this book
is available from the British Library.

Published 2016 by Tricorn Books
131 High Street, Old Portsmouth,
PO1 2HW
www.tricornbooks.co.uk

Printed in UK

VILLAGE BOYS STILL

Thirty-one men from the Parish of Tillington who gave their lives in the Great War

Dedicated to the memory of
Joan Violet Castle
1925 – 2016

A true friend and supporter

CONTENTS

.

ACKNOWLEDGEMENTS

The writing of this book would not have been possible without the help and advice from so many people. Following the The Great War exhibition in All Hallows' Church, Tillington in 2014, several relatives of the fallen soldiers have contacted me, generously providing photographs, letters and advice. It is my pleasure to thank Nick Duder of Jakarta, Indonesia for images and letters of the Barrington-Kennett family and the family tree; Nigel and Barbara Wood (Barrington-Kennett family); Charles Thompson (T G Bridgewater); Melvyn Bridger (A J Bridger); Judith Bartley (William Wadey); Mark Stocker (Thomas Daniels); David Lewis (Percy Boxall); Diana Watt (Reg Pratt) and Sharon Baker (Joseph Dummer).

During the course of my research I have visited Commonwealth war graves, MOD establishments, RAF bases, museums, county archives, National Trust properties, attended numerous lectures and purchased perhaps too many books, but above all I been privileged to meet or correspond with so many erudite people who willingly shared their knowledge with me. I am indebted to all of them. In particular I would like to thank Monsieur André Brochec, Président de l'Office de Tourisme d'Etretat, France, who within one hour of my contacting him had visited and photographed Captain Charles Wilson's headstone in Etretat Cemetery and sent me the image by email; Norman Parker and the Officers' Mess of the Empire Test Pilots' School, MOD Boscombe Down, for allowing me to photograph the Barrington-Kennett silver wedding presents; Rosemary Hibbs for her permission to use images of poppies on the South Downs; Lord Egremont for permission to access the Petworth House Archives and his Archivist, Alison McCann, for generous advice and assistance in locating relevant files. My thanks are also due to the staff at West Sussex Record Office for their good humour, patience and efficiency.

I am greatly indebted to Hugh Rolfe for agreeing to write the Forward to this book. I would also like to express my sincere thanks to those living in the Parish of Tillington who have consistently shown their support and encouragement for this project, most notably Barbara Biddell, George Warren, Joan and Gerry Castle and Fran and Peter Rhys Evans.

My grateful thanks are due to the many unknown people who regularly share their knowledge on the internet including The Great War Forum, De Ruvigny's Roll of Honour 1914-1919, The Long Long Trail, The World War I Message Board - Alan Greveson, Commonwealth War Graves Commission, Army Service Numbers 1881 – 1918, Findmypast.co.uk and to Ancestry.co.uk.

As always I am deeply grateful to my longsuffering wife, Carolyn, for her unceasing encouragement over the past two years, for her help with my manuscript and for being a truly wonderful companion on our many outings, particularly on the several visits to the war graves of France and Belgium.

I have tried diligently to trace all copyright holders, but if I have missed any or wrongly attributed images, then I sincerely apologise. If they would like to contact me through www.tillington.net then I will make the appropriate corrections in any future edition of this book.

FOREWORD

The novelist L P Hartley wrote 'the past is a foreign country: they do things differently there.' The Great War now seems a long time ago, even to us older villagers. Of course many of us know of a member of our family who died in the conflict, but we probably never met them. We remain shocked by the horrors of trench warfare and the killings on an unprecedented scale. We try and understand how the world could possibly have become caught up in such a disaster, and some of us may even wonder if, had we been part of that generation, we would have had the courage to go 'over the top'!

In focusing on a very small village, Trevor Purnell has enabled us to see the effects of this epic tragedy from a human perspective. No doubt what happened to the people of Tillington also happened in every other village and town in the United Kingdom. He has painted a vivid picture of our parish as it was at the outbreak of war which enables us to re-connect with this generation. We are their successors as villagers and parishioners, even though they would not recognise the social world in which we live today. We can be immensely proud of them.

Above all, this is a formidable work of research which has taken several years to complete. Trevor has gone to great pains to collect every scrap of information available on each of our soldiers who perished in the Great War. Where possible he has contacted their families, consulted many records and archives and visited their resting places. All this has enabled him to tell their story from birth, through education and civilian employment, and on to their enlistment in the armed forces and their subsequent adventures leading to their fateful end. I have been fascinated by all the stories and in each case have been left with a great sense of sadness and sympathy.

Trevor is to be congratulated on producing such a detailed and valuable account of our village history at that momentous time; thanks to him this part of our past is no longer such a foreign country. Every home in the parish should have a copy of *Village Boys Still*.

Group Captain Hugh Rolfe C.V.O., C.B.E. (R.A.F Retd)
Kimbers Cottage , 2016

INTRODUCTION

My wife and I came to live in Tillington in October 2000 and so perhaps we are still relative newcomers. We were, nevertheless, made very welcome and soon joined in with many of the village activities including those at All Hallows' Church. One of the really special church services for me is the Service of Remembrance each November. For many years a wonderful old soldier from the Burma Campaign, Jack Holloway, read the names of the fallen from both wars. Sadly no longer with us, Jack had a deep, authoritative voice, ideal for his poignant duty. The list began with the three Barrington-Kennett brothers lost on the Western Front and, although just names, I could not help but be deeply moved by the thought of their parents coming to terms with such devastating loss.

I soon felt that I wanted to research the brothers to learn something of their lives and personalities. I began with the oldest brother, Basil, and quickly discovered that he was a significant pioneer of the fledgling Royal Flying Corps from 1912; more importantly everyone who came into contact with him loved and respected him.

As the centenary of the outbreak of the Great War drew closer I became determined to find out more about all thirty Tillington men who made the ultimate sacrifice. This work was partially completed in time to mount an exhibition in All Hallows' Church in 2014. Since that exhibition my research has continued and numerous people have contacted me offering letters, photographs, memorabilia and other forms of assistance. I am indebted to them for allowing me to use their family information in this book. Most of the records for the 1914-18 soldiers were destroyed in World War II when an enemy bomb fell on the building in which they were stored. The surviving papers (known as the 'burnt records') give a fascinating insight into the character of each soldier - his physical appearance, promotions, postings and personal conduct - but sadly the records for only nine of the young men from our parish survived. Battalion war diaries and regimental histories, however, provide valuable details of the whereabouts of each soldier, the battles in which they fought and the conditions they endured. My main aim in writing *Village Boys Still* is to ensure that a record of each man's life remains for posterity and that we and future generations who come to live in Tillington will continue to honour the memory of each one of these eager young soldiers who courageously went to war and never returned to our green and pleasant parish. I hope that it will be read with interest and that readers will conclude, as I have, that it has been a privilege to learn something of this gallant group of young men who no doubt felt that they were only doing their duty.

The book has little pretention to a work of literature but, in addition to recording the lives and military service of the soldiers, I have tried to portray where possible something of their individual personalities. In the years leading up to the outbreak of The Great War these same young men were the life and soul of our parish, working hard and - one suspects - playing hard. When war came most did not hesitate to join up but others delayed enlisting until the local harvest was safely gathered in. These fresh young soldiers were real people who lived in the houses we now occupy, worshipped in same church and walked the same paths on a summer's evening. With these personal insights they can become once again heroes of our village who fought for freedom - no longer just names and initials, without rank or regiment, cut into the gleaming brass memorial plaques on either side of the chancel arch in our parish church.

Although this book is concerned only with our soldiers who died in the Great War, it is fitting that we should also acknowledge with gratitude those who returned but for whom there are no memorials: with the passing of time most of their names have been lost. Sadly these would not be the same laughing, adventurous young men who had left the parish just four short years before, neither would they come back to the same England for which they had endured years of suffering and hardship. When they finally reached home some men would be fit whilst others undoubtedly would carry the physical and mental scars of war. They too were heroes and should not be forgotten.

The author and scholar John Buchan lost several close friends in the Great War. Deeply saddened by their death, and haunted by a sense of guilt that he had survived, he began, towards the end of 1918, writing a small book remembering six friends in happier times. The book, *These for Remembrance*[1] is not well known as it was written for his children, Alice, John, William and Alastair. The preface begins: 'This book is written for you to read but not yet. It is for you as you grow older, for I want to tell you something about my friends who fell in the Great War'. In writing *Village Boys Still* I have similar feelings. The young men from Tillington who lost their lives in the same war were not my friends but have become very close to me and are often in my thoughts.

Few, if any, parishioners realised that the tranquility and traditional ways of their community were about to be lost forever when on 28 June 1914 the Austrian Archduke Franz Ferdinand and his wife were assassinated by a Serbian nationalist during a visit to Sarajevo in Bosnia. The death of the heir to the Austro-Hungarian throne set in motion a chain of events that led to millions more deaths and the horrors of trench warfare that was to be the Great War.

Austria-Hungary held Serbia responsible for the assassination and following the rejection of an ultimatum, they declared war on their neighbour. Russia was bound by treaty to defend Serbia and so mobilised her vast army. Germany, allied to Austria-Hungary, viewed this mobilisation as an act of war and declared war on Russia. France was bound to Russia by treaty and hence Germany also declared war on France. Germany invaded neutral Belgium as the quickest route to France and its capital, Paris. This remarkable sequence of events culminated when Britain, obligated to defend Belgium by the 1839 Treaty of London, declared war on Germany on 4 August 1914 - little more than a month after the Sarajevo assassination.

One can only imagine the reaction of Tillington parishioners to the news of Archduke Ferdinand's assassination. Certainly few would have foreseen the consequences and most probably would not even have been aware of the tragedy as they went about their daily lives in the pleasant Sussex countryside. Nevertheless, as news of impending war filtered through to the smallest of hamlets, the consequences for a generation of young men began to dawn. On 5 August 1914 Lord Kitchener was appointed Minister for War. He knew that the war would be long and costly and never entertained the widespread belief that it would 'be over by Christmas'. Britain needed many more soldiers if Germany was to be defeated and he quickly organised his legendary recruitment campaign.

Encouraged by this campaign an outpouring of British patriotism emerged during the summer of 1914. Young men everywhere believed instinctively that it was their duty to defend the very fabric of Britain against the German foe. Thousands volunteered, from public schoolboys to agricultural labourers, all prepared to lay down their lives for King and Country, or perhaps more importantly for the village or town of their birth and their 'mates'. For the agricultural labourer there was another compelling reason to enlist; in 1914 almost all of them lived below the poverty line in inadequate conditions with non-existent prospects. Enlistment offered more money, sufficient food, the chance to travel overseas and the prospect of an adventure with new and old friends.

The Petworth Armoury served as the main recruiting centre in the area for the 4th Battalion, Royal Sussex Regiment and over the next few years many young men, including those from Tillington, Upperton and River, found their way to the armoury and most were eager to enlist in this battalion. These fresh-faced recruits, along with hundreds of others, soon found themselves in regimental training camps in different parts of Sussex or further afield. Sooner or later, however, they were on their way to Gallipoli, Flanders or France.

The Weald had been the world of my youngness, and while I gazed across it now I felt prepared to do what I could to defend it. And after all, dying for one's native land was believed to be the most glorious thing one could possibly do.[2]

Soon after writing these words Siegfried Sassoon enlisted in the army and on the day Britain declared war on Germany, Tuesday 4 August 1914, Trooper Sassoon was in the uniform of the Sussex Yeomanry.

There were very few rules governing recruitment; eighteen was the minimum enlistment age and, in theory at least, young men had to be nineteen to fight overseas. In 1914 the average age of the thirty-one men from the parish (including Captain Charles Wilson from Petworth) was twenty-two, but in spite of the rules five of these were under age when they enlisted. There seems to have been an enthusiastic response to the call-to-arms with seventeen men enlisting between August and December 1914 and all thirty-one in training before the end of 1916. Thirteen young men had been born in the parish and a further eight in nearby villages; fourteen joined the Royal Sussex Regiment and others either trained with it and were later posted to regiments outside the county or chose to join other regiments from the start.

As expected the recruitment list reveals a spread of pre-enlistment trades, but is dominated by eleven agricultural labourers/gardeners, followed by three carpenters, the same number of bricklayers, and two bakers' assistants. Amongst the others there are three career soldiers, a doctor and a solicitor's clerk. These brave men entered the war for excitement, adventure and to do their duty but instead encountered filth, disease and death. The average life of our men from enlistment to death was two years, but ten soldiers fought only for one year or less and four young men were killed within two months of the Armistice on 11 November 1918. No doubt these statistics were common in many towns and villages throughout the land. A high price was paid for our freedom and that is why we must never forget.

1

The Parish in the years before the War

The parish of Tillington, consisting of the village and two hamlets, Upperton and River, lies to the north and south of the A272 one mile west of Petworth in West Sussex and is within the South Downs National Park. At the time of writing, the population was around 500 people living in 227 households, but in 1911 the population was 852 living in less than 200 dwellings.[1] The land area is approximately 3,790 acres, much of which is agricultural land lying within the historic estates of Leconfield and Pitshill.

The parish rises gently from the banks of the River Rother in the south, through open fields where once corn and potatoes grew and cattle grazed the rich, green grass. The land then begins to flatten out a little where today the busy A272 carries traffic through the lower part of the village. In 1912 this major

The A272 c1910. Unknown

Road up to Tillington – The Rectory on the right. Unknown

road was a mere country lane and children from the local dwellings would play happily beneath the large trees that once bordered it.

From the A272 the land rises quickly to the north with cottages nestling amongst numerous fine houses as the small road from Tillington to Upperton ploughs a straight uphill furrow. At the junction with the A272 stands The Rectory (now The Old Rectory), a fine Georgian house that has seen some eminent rectors including Reverend James Stanier Clarke (1789-1816), Reverend Robert Ridsdale (1816-1834), and Reverend William M Goggs (1911-1930), the latter being a popular incumbent during and after the war years. The beautiful 900-year-old All Hallows' Church with its impressive Scots Crown overlooks the rectory from the north. To its west stands the historic Horse Guards Inn, where in 1914 no doubt many of the local young men met for a pint of ale and excitedly discussed their impending enlistment. On the same side a little further along the road once stood the village school, opened in 1838, and where most village children received a rudimentary education until the age of fourteen. Regrettably this imposing Victorian building was demolished around 1963. Past the school is a long line of cottages called Park Terrace, the first of which was, for many years, the home of the schoolmaster. Halfway up the rising Upperton Road is the fine Victorian Tillington Hill House and the older Podmore's Farm. On the east side the walls of Petworth Park, with its fine trees and deer herd, bound the road. No doubt the Park was a popular venue for courting couples in the summer evenings before the outbreak of the Great War and perhaps where many tearful goodbyes were exchanged. Thereafter a wonderful uninterrupted view over rich farmland to the South Downs unfolds - one that surely our soldiers would vividly recall during their horrendous days in the trenches of the Western Front.

Before Upperton the road bends to the left and passes through a deep sunken lane with houses overlooking both sides before the hamlet proper is reached. In 1914 this hamlet provided several eager, adventurous and patriotic young men for the 4th Battalion Royal Sussex Regiment. Many of the dwellings in the hamlets, and some in Tillington, were owned by the Leconfield or Pitshill estates and rented to

The Upperton Road c1912. Unknown

their workers - most of whom were agricultural labourers employed on the estate farms or in their woodlands.

Farm dwellings were usually small cottages (perhaps a sitting room, kitchen and two bedrooms), in which families lived in extremely cramped conditions. James and Ellen Gumbrell lived with their eight children in a three-roomed cottage at River Common and would perhaps have been envious of nearby River House where seven people lived in fourteen rooms.

A typical village cottage c1912. Unknown

In the first decade of the twentieth century most of the farms were rented from the estates by tenant farmers. These included Parkhurst Farm (James Britten) in the north; Netherlands Farm (William Perry) to the west; Grittenham (Herbert Duck), Rotherbridge (William Bridger), Sokenholes (Arthur Brook) and South Dean (George Duck) in the south. In a statistical survey covering 1881[2] it was shown that just over 50 percent of working men were engaged in agricultural labour employed by some ten farmers. There was probably little change with the advent of the twentieth century. In 1909 the average weekly wage for a farm labourer was eighteen shillings, with carters (responsible for caring for the horses and their work e.g. ploughing, reaping and carting) and cowmen earning 1s 6d above this.[3]

Kelly's Directory for 1908[4] states that the chief crops grown within the parish were wheat, barley, oats and turnips. The cultivation of oats and turnips suggests that a good deal of land was put down to pasture for sheep, dairy and beef cattle.

The 1911 census shows several cowmen living in South Lane, Tillington and it is likely that they worked for Mr George Duck, tenant farmer of nearby South Dean Farm. Mr Duck built up a fine herd of Shorthorn dairy cows, giving excellent milk yields from the rich pastures close to the River Rother, and a good flock of Southdown sheep. Perhaps not content with this workload he also kept Large Black pigs, shire horses for farm work and a few chickens.[5] In his spare time he would hunt with Lord Leconfield and was always in demand as a judge at agricultural shows. There was also a Mr Herbert Duck farming with his sixteen-year-old son, William, less than a mile from South Dean Farm at Grittenham Farm, but he was apparently unrelated to George.

The new Smythe drill at Tillington. Tillington WI Collection

In addition to the large farms within the parish there existed several smaller farms, but size was no measure of efficiency. Sometime around 1830 Edward Barham moved from Suffolk to Little Common Farm, Tillington. He brought with him an early Smythe Seed Drill[6] that soon attracted the attention of other local farmers when he demonstrated the drill at the weekly markets in Petworth. This led to him transporting six additional drills from

The Horse Guards Inn c1912. Unknown

Suffolk to his farm in Tillington from where they were hired out to his neighbours. The Barham family continued to farm and hire agricultural machinery from Little Common Farm into the early part of the twentieth century.

After Edward Barham's death in 1900 his two sons - Cuthbert and Ernest - and their mother Ellen took charge of the farm. When the Great War broke out both boys, now in their late twenties, wanted to volunteer for the army, but one had to stay on the farm. Apparently the decision was made by the toss of a coin and hence Cuthbert joined the Sussex Yeomanry and fought in Gallipoli and France. While he was away Colonel Mitford of Pitshill asked the Barhams to take over Grittenham Farm, which by now was becoming neglected. They agreed and, when eventually Cuthbert was welcomed home, they farmed their tenanted land very successfully and were amongst the best farmers in West Sussex.

Their cousin, Frederick Barham, was the innkeeper of the Horse Guards from 1895 until his death in 1907. His wife Constance (née Bridger) took over the licence until 1913 when it was transferred to her daughter Maude. Unlike Maude many of the other women in the parish were employed as domestic servants, mostly in smaller houses, but several held a variety of positions in large houses. Pitshill had eight female servants (and a footman, hall boy, groom and 'motor car driver'); River House had four female servants and a companion, and the Reverend Goggs at the rectory had three female servants.

Just to the north-west of the hamlet lies Upperton Common, traditionally used by local farmers to graze sheep and cattle but much of it had become overgrown with brambles and bracken and, by the early twentieth century, it was largely used for recreation as evidenced by the records of Petworth House:[7] 'March 19th 1914 - Grass seed was purchased for Upperton Common cricket ground at a cost of 6s. 1d'. By mid-June the turf was established and at a cost of 11s. 3d the wicket and outlying field were rolled with a horse-drawn roller.

Cricket was an important part of village life and matches against neighbouring teams were eagerly awaited with much discussion focused on the likely strength of the opposition. Most of the village would turn out to watch

Tillington House c1930. Courtesy Peter Rhys Evans

the matches and to enjoy an impressive tea. Cakes and sandwiches of every description would be laid out on trestle tables covered with white tablecloths. On special occasions there might even have been a marquee to house the teas and later in the evening a dance. No doubt several young men of the parish played their last game of cricket on the new ground at Upperton Common.

Basil Barrington-Kennett lands his Boxkite in Tillington.
Tillington WI Collection

In addition to the parish farmers, the 1908 Kelly's Directory listed other notable residents including Lt Col Brackley Barrington-Kennett living at Tillington House. This is the earliest record of the family being resident in the village. Their eldest son Basil joined the Grenadier Guards in 1906 and later transferred to the Royal Flying Corps. In 1911 on one memorable Sunday afternoon 'Mr Basil' flew his Bristol Boxkite aeroplane from Aldershot and, after circling around Petworth church several times, landed safely in the ten-acre field below Tillington House. News spread quickly through the village and it is said that people rushed from church to see their first ever aeroplane and many signed their names on the wings.

Edward Verrell Lucas, the versatile and popular author of nearly one hundred books, came to Tillington in late 1913 or early 1914. With his wife Elizabeth and daughter Audrey they set up home in Tillington Cottage.

> The house, very trim and pretty with a grand view of the Downs, was called, officially, Tillington Cottage, but because of a sign just beyond the front gate announcing DANGEROUS CORNER, E.V. insisted on taking the warning as the name of the house and even had it printed on his notepaper.
>
> All the local conversation centred, rather in the Trollope manner, around Petworth House and the Leconfields. For the first year or so at least we did not know them, and the only active notice taken by E.V. of the 'great house' was in reference to chicken livers. The poulterer supplied us with birds, admirable birds in every respect save one - they had no livers. When at last, utterly exasperated, E.V. called on the man in person to inquire the reason for this deformity, he was told that all the livers of all the chickens on sale in Petworth were reserved for Petworth House.[8]

Life in Tillington for Edward Lucas was very sociable and the family entertained many houseguests and a stream of callers, including J M Barrie, A E W Mason - author of 'The Four Feathers' and several other books, who was also living in Tillington at the time - Reverend William Goggs, the local rector, and (probably) A A Milne and E H Shepherd. George Llewelyn Davies, the inspiration for J M Barrie's Peter Pan was also a regular visitor to this apparent literary retreat.

Kelly's Directory for 1911[9] lists the trades-people in the parish. In addition to the many farmers, Maurice Yeatman was a baker and grocer in Upperton, Constance Barham was landlord of the Horse Guards Inn, James Boxall, W Bryder and Charles Leazall were builders/carpenters and Emma White was a shopkeeper

The old sweet shop. Unknown

(it was in fact a sweet shop, conveniently located just a stone's throw from the village school, and one can imagine how often the schoolchildren must have stood excitedly waiting to spend a halfpenny on an ounce of aniseed balls or two liquorice sticks). Additionally noted are a chimney-sweep, wheelwright, rustic furniture manufacturer, police constable and the local postman.

The 1911 census provides additional information - The head teacher at the school was Albert Stringer, living at 1 Park Terrace and Mary Street was the postmistress. There was also a professor of music and a solicitor's clerk living further along the Upperton Road. There were at least two dressmakers in the parish, a laundress and a painter in Upperton, a wheelwright and blacksmith in Dean and numerous market gardeners, particularly around River. Charles Walker and his family of River Common appear to have converted their large house, Rock House, into a knitting factory where they produced and sold knitwear commercially. The Tillington Women's Institute 'History of Tillington'[10] written in 1965, notes of the knitting factory:

> Mr Walker came here from Pulborough. Mrs Felix Wadey was a girl of eleven when she started work there in 1912, and by the time she was twelve she started on the machines. For fourteen years she was employed there. During the 1914-18 War a great deal of work was undertaken for the Government. There were four machines for making garments and three

stocking machines. Mrs Wadey earned 7/- [shillings] a week but had her board and lodging. The hours were eight in the morning till eight at night.

Dr Charles Wilson from Petworth was the parish doctor and was well known and loved for the way he tended the sick throughout the parish and particularly the many poor folk.

With the trades-people and the availability of farm and garden produce, no doubt supplemented by nature's own bounty from fields and hedgerows, the parish must have been almost self-sufficient. Petworth railway station was some miles away and Petworth was the nearest town within walking distance for any supplies that were not delivered. There would be little need to travel as far as Chichester or Guildford - let alone London, which for many might as well have been in a foreign country.

The National Society built Tillington School in 1838 and in the early years a fee of one penny or two was charged. Originally it had only one big room that was divided into two parts, boys and girls each having a separate porch and entrance. The room was heated by one big stove in the middle. Later a room at the back was added for infants and this included a gallery. The big room was enlarged by an addition at the church end and large windows were installed at both ends. The garden was taken from the cottage next door and made into the playground. The school records provide an interesting glimpse into school life during the early years of the twentieth century.

During 1912 the school had a roll of 111 pupils and the average attendance was around 70 percent.[11] The main cause of non-attendance was illness or infection of various kinds, but in autumn it was noted that several children were absent because they were 'stopping'. This term was used in pheasant shooting circles in the days of the big driven

Tillington National School. Tillington WI Collection

shoots. Men and boys would have been 'on stop' all morning from first light, making sure that the birds did not escape from their particular drive. Waiting for the signal to release their birds was a cold, often wet, job and to keep warm fires would be lit. In addition boys often went potato picking and harvesting when the squire needed extra labour.

The School Log Book records that on 29 January 1912 the school reopened after a closure of six weeks following an outbreak of scarlet fever. During this time the school was disinfected. Normality soon returned and on 22 February the Reverend Goggs handed out watches and medals for good attendance. From his will made just before he went into his first battle, we know that Thomas Daniels received such a watch. Unfortunately the school only remained clear of infection until June when by order of Dr Cameron, Medical Officer of Health for Chichester Council, it was again closed from 3 June to 24 June due to an epidemic of whooping cough. It appears that the parish was dogged by a variety of illnesses for on 22 February 1913 a further five-week closure followed the start of a measles epidemic.

School subjects included arithmetic, English composition, scripture, drawing, gardening, nature walks and drill instruction. There was also cookery for the girls but this subject required travel to Petworth School.

In early 1912 the large, main room of the school was deemed to be poor use of space and it was very difficult to heat in winter, when temperatures were often not much above freezing. It was decided to divide the room into two smaller classrooms and to make other improvements. In July 1912 Messrs J Boxall and W Bryder each tendered for this improvement scheme. Mr Boxall tendered £387 and Mr Bryder £415. 'It was unanimously agreed to accept the lower tender'.[12]

The beautiful village church of All Hallows has always been at the heart of the parish and has marked countless births, marriages and deaths over nine hundred years. Since the late eighteenth century it has been under the patronage of the Earls of Egremont.

The Reverend William M Goggs came to Tillington in early 1911 and the Bishop of Chichester conducted his induction service on 11 January. William held his first service a few weeks later on 26 February at 8am. Throughout 1911 the number of communicants was low, generally ranging from four to seventeen

All Hallows' Church from Hilltop. Unknown

for most services. As always, however, Easter and Christmas were more popular and in 1912 sixty-six attendees received Easter Communion. In 1913 the total attendance was 847, with 129 on Christmas Day and 119 at Easter. There is no evidence that church attendance increased during August and September 1914, indeed the Christmas services for that year showed a fall in numbers. In spite of this disappointing church attendance the number of young people being confirmed was excellent for a small village. In 1912, for example, there were thirty (twenty-three of whom were aged sixteen or younger) including William Bryder and Thomas Daniels, both of whom were to be killed a few years later.

In the church service record[13] the Reverend Goggs had a wonderful habit of making observations in the margins of each page: 'very rough weather Dec 10th 1911 - Dec 24th 1911. Late May 1912 School closed on account of whooping cough'. In April 1912 Tillington was suffering a severe drought that continued into May. During this period the vicar regularly prayed for rain at his Sunday services. It seems that by June 2 his prayers were being received sympathetically since his margin notes recorded 'very wet', but it was not until the following Sunday that his plea for rain was really taken seriously. He recorded 'no service too wet'. Happily a month later he was able to record 'very hot weather'.

A photograph of the 1912/13 church choir shows the Reverend Goggs seated centre, with his churchwardens, Colonel Mitford and Colonel Barrington-Kennett to his left and right, surrounded by the choir, an all-male membership of over thirty, several of whom eagerly enlisted at the outbreak of the Great War. Some returned but sadly most did not.

On Saturday 1 August 1914 much of Britain awoke to a sun-drenched first day of the Bank Holiday and looked forward to enjoying themselves. Crowds flocked to the seaside all along the south coast and young boys eagerly waited to pay 4d to jump off the end of Worthing pier. For others the only place to be was The Oval where they were to witness the great Jack Hobbs score a double century for Surrey against Northamptonshire. The rest of the country enjoyed village fêtes, day trips, picnics and games or just lazed in the sunshine, many oblivious to the disastrous events unfolding in France and Belgium.

On that Saturday morning under the cloudless skies above Petworth Park the final preparations were being made for the National Service League Fête beginning in a few hours. The marquees were erected, tables were laid in the tea tent, stallholders were excitedly comparing notes about their expectations for the afternoon and the military band, paid for by Lord Leconfield, was beginning to tune up to entertain the crowds. This was going to be a fête to remember and surely everyone had a wonderful time, the young men with their friends, not venturing very far from the beer tent and the lucky ones with their girlfriends, strolling through the colourful stalls and resting in the tea tent. Perhaps as the sun went down it was time for the dance in the marquee on the main lawn of the Park. Finally came the 'goodnights' when some went home together and others made their parting last as long as they could.

The Church Choir 1912. Courtesy Tillington PCC

Back. Row L to R: C Bryder, N Dummer, D Dummer, B Pullen, W Bryder, P Pullen, T Daniels.

Third Row L to R: J Wadey, G Knight, P Boxall, B Barrington-Kennett, J Daniels, ? Street, J Boxall, H Starker, J Pullen.

Second Row L to R: Unknown, W Boxall, ? Stringer, Col Mitford, Rev'd Goggs, Col Barrington-Kennett, A Barrington-Kennett F Whitcombe W Bryder,

Front Row L to R: A Howard T Bryder, ? Howard, ? Howard, B Goggs, B Moddy, F Randell, I Yeatman.

On Tuesday, the day after the Bank Holiday, in the warm evening air His Majesty's Government declared to the German Government that a state of war existed between Great Britain and Germany as from 11pm on 4 August.

View over Petworth Park and lake. © The Francis Frith Collection

During November 1914 troops of the 9th (Service) Battalion Rifle Brigade and 9th (Service) Battalion Kings Royal Rifle Corps began to arrive in Petworth from training at Aldershot. Here the soldiers underwent further field training, long route marches and assembly with other units of the 42nd Infantry Brigade. After several months of very hard training at Petworth the battalions returned to Aldershot in February 1915. Three months later, fully trained and in high spirits, they set off for the battlefields of northern France.

The residents of Petworth made the men and their officers very welcome and many friendships were formed. Officers were billeted in a wing of Petworth House and some soldiers were billeted in the town, but most were housed in canvas bell-tents in the Park and fields surrounding the town. One local person recounted that the soldiers were not allowed to use her beds. They had to sleep on the floor to get them used to living rough when they were on active service.[14]

As these troops arrived in Petworth, and the Parish of Tillington gave up its young men to the Western Front and beyond, so the pre-war life of this close-knit community began to ebb away. The large houses lost many of their servants and farmers lost not only their farm hands but also most of their horses. Girls lost their amorous companions and for some, walks in Petworth Park would never be the same again while soldiers' families would dread the steps of the telegram boy. Then the whole community would share their grief and rally round because, even today, that is what a community does best.

2

Recruitment

Lord Kitchener made his first national appeal for 100,000 recruits on 4 August 1914, initially using newspaper advertisements, but by early September these were replaced by the series of famous war posters. These featured Lord Kitchener himself with a range of slogans including 'Join Your Country's Army' and 'Your Country Needs You'. This campaign was hugely successful and by the end of September some 750,000 young men had enlisted.

The Royal Sussex Regiment sent one battalion (2nd Battalion) to join the four divisions of the British Expeditionary Force in early August 1914. The Sussex authorities, however, responded quickly to Kitchener's campaign with the formation of new battalions for the 'New Armies'. The 7th (Service) Battalion was the first to be formed at Chichester, but this was filled within weeks and followed in September by the 8th and 9th Battalions also at Chichester and the 11th, 12th, 13th Battalions at Bexhill during the same month.

At the same time the County Territorial Force was being expanded with the formation of the 4th Battalion at Horsham, the 5th at Hastings and the 6th (Cyclist) Battalion at Brighton all during August 1914. Men in these battalions had only signed on for service on the Home Front but were soon expected to sign the 'Imperial Service Obligation' allowing them to be sent overseas. Hence these battalions were soon mobilised, the 4th to Suvla Bay, Gallipoli in August 1915 and the 5th to France earlier in the same year. Only the 6th remained in UK throughout the war. With these senior battalions overseas, new training units were needed to maintain the supply of reinforcements. The 2/4th and 2/5th Battalions were formed in January 1915 and November 1914 respectively, quickly followed by the 3/4th and 3/5th Battalions.

The recruitment posters soon reached the Petworth area but, in the early days, they did not seem to reflect the success of the national campaign. On 14 August Captain Basil Constable, Commanding Officer of D Company, 4th Battalion, Royal Sussex Regiment, then based at Newhaven, wrote to Mr Pitfield, a well- known Petworth solicitor:

I wonder if you could do anything for us in the way of recruits. This company is very short still and they are drafting in men from other districts to fill our ranks, this seems to me to show that the men of Petworth district are somewhat lacking in energy. Hundreds of recruits are coming forward for other companies except ours. I am writing to Sydney Vincent who has just left us, to see what he can do to help you if you will take this up.[1]

It is not known why Captain Constable chose Mr Pitfield out of all the Petworth dignitaries, but it may have been that as a solicitor he was well-respected and not without influence. Sydney Vincent, another recipient of the letter, was a local tradesman and long-time member of the local Territorial Force. The letter suggests that Mr Vincent had just left D Company, perhaps as a recruiting officer. There is no information on whether the two gentlemen accepted the challenge and if they were successful.

In spite of the pessimistic tone of the letter, it appears that by September 1914 any recruitment crisis was beginning to pass. Indeed letters found in a 1914 file in Petworth House archives, suggest a much more upbeat recruiting campaign spearheaded by the Leconfield Estate and Lord Leconfield in particular. This is illustrated by the short exchange of correspondence between Mr Watson of the Leconfield Estate Office and Reverend William Goggs of Tillington. On 4 September Mr Watson sent the following typewritten letter:

> Dear Mr Goggs,
> I am sending you 4 posters as to recruiting. Lord Leconfield would be very glad if you would give them out and get them fixed in public places in Tillington. The Public House is to have two. I am sending you these as although Tillington belongs to Midhurst the recruiting station at Petworth is nearest and handiest for the men.
> Yours very truly.[2]

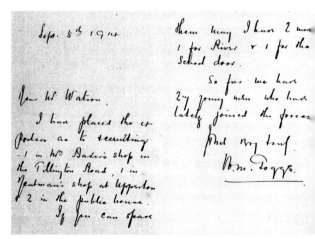

Letter from Mr Watson to Reverend Goggs. Courtesy Petworth House Archive

Reverend Goggs's handwritten reply. Courtesy Petworth House Archive

Reverend Goggs replied the very next day with a handwritten letter:

Dear Mr Watson,
I have placed 4 posters as to recruiting – 1 in Mrs Baker's shop in the Tillington Road, 1 in Yeatman's shop at Upperton and 2 in the public house. If you can spare them may I have 2 more, 1 for River and 1 for the School door. So far we have 27 young men who have lately joined the forces.

Yours very truly
Wm Goggs.[3]

It is clear from the archive file that Lord Leconfield also played an important role in the recruitment of local men, encouraging his young employees to enlist. A letter dated 9 September 1914 states:

Lord Leconfield is in charge of recruiting here and is spending his days enlisting men at the recruiting office here and holding meetings all round the neighbourhood and we have the district well posted with War Office and other placards. Men are coming forward fairly well – I don't think many unmarried men are left in the villages around here.[4]

In 1914 the Petworth Armoury, situated in Tillington Road (opposite the entrance to the present day Sylvia Beaufoy car park), served as the main recruiting office for D Company of the 4th Battalion Royal Sussex Regiment. Young men below the age of nineteen years could not serve overseas but could be trained as fighting soldiers so that, on reaching this age, they could be transferred to a senior battalion.

The Petworth Armoury. © Author's collection

The Armoury, which is built into the wall of Petworth Park, is of stone construction and is relatively small (50 feet x 24 feet) compared with most drill halls. There are three large sash windows on both the north and south sides providing excellent natural light. Interestingly in the centre of the ceiling there is an alabaster rose, perhaps suggesting that it may have been a dwelling at one time. At the east end, separated from the main hall, is a covered passageway leading from the A272 door, past an entry into the Armoury and on to another door leading to a large grassed area and to the long-established covered miniature rifle range.

One can imagine the recruiting sergeant sitting at a table at the west end of the hall dealing with an eager recruit, who holds his well-worn flat cap respectfully in his hand, perhaps stuttering a little when asked his age. Behind him, stretching out on to the road, there is a long queue of young men, including groups of friends, eagerly awaiting their turn to enlist. No doubt in August 1914 and at other busy times the grassed area was used to hold the excited, vociferous young men.

Not only did Lord Leconfield spend his days at the recruiting office but he also spent many evenings and weekends organising, chairing or speaking at 'Call to Arms' meetings. One such meeting, chaired by his Lordship, was held in the Market Square at Petworth on Saturday 19 September at 8pm. The visiting speaker rallied the young men gathered there with 'The Causes of the War and the Present Need for Recruiting'. No doubt a good number of these men were to be found queuing outside the Armoury on Monday morning.

Another well-attended recruitment meeting was reported in the *West Sussex County Times* for 9 September 1914:

> Stirring scenes have been witnessed day after day this week at the headquarters of the 4th Battalion of the Royal Sussex Regiment in Park Street [Horsham]. On Monday the building was totally inadequate to meet anything like the demands and the process of recruiting required the utilisation of another building.[5]

The 4th Battalion also used another ingenious way of attracting new recruits. Before any uniforms were issued to new groups of volunteers they were often required to take part in recruitment drives in civilian clothes. Private Albert Baker of Horsham recounted his experience in a delightful audio recording made for the Imperial War Museum in 1982.[6] No sooner had he joined the 4th Battalion Royal Sussex Regiment in August 1914 at Horsham than he was on a recruitment march with fellow fresh-faced recruits to find more volunteers to make up a reserve battalion. He recalled setting off from Horsham towards Henfield then across the Downs to Worthing, where they were accommodated in a seafront hotel, then on to Chichester and Petworth, finishing their trip at Midhurst. At each stop meetings were arranged where men would be encouraged to join the reserves. Albert remembered clearly that the week-long march, covering some fifty miles, successfully recruited six hundred men. They all began their Army life at Denne Park in Horsham, moving on to Belhurst Park in Essex for more specialised training part of which was to guard the Woolwich Arsenal. The 2/4th Reserve Battalion remained in the UK, providing much-needed reinforcements for the senior battalion as the war took its dreadful toll.

Over the next few years more young men responded to the call. Most enlisted in the local battalion, at least for their initial training, but as fully trained soldiers they may have been posted to other battalions of the Royal Sussex Regiment or to any other regiment in Kitchener's New Army.

Young men who volunteered early in the recruitment campaign of 1914 could often choose the regiment they wanted to join and groups of friends could sign up together for the same regiment. As the war went on, and recruits were urgently needed in particular regiments, freedom of choice became very limited. This is shown in a letter written home by Egbert (known as Reg) Pratt of River on 23 January 1916. Reg made his way to Chichester eager to enlist in a branch of the artillery. He writes:

> …. all the artillery was closed; there was the Cavalry open. I did not want to go in that and the Engineers was only open for trades so I thought it was no good trying for that. Nearly all the chaps have been put in the 14th (Reserve) Battalion Sussex today.[7]

When the Great War broke out there was also a great demand for horses. Hunters were needed for officers, dray horses to haul wagons, and mules and ponies to carry loads. To address the problem Remount Depots were set up around the country and the Army Service Corps was responsible for the compulsory purchase of thousands of animals across the United Kingdom. It is said that local tradesmen, carts, vans and wagons were stopped in the street and the animals removed from their shafts.

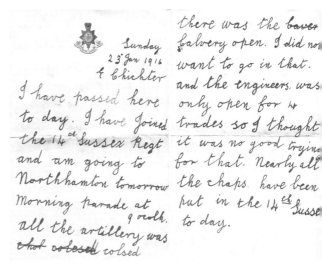

Original letter from E R Pratt 1916. Courtesy Pratt family

During August 1914 the extensive Swaythling Remount Depot was built on the edge of Southampton and became the centre to which nearly all horses and mules from England were sent before being dispatched to the Western Front. These animals were collected at local Remount Depots before being prepared and transported to the south coast.

One such location was in Petworth Park where workers began preparing a 'Remounts Depot' in late August 1914 opposite the almshouses on the edge of Tillington. The estate accounts show receipts from the War Office on 1 October to cover:

25th August 1914 – Erecting stalls for war remounts in park - £6 18s 8d.

22nd September 1914 – Laying picket lines for war horses, park - £4 8s 4d.

… for men's time and materials used in fixing stalls, tents, laying on water, pickets and stumps for horses in park £64 0s 1d.[8]

In the same month £36. 9s. 6d was also received for oats, hay and straw.

Writing to Mr Pitfield on 16 August 1914, J B Watson, Lord Leconfield's land agent, laments that his lordship's cub hunters and coach horses had already gone.

The hunters will no doubt go shortly. They have taken my two cobs, so far I have saved my old horse and the missus' pony.[9]

The Howick family of Tillington had two soldiers billeted with them from the Remounts Depot. In addition a gentleman, Lionel Trower (uncle of the future Mrs Basil Barrington-kennett), lodging at Tillington Hill House, gave his occupation as 'Remounts'. Many of the Remount officers were drawn from the mature landed gentry who had experience with horses in civilian life, thus avoiding withdrawing Army officers from their normal duties. The Petworth Park depot closed in 1916.

In August 1914 a training scheme originated by the Eastnor Castle Estate in Herefordshire was commended to Lord Leconfield. The purpose of this scheme was to train all local men not already in the army to use a rifle. This would provide some preparation for those who later enlisted and the men who for one reason or another were not eligible for the army could be formed into a local defence force. It is perhaps no surprise that Lord Leconfield had pre-empted the need for such training so clearly detailed in Mr Watson's confident reply to the Eastnor Castle Estate.

… I may say however that we have a miniature rifle range on the estate and that very considerable use is being made of it for the instruction of those not eligible immediately for recruiting. These men are not formally enrolled but 60 or 70 are practising 3 or 4 nights a week at the range and ammunition has been provided by private donation for those not able to pay the small cost of their own ammunition. Besides this we have about 150 members of the Civil Guard who are drilling twice a week under efficient instruction, but the greatest effort has been towards encouraging recruiting of those fit for service.[10]

For many years a simple, oak board hung in the old Armoury at Petworth, commemorating the soldiers of D Company, Royal Sussex Regiment, who gave their lives in the Great War. The board still exits and Melvyn Bridger (great nephew to Arthur Bridger) recalls its whereabouts:

> The Armoury has for some years now been used for rehearsals and storage by the Petworth Players. Some of my family were members of the Players and I have known it [the memorial] for eternity. I presume it had been there since the First World War. In 1990 my father, Owen Bridger, who was Secretary of the Midhurst branch of the Royal Sussex Regimental Association wrote to Lord Egremont asking for permission to remove the plaque, which was given. I removed the plaque and my father passed it on to the Regimental Museum at the Roussillon Barracks, Chichester. When the barracks closed, I understand that it was taken to the Redoubt Museum at Eastbourne.[11]

Indeed it was found safe and well at the Regimental Museum there and, although the memorial maker has long been forgotten, somehow this simple rustic board, fashioned and painted from the heart by an unskilled hand, is a fitting memorial to the never-ending debt we owe to the thirty men who never returned to their loved ones in the parish.

The simple oak memorial to the 4th Battalion, Royal Sussex Regiment. Courtesy Redoubt Museum, Eastbourne.

~ 3 ~

The Barrington-Kennett Family

In March 1828 Vincent Kennett married Arabella Barrington at St Ann's Church of Ireland, in Dublin. Their first son, born on 3 September 1844 near Lucca in Tuscany, was christened Vincent Kennett-Barrington (later to become a distinguished diplomat and statesman, an early pioneer of international medical aid and a knight bachelor). Interestingly their second son, born 29 March 1846 near Calais, was christened Brackley Herbert Barrington-Kennett with the hyphenated surname being transposed.

At the age of twenty-one Brackley was commissioned into the 51st Light Infantry on 21 August 1867 and by 1883 he had been promoted to Major. He served both in the UK and in the East Indies taking part in battles against the Jowaki Afreedis tribesmen. He also fought in the Afghanistan campaign of 1878-1880. Major Barrington-Kennett was wounded at Hissarak on 16 June

The young Barrington-Kennett Brothers. L to R: Aubrey, Victor, Godwin, Basil. Courtesy Nick Duder

1880 and returned to England, where for the next five years he was the adjutant of the 1st Durham Light Infantry.

Brackley married Ellinor Frances Austen in Brighton early in 1884. They remained there for a short while, probably in Ellinor's family home. Her mother died in 1885; that same year Basil Herbert was born and his brother Godwin Austen made his appearance a year later. Soon after the birth of Godwin the family moved to London and the 1891 census shows them settled into 23 Sloane Gardens, Chelsea, now with four sons, Basil Herbert (6), Godwin Austen (5), Victor Annesley (3) and Aubrey Hampden (seven months). Their Sloane Gardens home was a wealthy household with two nurses, a housemaid, a cook and a manservant, but by 1888 they had moved into the more prestigious Eaton Square, London.

The youngest of the Barrington-Kennett brothers, Aubrey, was born on 8 September 1890 at Norrysbury, Cockfosters Road, East Barnet, the home of his mother's sister Catherine Malcolmson (née Austen). Catherine was the wife of George Malcolmson, a city banker and the mother of Helen Matilda, the eldest of their six children. In late 1892 Helen married Arthur Tempest Blakiston Dunn, schoolmaster, all-round sportsman and captain of the England football team. In early 1892 Arthur left his teaching post at Elstree School and in May of the same year he established his own preparatory school, Ludgrove, at Hadley Common, East Barnet, close to his future in-laws. It is, therefore, not surprising that the Barrington-Kennett boys all started their education at this preparatory school. The 1901 census shows both Victor (13) and Aubrey (10) boarding at Ludgrove School.

Brackley next appears in 1895 as a Lieutenant Colonel in The Honourable Corps of Gentlemen-at-Arms, a Royal bodyguard. This is a ceremonial

The Lying in State of King Edward VII 1910. Courtesy Nick Duder

The Barrington-Kennett family with two visitors L to Right: Aubrey, Majorie Sawyer, Basil, Victor, Doris Sawyer, Ellinor, Godwin and Brackley. Courtesy Nigel and Barbara Wood

position that still exists today; the retired military officers of the Corps wear the uniform of a Dragoon Guards Officer of the 1840s. During the lying-in-state of Edward VII in Westminster Hall in May 1910, each corner of the catafalque was guarded around the clock by members of the Sovereign's Bodyguard and the Grenadier Guards or Household Cavalry. Brackley and Basil Barrington-Kennett shared this honour when they mounted the guard together.

By 1901 the family had moved to Burton Firs, Barlavington, West Sussex, but the census of that year shows that only Basil and a number of servants were at home with mother and father. By 1911 the family was living in Tillington but by this time the three eldest boys had joined the army and were with their new regiments whilst the youngest, Aubrey, was finishing his Oxford education.

We know from Kelly's Directory for 1908 that the family came to live at Tillington House around this time. The Petworth House archives record that 'Colonel Kennett' purchased building materials from the Estate during the period 1908-1914. He also paid an annual rent of £80 for Tillington House and seven acres of land over this period. The family settled into village life very quickly and on 5 August 1909 Colonel Brackley became a churchwarden of All Hallows' Church, replacing Mr Colebrook. At the 1911 Annual Vestry Meeting,[1] Mrs Barrington-Kennett, Victor and Aubrey were also present. At the same meeting in 1912 Colonel Mitford (the rector's churchwarden) 'wished to thank Colonel Barrington-Kennett for energy and business like method of carrying out his duties during his absence in India'.

The Barrington-Kennett family remained at Tillington House until the late spring of 1914. All the sons were now fighting for their country and Colonel and Mrs Barrington-Kennett decided to move permanently to their London home in Chelsea. In the minutes of the Easter Vestry Meeting[2] thanks were expressed for the contribution made by Colonel Barrington-Kennett to the village church.

> Colonel W Kenyon Mitford wished on behalf of himself and the whole parish to express his gratitude to L Colonel Barrington-Kennett for his unfailing energetic work and for many hours spent in the performance of his duties as his colleague. No one could have worked harder or taken a deeper or more hearty interest. Also he wished to say on behalf of all, how truly sorry all are at his leaving the parish and the same as regards Mrs Barrington-Kennett and the family.
>
> Colonel Barrington-Kennett expressed his feelings of deep gratitude for the kind words addressed to him and assured him that his work as one of their churchwardens had always been a source of joy and satisfaction to him. During the five years he had always tried his upmost to perform the duties conscientiously and to the best of his ability. Mr James Boxall was elected people's churchwarden in his place.

Whilst at Eton, Victor Barrington-Kennett met George Butterworth, then a fledgling composer; they became the greatest of friends, a friendship which endured through their days at Oxford and into the war years.[3] George's parents lived at 19 Cheyne Gardens, Chelsea, but after his mother's death in January 1911 the house felt an empty place with just father and son living there. George suggested to his father that they should share their home with the Barrington-Kennetts when they were in town. It would also provide a base for Victor who, following Oxford, joined the Canadian Agency, a semi-private financial house in London. In early 1914 the Butterworths moved from Cheyne Gardens leaving the Barrington-Kennetts to continue the lease.

So it was that the family moved from Tillington to 19 Cheyne Gardens, which was, and remains, a fine five-storey property in fashionable Chelsea, where in early March 1919 the Colonel died at the age of 72 years. He was laid to rest on 17 March following a service in All Hallows' Church conducted by Reverend William Goggs. Ellinor died aged 84, in spring 1933, at 71 Onslow Gardens, Kensington and was buried on 16 May. Her burial service was also conducted in All Hallows' Church when the Very Reverend Wilfred W Youard, Dean of Battle, officiated at the service. It is interesting to note that Dean Youard was married to Evelyn Constance, daughter of Catherine Malcolmson, sister of Ellinor. Although in life the Colonel and Mrs Barrington-Kennett were used to the bustle and grandeur of London, in death they chose to be laid to rest, together, in the peaceful, rural cemetery of Tillington beneath a simple stone cross that also acts as a memorial to their three boys. It is also perhaps an indication of the regard and warmth they both felt for the village.

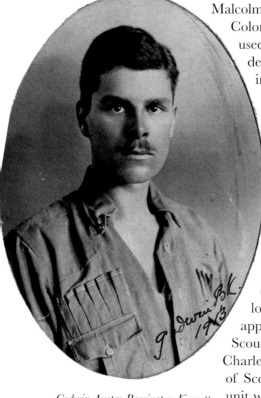

Godwin Austen Barrington-Kennett 1913. Courtesy Nick Duder

All four boys fought in the Great War, but only Godwin survived. He joined the 4th Battalion Royal Sussex Regiment during the first decade of the twentieth century and on 1 December 1909 Godwin Austen Barrington-Kennett was promoted to 2nd Lieutenant (*London Gazette* 28 January 1910). We then lose him until 1914 when, surprisingly, he appears in Africa where he has joined Ross's Scouts. On the declaration of the Great War Charles Ross was appointed to set up his own unit of Scouts and in November 1914 a forty-strong unit was formed. This 'private army' comprised a rough bunch of lads and, perhaps because of this, the unit was disbanded in January 1915. Before the end of the month Godwin Barrington-Kennett was posted to C Squadron of the East African Mounted Rifles with the rank of private, service number 500. By the end of 1916, however, he had been promoted to temporary Lieutenant and transferred to the Kings African Rifles. He remained on active service in East Africa with this regiment until the end of the war.

In the summer of 1918 Godwin travelled to London where he married Beryl Malcolmson. Together they returned to Africa, but after a short time Godwin contracted Blackwater Fever and was advised to return to England. The *London Gazette* 7 January 1919 reported that G A Barrington-Kennett had relinquished his commission on account of ill health contracted on active service, but retained the rank of Lieutenant. Arriving back in early 1919 they settled close to Haywards Heath in West Sussex where their daughter Jean Violet was born on 23 March 1920. Her father told such wonderful stories of Africa and from an early age she knew it was the only place she wanted to live. Jean married three times and spent most of her life in Kenya. She married her second husband, Alexander Hyde Duder, in Nairobi on 20 December 1952. They had two sons, Michael and Nicholas. Jean was the last of the Barrington-Kennett line and sadly the name has now been lost. In 2016, Nicholas was living with his wife and two sons in Jakarta, Indonesia. Barrington is a forename of his elder son complemented by Kennett being included in his younger son's name.[4]

Godwin died aged 85 in 1971 in Worthing, Sussex, and when Jean died in 2008 her ashes were scattered in the Nairobi Game Reserve.

Among Ellinor's many talents she was something of an author and in 1916 she wrote a small book called *Four Little Brothers*[5] about the childhood exploits of Rex, Godfrey, Lionel and Humphrey. There are a number of simple tales within the book that are clearly based on Ellinor's own children. One story is called 'The Accident' and tells the tale of Godfrey and Lionel who one day found their way to the hayloft in the coach-house where 'in one corner stood a funny looking machine with a handle to turn'. This was a chaff-cutter with exposed sharp blades. Unfortunately in the story Godfrey severed two fingers playing with the machine. Whilst mother and father were very loving and sympathetic to their son's accident, father made the comment: 'I am afraid this puts an end to either of the Services for him. We always meant to make a sailor of him, but they are so strict in the Navy, I am sure it would be hopeless to try'.

We know that Godwin had an unfortunate accident in which he lost two fingers in an identical machine and his military career did suffer. The very last page of Ellinor's book is deeply poignant and gives us a glimpse into the grief of two parents who lost three of their four sons in war.

Since this story was written the great war has come, and first "Baby Humphrey", then "Rex", and then "Lionel" have all been called on to give their lives in action for King and Country and the cause of Honour and Truth. Godfrey is still on active service, fighting with a sad heart for the dear brothers who are gone. Daddy mourns for his three brave sons, and Mother feels that life can never be the same without them; she looks forward to meeting them in the land "where there shall be no more death, neither sorrow nor crying", and where "God shall wipe away all tears from their eyes".

July 1916

MANY YEARS AFTER

SINCE this story was written the great war has come, and first "Baby Humphrey," then "Rex," and then "Lionel" have all been called on to give their lives in action for King and Country and the cause of Honour and Truth. Godfrey is still on active service, fighting with a sad heart for the dear brothers who are gone. Daddy mourns for his three brave sons, and Mother feels that life can never be the same without them; but she looks forward to meeting them in the land "where there shall be no more death, neither sorrow nor crying," and where "God shall wipe away all tears from their eyes."

July 1916

The final page 'Four Little Brothers'. © Author's collection

4

Major Basil Barrington-Kennet

Grenadier Guards and Royal Flying Corps

Basil Herbert Barrington-Kennett was born in Hove, Sussex in 1885, the son of Lieutenant Colonel Brackley Herbert (Royal Body Guard) and Mrs Ellinor Frances Barrington-Kennett. Basil was the eldest of four sons, followed by Godwin (1886) Victor (1887) and Aubrey (1890). At the time of Aubrey's birth the family had settled into 23 Sloane Gardens, Chelsea, but the 1901 census shows that they had also rented a country home, 'Burton Firs', at Barlavington in Sussex. Basil was sixteen years old and living at home with his parents, having left Eton in 1900. In 1908 the family left Barlavington to rent Tillington House just a few miles away.

Basil entered Sandhurst Military Academy in 1905 where his records show that he was an average student, but did well in History and Geography, Tactics and Riding.[1] He left the Academy in 1906 to join the Grenadier Guards. The *London Gazette* Tuesday 23 August 1906 reports: 'The under-mentioned gentlemen cadets from the Royal Military College to be second lieutenants: Foot Guards: B. H. Barrington-Kennett in succession to Lt D.C.L. Stephen'.

At this time the army was very much involved in developing the use of balloons for aerial observation purposes and ballooning soon attracted the attention of the adventurous Lieutenant Barrington-Kennett. Unfortunately one of his early flights, in which he was a passenger, nearly led to disaster as recorded in *The Cornishman* newspaper of 17 September 1908:

Lieutenant Barrington-Kennett in the uniform of the Grenadier Guards 1910.
Ⓒ *Copyright expired*

BLOWN OUT TO SEA - NARROW ESCAPE FOR BALLOONISTS

The pilot steamer Hoek Van Holland has rescued in the North Sea two balloonists who ascended in London at ten last night, and were driven out to sea by the strong wind. When the steamer came to the rescue the balloon was only about ninety feet above the sea.

It was ten-o-clock in the morning when the balloon with its two passengers, Messrs Barrington Kennett and Short was first sighted about fifteen miles to the north of the northern breakwater at the Hook of Holland. The balloon was coming down at the time, and was in danger of falling into the water. A salvage steamer and the pilot vessel set out immediately, and the latter took the balloon on board with its two passengers. The gentlemen stated that they had intended to cross the North Sea to Belgium, but when at a height of 4,500 feet they were caught in a snowstorm and driven towards the Dutch coast. They were both suffering slightly from the effects of their trying experience, but received every attention at the Hook of Holland.

They stated in an interview that they started from Battersea Gasworks last night at ten-o-clock intending to go to Belgium. The first part of the voyage was made in beautiful moonlight and with a favourable wind. Later the wind veered to the north-west and then to the west-south-west and drove them towards the coast of Holland. They could not make the coast, for the wind changed again driving them towards the North Sea. At seven-o-clock they were caught in a snowstorm, and later, seeing boats in the distance and their ballast being exhausted, they employed white scarves to attract the attention of a pilot tug. The vessel steamed under the balloon and put out a small boat which caught the trail rope attached to the balloon's water anchor. The sailors took the balloonists on board and saved all the instruments in the car. The balloon was then ripped with a knife, as the ripping apparatus was in the water. Although the aeronauts carried lifebelts it would have gone hard with them if the boat had not been on the spot. Both gentlemen highly praised the conduct of the tug's crew. They return to London from the Hook tonight to Wellington Barracks.

By 1909 Basil had joined the Royal Aero Club and quickly became a member of the 'Balloon Committee'. He entered balloon races organised by the club, at first as a passenger but it appears that he soon purchased his own small balloon called 'Comet'. The Aero Club report for 19 June 1909 notes:[2]

About half-past five the little "Comet" [2,500 cub. ft.] was sent off with Mr. B. H. Barrington Kennett in charge and a passenger. Then the new balloon, "L'Esperance", of 52,000 cub ft capacity, which has just been made by Messrs. Short Bros, for the Baroness von Heecheren, got away, the Hon. C. S. Rolls [Rolls Royce] being in charge…. "L'Esperance" was brought down at Littlehampton, as close to the sea as it was safe to venture. Pulborough was the stopping-place of the "Lotus", and the "Comet" came down also in the same neighbourhood.

After several years of indecision the War Office finally accepted in 1878 that there was indeed scope within the British Army for the employment of balloons. An army balloon was designed and built at Woolwich Arsenal, East London, by the men and officers of the Royal Engineers. Over the next two decades development continued apace and a Royal Engineers Balloon Section was formed to operate these balloons in the field. The Section saw action for the first time at the outbreak of the Boer War in 1899. Although the development of powered flight in the early 1900s began to marginalise the balloon, the army continued to believe that aeroplanes had no place in war and would only frighten the horses. They kept a sceptical eye, however, on the early flying machines and when - in the summer of 1909 - Louis Blériot made the first airborne crossing of the Channel, the Army's attitude began to change. On 1 April 1911 the Balloon Section, Royal Engineers became the Air Battalion of the Royal Engineers. No 1 Company retained responsibility for airships kites and balloons whilst No 2 Company became devoted to 'heavier-than-air-flying'.

It was perhaps with a clear view of the future that, in autumn 1910, Basil enrolled in the then famous McCardle & Drexel flying school close to Brockenhurst in the New Forest. *Flight* magazine was, at this time, the official voice of the Royal Aero Club and maintained a regular series of articles on the training of new pilots. Basil's training exploits appeared regularly in these articles:

> September 1910 – The New Forest Aviation School commenced operations after the Bournemouth International Meeting and at present is going along at full swing. Major Cooke, R.A., and M. Poggioli have both managed some short flights in a straight line, and Messrs B. H. Barrington Kennett [Grenadier Guards], A. Aitken, and St. Croix Johnstone [Chicago], are "rolling" whenever the weather is suitable which has been the case almost daily for the past fortnight.[3]

> October 1910 - Mr Barrington-Kennett, made some excellent straight flights up to a distance of half a mile. His first experiment at turning, however, was not attended with success, for banking over rather steep, the machine came down sideways, his nearness to the ground not allowing sufficient time or space for righting, and consequently a somewhat complete smash ensued. The pilot was entirely unhurt, and did not seem at all disheartened by the mishap, which he laughingly attributed to "excessive ambition".

November 1910 - During the three fine days at the end of last week, Barrington-Kennett, Cook, Wilson, and Kempton Cannon were busy on the School monoplanes, the first-named couple making excellent flights which would have enabled the pilots to pass their tests for certificates had they arranged for an official observer to be present. [4]

After £80-worth of lessons and following a flying test at the Royal Aero Club, Basil gained his Aviators Certificate on 31 December 1910, only the 43rd person to do so. His success was reported in the early January 1911 edition of *Flight*[5] and soon afterwards Basil was seconded from the Grenadier Guards to No 2 (Aeroplane) Company of the Air Battalion, Royal Engineers. The Air Battalion was formed on 1 April 1911 at Lark Hill on Salisbury Plain. Four Bristol Boxkites had been ordered for delivery in May but by August five more assorted aircraft had arrived at Lark Hill.

Aviator's Certificate No 43, 31 December 1910.
Courtesy Empire Test Pilots School, Boscombe Down.

Lieutenant Barrington-Kennett's flying exploits, particularly his pursuit of records, continued to be reported in *Flight*:

> Lark Hill, Salisbury Plain, September 1911, Air Battalion:
> Capt. Fulton, Lieut. Barrington Kennett and Lieut. Conner, all three again flying on Sunday morning, Lieut. Conner carrying a passenger. On Monday they were practising in view of some despatch-carrying and bomb-dropping experiments which will shortly be carried out. [6]

Although with limited resources, the Company soon began work testing their aeroplanes' suitability for lengthy cross-country flights. The first trip to Aldershot was a success with all four pilots landing safely after a flight of about one-and-a-half hours. This was perhaps a practice for the Army manoeuvres at Cambridge in August 1911. No 2 Company was given the task of providing support for this event, which firstly required a number of aeroplanes safely to reach Hardwicke Farm, near Cambridge; a distance never before attempted. Although the manoeuvres were cancelled shortly before the planned date, it was decided that the Air Company should continue with its plans in order to improve training.

On 16 August four Bristol machines left Lark Hill with at least one pilot navigating with the aid of a *Bradshaw Railway Guide*.[7] Basil flew his newly built machine, bearing the inscription 'Air Battalion F 8 No 38. The Bristol'. Most completed the first stage to Oxford successfully, but Basil landed some twenty miles short with a broken tailskid. Lt Reynolds had less success, when over Bletchley the weather took a turn for the worse. In his own words:

> I scarcely had occasion to move the control lever at all until I got to Bletchley, where it began to get rather bumpy; at first I thought nothing of this, but suddenly it got much worse, and I came to the conclusion it was time to descend … I began to glide, but almost directly I had switched off, the tail was suddenly wrenched upwards as if it had been hit from below …. I was not strapped in … the next thing I realised was that I was lying in a heap on what ordinarily is the underside of the top plane [wing]. The machine in fact was upside down … Then it went down tail first, turned over upside down again ... as we got close to the ground I made up my mind that the only thing to do was to try and jump clear of the wreckage before the crash … Fortunately I hung on practically to the end, and, according to those who were looking on, I did not jump till about 10ft from the ground. Those who were looking on were two men, stark naked, who had been bathing nearby. About fifty or sixty people soon collected, and some time passed before it occurred to anyone to remark that these two men had no clothes on.[8]

With the tailskid quickly replaced, Basil continued his flight to Oxford the following day. He remained at Oxford until Saturday 19 August when he set off once again. Soon after 7pm the same day the inhabitants of Aspley Guise in Bedfordshire excitedly heard the buzz of the 50 hp Gnome engine of the Boxkite. According to *The Bedfordshire Times* of 25 August 1911[9] it was evident that the pilot was having trouble:

> The machine, after some difficulty with telegraph wires, eventually settled very easily in Mr Barker's field, near Higgins's brickworks. The airman Lt B. B Kennett was pleasantly communicative and explained that he had hoped to reach Bedford that night, but owing to a squall after leaving Bletchley, he was obliged to come down.

Perhaps not surprisingly Basil dined that evening with Mr and Mrs Downes of Aspley House and returned to his aircraft at 6am the following morning, heartily greeted by an assembled crowd that had risen early to see him off. He reached Blunham in Bedfordshire the same day where he landed and remained until early on the morning of 21 August. He was overhead Sandy by 7am.

The shout "A flying machine" quickly brought those who had risen from their beds, into the streets …. as the machine skimmed smoothly by at no great altitude.

It came down on Biggleswade Common where it remained until about 5pm. *The Bedfordshire Times* takes up the story once again:

The news soon spread and in spite of a heavy rain hundreds of persons visited the scene. The officer spent the day in the town, made the ascent at 5.40 pm in the presence of a large excited crowd. The biplane rose splendidly, and a demonstration lasting 10 minutes was given by the gallant officer, who was heartily cheered each time he passed over. At 5.50 the airman waved his hand and flew off in the direction of Potton, following the L.N.W.R. railway line to Cambridge … It was a never to be forgotten scene, as this was the first flying machine that had come into the parish.

Lieutenant Barrington-Kennett, RFC at Hardwicke Farm, Cambridge 1911. Courtesy Nick Duder

Basil safely reached the final destination, Hardwicke Farm, Cambridge. During the return flight to Lark Hill, he landed near Huntingdon:

Lt B.H. Barrington-Kennett flying Bristol Boxkite No. F8 of the Air Battalion, R.E., landed on Portholme, [airfield] Wednesday, 30 August 1911. His aircraft was serviced by Portholme's mechanics that afternoon. After a test flight Kennett made the first passenger flight from Portholme with local enthusiast Dr. Whitehead seated behind him. After the passenger flight Kennett took off in the direction of Oxford.[10]

In his book *Flying with the Larks*[11] Timothy Brown recognised that these early flying aces acquired a certain celebrity status:

The pilots in particular were welcome guests at parties and gatherings across the country. It was commonplace for them to fly off to country houses for shooting and hunting weekends, where well-to-do families would entertain them, and it is said they were popular with the wives and daughters. On at least one occasion, Reynolds and Barrington-Kennett got into trouble for being away from Lark Hill for a whole week, ostensibly with mechanical problems.

At the end of 1911 the Air Battalion had four new French aircraft including a two-seater Nieuport IVG and a Breguet. It was not long before Basil claimed the former as his personal machine and went on to achieve greatness in it. By early January 1912 the officers of the Air Battalion were forbidden from flying cross-country. *The Pall Mall Gazette* in January 1912 informed its readers that:

> Flights further afield may entail expense in petrol and oil … and the funds of the Air Battalion do not admit such generous expenditure.[12]

This ban, however, was not taken too seriously, at least by some since in late February Basil made a rather long cross country flight.

> Although the weather was very dull on Wednesday of last week, Lieut. Barrington-Kennett had his Nieuport monoplane brought out and after three flights to test the engine took Corporal Ridd, R.E [his mechanic] on board and started off for a second attempt on the Mortimer Singer prize. He was flying for 4 hrs. 51 mins and covered a distance of 249 miles 840 yards at a height of 250 feet. This distance, however, does not include the flying from Salisbury Plain to the course so that the flight completely puts into the shade his previous attempt and constitutes a world's record. The Royal Aero Club has applied to the Federation to have this record officially recognised.[13]

Lieutenant Barrington-Kennett and Corporal Rudd prepare to take off for their record breaking flight.
Flight 24 February 1912

The record was verified and Basil was awarded the Mortimer Singer Prize for long-distance flying and the sum of £500. He wrote in the log book of Nieuport No B4:

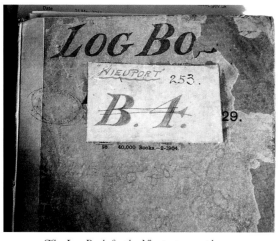

The Log Book for the Nieuport monoplane No B4. Courtesy Empire Test Pilots' School, Boscombe Down.

Went out for a short flight to test machine. Found same flying with left wing down. Ridd altered same & after satisfactory test we started away for Mortimer Singer. Rather rough for first 2½ hours, then wind dropped by degrees and it was perfect going. Petrol lasted out, but was compelled to return to sheds owing to approaching darkness, otherwise could have gone on for another hour, the engine running beautifully - 249 miles counted for M.S. I fancy this flight constitutes a world record for duration and distance for a flight with a passenger.[14]

Flight of 18 May 1912 reports from the Royal Flying Corps:

> No work was done on Saturday owing to Lieutenant Barrington-Kennett taking a party of non-commissioned officers and men to London to celebrate the winning of the Mortimer Singer prize. They had dinner at the Holborn Restaurant at which Capt Loraine was in the chair and several other officers of the R.F.C. were present. A visit to the Palladium wound up an enjoyable day.[15]

With this world record and his dashing good looks, Basil was in great demand as a speaker, as this notice in *Flight* of 16 March 1912 illustrates:[16]

> ARRANGEMENTS have been made by the Ladies Automobile Club for a lecture to be given at the Club Rooms at Claridge's Hotel by Mr B.H. Barrington-Kennett on Tuesday, April 2nd at 3.30 pm, the subject being 'Aviation at Home and Abroad'. The lecture will be illustrated by lantern slides and cinematograph view

The Air Battalion enjoyed only a short, but eventful, life since on 13 May 1912 the Royal Flying Corps was formed. No 2 Company Air Battalion evolved into No 3 Squadron RFC, the first to use aeroplanes. B-K [as he was always known in the RFC] became one of the first army pilots to be attached to the Royal Flying Corps and one of the most prominent aviators in the British Army. Captain F H Sykes was given command of the RFC and his first adjutant was Lieutenant B H Barrington-Kennett who made a vow that the Royal Flying Corps should combine the smartness of the Guards with the efficiency of the Sappers.

In his memoirs *'Flying Fury'*,[17] written before his death in 1918, the flying ace James McCudden VC wrote of Basil:

> The RFC at this time [June 1914] was very efficient and highly disciplined. This is due to the fact that the original N.C.O.'s of the RFC were largely transfers from the Guards, the Adjutant, Lieutenant Barrington-Kennett being a Guardsman.

Flight 25 May 1912 RFC reports:

> On Friday, the King specially visited the headquarters of the Royal Flying Corps [Aldershot] and the Royal Aircraft Factory [Farnborough]. Their Majesties were received by Major Sykes, the new Commandant of the Military Wing of the Royal Flying Corps, who presented Capt. Burke, Capt. Loraine and Lieuts. Fox, Reynolds, and Barrington-Kennett, together with Mr De Havilland.[18]

Basil married Rhoda Violet Hargreaves, the eldest daughter of Captain Hargreaves of Remenham Park, Wraysbury, Buckinghamshire [now Berkshire] on Wednesday 8 January 1913. The wedding ceremony, which was conducted by the bride's uncle, the Reverend Cuthbert Trower, was held in St Andrews Church, Wraysbury and the reception at the bride's home. One newspaper article[19] records that there was a large number of guests, which included many of Basil's RFC colleagues and 'Colonel' Samuel Franklin Cody, one time showman and aeroplane inventor, who was to be killed only a few months later whilst demonstrating a new aeroplane at Fleet in Hampshire.[20]

War followed quickly and by August 1914 B-K was in France as Adjutant and Quartermaster-General of an RFC advance unit. He was clearly extremely competent for during the same year he was promoted to Staff Captain and then to Brevet Major.

The first RFC Commander was General Sir David Henderson and in 1914 his friend Maurice Baring (poet, author and man of letters) persuaded the General to take him to France as his Private Secretary. General Hugh Trenchard took over from Henderson in 1915, but Baring remained at headquarters as Trenchard's right-hand man until the end of the war. Baring kept diaries and letters from those historic years and in 1920 wrote *Flying Corps Headquarters 1914-1918*, a detailed account of the daily life at RFC headquarters as it moved around northern France.[21]

During his time in France, Maurice Baring became great friends with Basil who was also based at headquarters. Adjutant Basil's responsibilities included personnel and discipline, but it was a desk job and he did not fly for the RFC again. Headquarters was moved from time to time and was often no more than a small house. The two friends regularly dined together and often shared a room, talking well into the night. They travelled together to buy food or to search for potential new aerodromes. They occasionally drove to Paris to visit the French War Office or one of the banks; they even went to Epernay to buy champagne for the officers' mess. On another occasion, as the HQ was being moved to Abbeville, the Daimler being driven by B-K with his passenger Maurice Baring broke down close to their destination. Baring records:

> We were held up for hours, B.K. slaving and toiling on his stomach under the car, and as it grew darker and darker the driver got keener and keener on pulling every bit of the engine to pieces. Finally we were towed into Abbeville by an ambulance, and arrived after eight and went to the Hotel de France, thoroughly exhausted and hungry.

Shortly afterwards they moved again to a little château close to St Omer where they remained until the end of the war.

> We sadly overcrowded this house. In the office B.K. used to sit at one table [a card table], Salmond at another rickety piece of furniture. Brooke-Popham had a second small card table for his work, which soon became littered with papers. The Sergeant-Major sat on a box in front of other boxes … The bedroom downstairs was Brooke-Popham's. Upstairs General Henderson had one big bedroom and a small office. Salmond, B.K. and I shared a second.

> I shared, as I have already said, a bedroom with B.K. and Salmond, and we often had a guest or two sleeping on the floor. After going to bed we used to brew tea in a small kettle, and we used to talk and talk till late in the night. We used to get up about seven, and we always sang songs while dressing.

On 7 February 1915 B-K caught influenza and was confined to his bed, but he insisted on continuing work. The next day he was moved to hospital and remained there until the 11th when he returned to England to convalesce. Together with his wife he spent his convalescence in a hotel at Sidmouth. Here he received a letter from his friend Major Geoffrey Salmond and on 25 February B-K replied in light-hearted mood:

> I saw the General [Sir David Henderson] when I first came back and told

him I wanted to leave. He was very nice and offered me a Squadron. The call of my Regiment is too strong, however. You see it is quite different for you, as there are plenty of Gunner officers to go round allowing for a nice surplus. I was offered the adjutancy of the Welsh Guards with the bait of considerable seniority, but I refused. It would have been interesting work in peacetime, but at the moment it would mean being tied to this country for at least three months. Hope to get out with the 1st or 2nd Battalion [Grenadier Guards] early next month. You must pay me a visit in my dug-out, and bring Victor and a select party. Yours ever B.K.[22]

Although clearly it was B-K's decision to return to his old regiment, in his diaries Maurice Baring suggests that:

When he [B-K] had fully recovered from his bad attack of influenza the doctor had told him that office work was bad for him. So he applied to go back to his old regiment.

The departure of B-K was undoubtedly a personal loss for Baring but perhaps a greater loss for the RFC. Again Baring writes:

B.K. had been one of the first pilots in the Flying Corps before the war. It is impossible to state too strongly what a loss his departure was to the whole Corps. He had himself laid the foundation of a certain tone; he had always been keen about instilling a certain spirit, and although there was nobody less of a martinet, he had always insisted on the extreme importance of discipline. He had recruited from the Guards a nucleus of excellent non-commissioned officers, and had thus established a solid frame-work of tradition and sound principles, which in a new Corps dealing with a new weapon, and a weapon such as the aeroplane and with all the qualities and defects which flying must necessarily entail, was, of course, of vital importance. His influence was great, and time and again I heard pilots say: "B.K. says we ought to do this or that".

Major Barrington-Kennett returned to the Grenadier Guards on 1 April 1915, joining the 2nd Battalion, which was in the 4th Guards Brigade, 2nd Division, in the Givenchy sector. On 16 April Maurice Baring went to Bethune to visit him:

He was out when we arrived at the billet. But we waited until seven o' clock, when he came in. We had a long talk. He wanted to know how to cook cauliflower. This was the last time I was to see him.

In early May B-K was commanding No 3 Company preparing for the Battle of Festubert. Early on the morning of 17 May the men were close to the front line awaiting further orders. These came through around 1pm when the 2nd Battalion was sent across country to another part of the line close to Le Touret. Progress through the maze of old British and German trenches was slow because after heavy rain the ground was deep in mud and the many shell holes were full of water. In addition they had to negotiate heavy shelling and raking machine-gun fire. It was dark before the battalion reached the front line, which was about 800 yards from the eastern edge of Festubert.

The following day the 2nd Battalion was ordered to attack the German line at Cour l'Avoue (a farmhouse bristling with German machine guns) at 9.30am, but bad weather delayed the attack until 4pm. Only No 3 Company was to attack the farmhouse, with advances to be made in short quick rushes by platoons. The ground was very flat, with no cover from the enemy machine guns, and the men had no real chance of reaching the German trenches some 600 yards in front. The first platoon was mown down before it had covered 100 yards and the second and third suffered similar fates. Leading his men in the first rush the thirty-year-old Major Barrington-Kennett was killed instantly with several other officers under his command.

Lt Oliver Lyttleton (subsequently an MP and President of the Board of Trade) with the 3rd Battalion Grenadier Guards was present during the attack and later wrote home:

> By looking over the top which I did sparingly, I could see the attack. On the extreme left, perhaps 800 yards away, I could see British infantry pushing forward in rushes of about a platoon extended to three or four paces. The Germans were bursting wooleys [high explosive shell] right on the parapet of the hastily thrown up trench: nearer to me I could see a platoon of Grenadiers doubling forward thirty yards at a time whilst two platoons kept up a hot fire from the trench to cover them. It was a stereotyped attack and as far as I could see perfectly executed …. An hour later heard: "Attack is held up by machine-gun fire, the Irish are not getting on on the left, no sign of the Canadians on the right. One company [No. 3] has got forward 250 yards but have been badly cut up. Major Barrington Kennet is killed".[23]

The official war diary of the 2nd Battalion Grenadier Guards[24] records both Major Barrington-Kennett's arrival and death totally without emotion. The diary also records that 'Major Barrington-Kennett was buried at Le Touret'.

In contrast his great friend Geoffrey Salmond - who survived the war, was knighted, and became Chief of the Air Staff in 1933 - wrote home to his wife:

> One of the saddest things has happened. Barrington-Kennett, the one

2nd Battalion Grenadier Guards war diary entry 1 April and 18 May 1915. The National Archives

I was with at the beginning of the war, has been killed. It is so distressing, he was such a good fellow. I do wish he had never left us … It is due to him and him only that the spirit of the men in the RFC is what it is, everyone is grateful to him for it … Poor Mrs Barrington-Kennett – I am so sorry. I wish she could know what we all feel about him… What a stamp his personality, élan, and work has put on the Flying Corps, how all his hard work which he put in at Farnborough and out here has done for our country. Our Flying Corps is recognised by all nations as being the best and this is principally due to BK, he was such a good fellow.[25]

Maurice Baring wrote:

If ever a man deserved a soldier's death, to die leading the men of his own regiment into battle, it was BK. But of all the bitter losses one had to bear throughout the war, it was, with one exception, this particular loss I felt the most, minded the most, resented most and found it most difficult to accept. He was not an old friend of mine. I had never seen him before the war. But he was bound up with every moment of my life during the first months of the war, and I had got to know him intimately and to admire him more than others and to delight in his company more than in that of others. He had left the Flying Corps, and I should probably not have seen much more of him, unless, as would have perhaps been possible later, he had returned to it. But when this particular piece of news came I felt the taste of war turn bitter indeed, and apart from any personal feelings, one rebelled against the waste which had deprived, first the Flying Corps and then the Army, of the services of so noble a character. He was the most completely unselfish man I had ever met: a compound of loyalty and generosity and a gay and keen interest in everything that life has to offer. Not long ago I heard a little boy of eight years old asked if he knew what the word gentleman meant. He said, "Yes, of course." On being pressed for a definition he said: "A gentleman is a man who loves God very much and has beautiful manners." This definition exactly fitted B.K.

In his book *Flying Fury* (1918) James McCudden VC wrote:

Major Barrington-Kennett died gallantly in France commanding a wing of the Guards Battalion, having thrown up an RFC Staff appointment, with the certainty of promotion to Brigadier General, in order to do his duty to the Brigade of Guards, to which he belonged.[26]

The bravery and leadership shown by Major Barrington-Kennett in the hours before his death did not go unrecognised and he was mentioned in dispatches, published in the *London Gazette* on 22 June 1915.

Following Basil's posting to France, his wife Rhoda (she preferred to be known by her middle name, Violet) lived at her family's home in Wraysbury and it was here on 21 May 1915 she received the tragic news by the customary telegram:

To: Mrs Barrington-Kennett, Remenham, Wraysbury, Bucks.
Deeply regret Major B H Barrington-Kennett Grenadier Guards reported killed in action 10th May. Lord Kitchener expresses his sympathy.
From: Secretary War Office.[27]

War Office telegram to Mrs V Barrington-Kennett (digitally enhanced).
The National Archives

Major Barrington-Kennett was buried in Le Touret Military Cemetery, Richebourg-L'Avoué. The cemetery is less than a mile from the village of Le Touret, close to Bethune in the Pas de Calais. The grave reference is II. D. 13. He was awarded the 1914-15 Star, the British War Medal and the Victory Medal. Since Basil was mentioned in dispatches an oak leaf clasp is attached diagonally on the ribbon of his Victory Medal.

The battalion's Commanding Officer, Lieutenant Colonel Wilfred R A Smith, positioned behind a mound of earth with the support troops, was watching Basil leading his men as they attacked Cour L'Avoue when he was struck in the head by a bullet. He is buried next to Basil.

On 18 August 1915, at the request of the War Office, Mrs Barrington-Kennett completed a declaration of lawful marriage to obtain the army pension due to her. One of the witnesses to her signature on this document was her uncle, Lionel G Trower, at the time living at Tillington Hill, Tillington and working at, or for, the Remounts Depot in Petworth Park.

Mrs Barrington-Kennett duly received her army pension, dated from 19 May 1915, of £140 per annum with an initial gratuity of £300. Her pension was increased to £168 in April 1920 and again in October 1928 to £180 per annum.

The couple were only married for two years, but for Violet, Basil was undoubtedly the love of her life since she never re-married. The immediate years after the war must have been very difficult for her, for she not only had to come to terms with the loss of both her husband and her young brother Sydney who fell in Picardy in 1918, but also the rehabilitation of her elder brother Reginald who returned with severe war injuries. Nevertheless it appears that she and Reginald remained positive and in 1922 they founded the Wraysbury Scouts by purchasing a war-surplus hut and erecting it on leased land. The Parish Council took responsibility for the Scout hut when, in the mid 1920s, Violet left the village to join her mother at Fulmer Grange in Stoke Poges, Buckinghamshire. It is likely that she remained here until the death of her mother in 1940, when she moved to 'The Little House', Barnsley, near Cirencester, Gloucestershire. This house was next door to the village school (now the village hall). By this time Violet was fifty-two years old and although she had a car she seems to have travelled everywhere by bicycle, including shopping trips to Cirencester, a distance of nearly five miles. The bicycle, a 1934 BSA Ladies Roadster Model 420A, is still in existence, has been lovingly restored and now resides close to Stonehenge.[28]

In 1919/20 Violet presented a trophy to the newly established RAF Halton in memory of her late husband. It was a sporting award presented twice a year to the wing of aircraft apprentices gaining the highest points in a winter and summer sports competition. The original 'Barrington-Kennett' trophy (which unfortunately was stolen) was a solid silver replica of a Great War SE5 fighter aircraft with a twenty-four inch wing span mounted on an ebony plinth. After the theft it was replaced with a half-scale trophy.

From 1928 Barrington-Kennett silver medals were introduced for members of each winning team and those in bronze for individual achievement. There were four series of medals presented over a period of eleven years, after which the award of medals ceased. The first three series were made from solid silver, but the fourth was cast in bronze and silver-plated. Each medal depicts the original trophy and bears the inscription 'Barrington-Kennett Trophy'. The trophy and examples of the medals can be seen today in the Trenchard museum at RAF Halton.

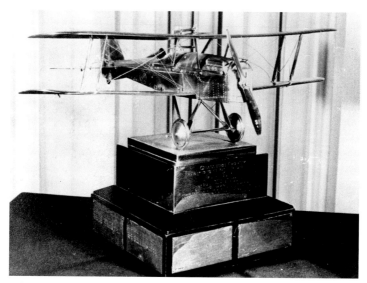

The original silver Barrington-Kennett trophy. Courtesy Derek Larkin, Trenchard Museum, RAF Halton.

In the early summer of 1953 Violet attended an RAF dinner at Boscombe Down in Wiltshire hosted by the Empire Test Pilots' School, based there since its inception in 1943. Air Chief Marshall Sir Robert Brooke-Popham, who was a squadron commander in the RFC contemporary with Basil, also attended the function. Violet presented the ETPS with some treasured momentos from her short married life with Basil - a beautiful silver slipper sugar bowl, a wedding present from 'Col' S F Cody; and a silver model of a Nieuport monoplane which was a wedding present from Basil's fellow RFC officers. On the tail is inscribed 'B4', the number of his monoplane. However, perhaps the most precious gift was the log book for the Nieuport monoplane B4. In his own handwriting this book records all Basil's training flights, together with his world record distance flight on 14 February 1912.[29]

Mrs Barrington-Kennett donates personal mementos to Empire Test Pilots' School 1953.
Flight 15 May 1953

In 1977 Violet died peacefully at her home in Barnsley, Gloucestershire at the age of eighty-eight and she lies in the village churchyard overlooking The Little House. The inscription on her headstone reads:

'In loving memory of
Violet Barrington-Kennett
1889-1977
And of her husband
Major Basil Barrington-Kennett,
Grenadier Guards and
Royal Flying Corps.
Killed in action in France 1915
Per Ardua ad Astra'

5

Major Victor Barrington-Kennett

Royal Flying Corps

Victor Barrington-Kennett was the third of four sons of Colonel and Mrs Brackley H Barrington-Kennett. He was born in London on 16 June 1887 and began his education at Ludgrove Preparatory School. He won a King's Scholarship to Eton (1901-1905) and accordingly lived in the most ancient part of the school, called College. He enjoyed an active school life and was a member of College Cricket Club and for two years played for College in the St Andrew's Day Wall Game. In his senior years he was elected to the exclusive club for elite prefects, the Eton Society (nicknamed Pop). Members wore a distinguished uniform to differentiate themselves from other students and those elected were often the College's top athletes.[1] Victor was certainly an excellent athlete and in the Wall Game it was said of him:

> a very weighty, strong third who has been quite invaluable in rushing loose bullies and kicks with great power.[2]

He became a great friend of George Butterworth, two years his senior. They had similar personalities and both were King's Scholars and members of the Eton Society and College Cricket XI.

In his final year at Eton, Butterworth became captain of the College Cricket XI and he was to oversee some excellent cricket performances, drawing one match and winning four. Butterworth's biographer, Anthony Murphy, notes: 'Butterworth usually opened the batting with a talented younger boy, Victor Annesley Barrington-Kennett, who was also now the regular wicket keeper'. In Butterworth's words the lad was 'a fine free bat, with a wonderful faculty of scoring off good length balls'.[3] A popular boy, tall fair-haired and athletic, Victor was one of only three Collegers elected to Pop in 1904, Butterworth's final year.

After leaving Eton in the summer of 1905, Victor was admitted to the Royal Military College, Sandhurst, as a 'Gentleman Cadet' for a course commencing at the beginning of 1906. After taking his summer examinations the records show that he was 'permitted to resign'.[4] He was an average student and no reason was given for his resignation but in late autumn 1906 Victor went up to Balliol College, Oxford. The college archive tells us something of his character and personality:

> Even at school he was big and impressive and in some ways grown up. He was intellectually, I suppose, behind the rest of his election, writes a friend and contemporary, but they all looked on him from the start as a sort of god - even strong minded people. I think he was quite amazingly unspoilt by the hero-worship he got; he had an odd, native kind of dignity, but he never carried any side.[5]

It continues:

> When he came up to Balliol in 1906, it was much the same. 'B-K' could take, whenever he wanted to, a leading position, though he cared little about it. With all his humour and boisterousness there was an odd shyness of manner which made his fun all the more infectious; there was also a good judgment and taste which prevented him going too far.

Victor Barrington-Kennett at Balliol College Oxford 1908. Courtesy Balliol College Archive

Surprisingly, since Victor did not row at Eton, he quickly joined the College Boat Club and soon made the first eight. At 6ft 1in and weighing 180lbs he was destined for the engine room of the boat, rowing at either No 4 or 6. According to Club records, 1907[6] was *an annus mirabilis* when, through the torpid races, the first eight won the title of 'Head of the River' and Victor's contribution

Victor Rowing in the College eight at No 6. Courtesy Balliol College Archive

was succinctly recorded: 'No 4 was a powerful oar with a good body swing and finish'. In 1909 the College fours won the Wyfold Challenge Cup at Henley with Victor rowing at No 2 and Hon Julian Grenfell, the poet, at bow. Victor continued rowing throughout his time at Balliol, eventually becoming Captain of the College Boat Club.[7] As soon as Victor had settled in to his new College he renewed his friendship with George Butterworth who was by now studying Classics in preparation for 'Greats' and to fulfil his father's ambition to see him train for the bar. George, however, wasted no time in taking advantage of the rich musical life in Oxford, including the University Musical Club, and he was swept up in the enthusiasm for the new folk-song movement. He had already been introduced to Housman's poignant verses in *A Shropshire Lad* by his friend Francis Jekyll, whose aunt was Gertrude Jekyll, and now wanted to collect more folk-songs. During the summer vacation of 1906 George and Francis searched the countryside of Sussex and Herefordshire for these old country songs. By this time Vaughan Williams had also befriended Butterworth and together they also would go on folk-song collecting trips.[8]

Butterworth had barely returned with Vaughan Williams from Norfolk when he was back in touch with Jekyll and the end of October found the two of them once again in Sussex. Using the Jekyll family home, Munstead, and their friend Victor Barrington-Kennett's family home near Petworth as bases, they went on to collect more folk songs from farm workers in Lurgashall and Rusper.[9]

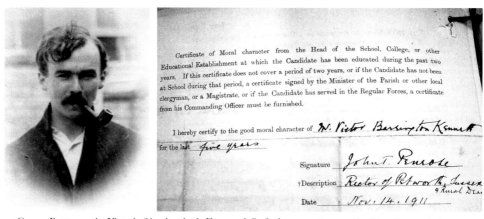

George Butterworth, Victor's friend at both Eton and Oxford. Photo by permission of Anthea Ionides.

Support for Victor's moral character. The National Archives

Victor graduated in 1910 and for a short period it appears that he was a banker with the Canadian Agency Ltd, living at 19 Cheyne Gardens, Chelsea. However, on 6 November 1911 he joined the London Balloon Company, Royal Engineers Territorial Force, as a Second Lieutenant. As part of his candidature for this commission the Rector of Petworth and Rural Dean, Reverend John T

Penrose, certified Victor's good moral character - a reference endorsed by the Master of Balliol.[10]

In early 1911 the Admiralty was becoming increasingly interested in 'powered flight' particularly at Eastchurch aerodrome on the Isle of Sheppey. It was soon offered the loan of aeroplanes to train Naval Officers to become pilots. Later in the year these facilities were extended to the London Balloon Company, RE Territorial Force, when two machines of the Farman type were lent to them.[11] This arrangement, however, failed to impress the War Office and on 5 February 1912 a letter was sent which included the phrase

> … it has been decided that personnel of the London Balloon Company should not be trained in aeroplane work.

Words which no doubt caused considerable embarrassment in the coming years. Fortunately Victor and three fellow officers managed to qualify before the restriction fully came into force.

Barely a month after joining the Balloon Company, *Flight* of 9 December 1911 records:

> Royal Aero Club flying ground ,Eastchurch,
> Mr. Barrington Kennett had his first experience of piloting from the passenger pilot seat of the new machine, from which, by a special dual control, a pupil is able to take charge at the will of the instructor. [12]

Just one week later the same magazine reports:

> Royal Aero Club Flying Ground, Eastchurch.
> On Wednesday there was an improvement [in the weather] and Mr. V. A. Barrington Kennett [of the London Territorial Balloon Corps] made his first solo flight on the 70-h.p. Short biplane. After making several short straight flights he took the machine up to about 70 ft., and at that height put in a complete circuit of the ground, making his first turn in a very neat manner, and finishing with only the slightest of "pancakes" quite close to some trees on the outskirts of the ground.[13]

After a well-earned break for Christmas, Victor lost no time in returning to his flying training:

> Royal Aero Club flying ground, Eastchurch,
> Mr. V. A. Barrington-Kennett, of the Territorials, and Mr. S. P. Cockerell were down on Saturday for the week-end, and got some fine practice on the School machine. Barrington-Kennett made what was really the "Territorial" flight of the week on Saturday, remaining in the air for nearly

three quarters of an hour, doing some sharp banking and figures of eight which would easily have gained him his pilot's certificate, and considering that he has only had charge of the machine on two previous occasions he has made wonderful progress.[14]

Royal Aero Club flying ground, Eastchurch, Lieut. V. A. Barrington-Kennett was down for the day and also flew for the last half of his pilot's certificate test on the Short dual-control biplane, completing the course in an excellent manner and landing very neatly.[15]

```
M.                                          190

  BARRINGTON-KENNETT, Victor Annesley.


Born  16th June, 1887,    at    London
Nationality  British
Rank or Profession   2nd Lieut. London Balloon
Certificate taken on  Short Biplane          Corps
At  Eastchurch
Date   5th March, 1912
```

Confirmation of Victor's Aviator's Certificate No190, 1912. The National Archives

On 5 March 1912 Victor qualified for Royal Aero Club Aviation Certificate No 190 flying a Short biplane.[16]

In her book *Too Close to the Sun, The Life and Times of Denys Finch Hatton*,[17] Sara Wheeler tells that in the summer of 1913 Denys met with an old friend:

That summer Denys took to the air himself. He went up with Victor Barrington-Kennett, a huge athlete and joker from a military family and a friend from both Eton and Oxford. Over the years Denys had enjoyed many days with Victor and his three brothers at the Barrington-Kennett home in South Kensington.

In later years Denys became an accomplished pilot himself, but it appears that his first flight was with Victor. Denys was immortalised in the pages of *Out of Africa* written by the Danish Baroness, Karen Blixen in 1937.[18] In the autobiography she tells of her love affair with Denys on the farmlands of Kenya; this was much later turned into a successful film with Robert Redford playing the part of Denys Finch Hatton.

In August 1913, Victor was appointed to the Royal Flying Corps Special Reserve and by August 1914 he was part of C Flight, No 4 Squadron.[19] The Squadron was based at Netheravon preparing to join the RFC Expeditionary

Force. The Squadron's A and B Flights made their way to the collecting ground at Dover and, with other squadrons, left for France on 14 August. Unfortunately C Flight consisted only of Maurice Farman 'Shorthorn' aircraft, which - because of their slowness and poor manoeuvrability - were not considered to be war machines and hence Victor and the rest of C Flight remained at Netheravon.

At the outbreak of war the Navy was responsible for guarding the British coast. As rumours spread about spies, mysterious vessels and potential Zeppelin raids the Navy realised that they could use the Maurice Farman machines left behind by the RFC to strengthen their patrols along the east coast of Britain. Hence C Flight moved to their new base at Dover as soon as the Expeditionary Force had left for France. It seems that a number of the transferring aircraft experienced trouble in making this journey. Two made forced landings somewhere near Dover and 'Farman 472 was wrecked by Second Lieutenant Barrington-Kennett whilst landing at Dover on August 21st'.[20] C Flight was used to patrol from North Foreland to Dungeness using their six Maurice Farman machines. The futility of these patrols was soon realised and they were abandoned after a few weeks.

Soon after the RFC Expeditionary Force began an active role in the war it was realised that more aircraft were urgently needed and in September 1914 the first major reinforcement began. Short of planes, the Maurice Farmans of C Flight were pressed into service. Four aircraft were shipped to France, probably via Southampton, early in the month, whilst two pilots flew their planes over the English Channel, re-joining No 4 Squadron at Fère-en-Tardneois close to Reims. Victor did not travel to France at this time because George Butterworth's diary for 28 September shows him to be at RFC Headquarters in Farnborough:

Sunday, September 27th.
A lovely day and pleasant rest. The morning casualty list contains the name of Aubrey Barrington-Kennett – the youngest and most loved of the family.

Monday, September 28th.
Another fine day: in the afternoon inoculations, the second dose. Afterwards I went over to Farnborough to see Victor BK, who is now at the Headquarters of the Flying Corps. We dined with his sister-in-law' [Violet].[21]

Sometime before March 1915, Victor joined the newly re-formed No 1 Squadron. During the winter of 1914-15 this squadron moved to Netheravon, received new planes and began training pilots. In January 1915 Major Geoffrey Salmond returned from RFC Headquarters in France to take command of the squadron. By early March it had been equipped with twelve new aircraft (four BE8s and eight Avros) and transferred to their new base at St Omer. Victor had also been promoted to Lieutenant.

We know that Victor was with the Squadron at St Omer because his brother Basil wrote to Major Salmond on 25 February congratulating him on his new command and saying:

> You must pay me a visit in my dug-out, and bring Victor and a select party.[22]

(By this time Basil had just requested that he be transferred from the RFC to rejoin his old Grenadier Guards Regiment).

On arrival at St Omer the Squadron was in action almost immediately in the battle of Neuve Chapelle. The first report of action contains the names of Capt. E R Ludlow-Hewitt and Lieutenants E O Grenfell, V A Barrington-Kennett and O M Moullin. Flying their B.E.8s, and carrying 20-lb bombs, they bombed the railway bridge close to Douai.[23] Soon after this mission Geoffrey Salmond wrote to his wife, Peggy:

> I am now staying with the Squadron, as I thought it best to live with them, though I was enjoying being at Wing HQ. I stay with 'B' Flight, i.e. with [Victor] Barrington-Kennett, Hewett and the others.[24]

In mid-April Nos 1 and 4 Squadrons left St Omer, moving forward to the airfield at Bailleul. By now No 1 Squadron was flying a 'rather mixed bag' of aircraft including three Avro 504s, four Morane Parasols and only one BE 8. This latter aircraft was in its final days of service when it took part in the first aerial combat recorded by the squadron. At the beginning of May whilst on a routine reconnaissance flight, Victor and his observer spotted an enemy aircraft over Lizerne. They chased after it but were unable to catch up, so climbed to 7,000 feet and dropped down on the aircraft when it turned. The observer fired several rounds with the plane's Lewis gun at close range. The enemy aircraft disappeared in a vertical dive towards a forest, but no claim was allowed because it was not seen to crash.[25]

From Maurice Baring's memoirs:

> On May 20th I went to No 1 Squadron at Bailleul commanded by Geoffrey Salmond. I had a long talk with Victor Barrington-Kennett.

(This was only two days after his elder brother Basil had been killed in action with the Grenadier Guards).

On 11 June 1915 Victor was promoted to Flight Commander, with the rank of temporary Captain, (*London Gazette* 25 June 1915), before being posted home at the beginning of July. So began a spell of instructing with No 2, No 1 and No 15 Reserve Aeroplane Squadrons (pilot training squadrons). Perhaps this return to England was a compassionate posting related to the death of Basil and to his younger brother Aubrey who was killed in September 1914.

In late 1915 Victor became the first (Acting) Squadron commanding officer of the newly formed No 15 RAS at Thetford in Norfolk, but before the end of the year he was preparing to return to the Western Front. In mid-January 1916 Victor was appointed Squadron Commander, 'to be Temporary Major whilst so employed,' and returned to France as Commanding Officer of his old No 4 Squadron which at the time was based at Allonville just to the north-east of Amiens. From the History of No 4 Squadron:

> January 17th 1916: received a new CO, Major V A Barrington-Kennett. Operations continued routinely until March 13 1916 when the CO Major Barrington-Kennett was killed in a Bristol Scout while in pursuit of an enemy aircraft. [26]

Although the Squadron was largely engaged in reconnaissance and artillery observation, it did have one Bristol Scout aeroplane to chase off enemy planes. Whilst pursuing a hostile aeroplane in his Bristol Scout No 4678, Victor was shot down and killed at 12.55pm on 13 March 1916. There is some confusion surrounding the exact cause of his death. The RFC Casualty Card states 'shot down by a direct hit from anti-aircraft fire', yet there is another report that suggests that he was brought down by rifle and machine gun fire. The report does not state whether this fire was from an enemy aircraft or the ground. There is, however, good evidence from a report in *Flight* that:

> … he was shot down by a German aeroplane during a fight in the air. He was flying alone when he met his death. [27]

Max Immelmann, the German Ace, always claimed that he shot down the Bristol Scout - referring to the aeroplane as his 10th victim. [28] This is now the most widely held explanation for Victor's death. Such was the sense of chivalry between opposing officers in the two flying corps that soon after Victor's death, a note was dropped from a German aircraft addressed to the RFC.

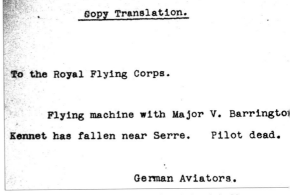

Message from German Aviators. The National Archives

To the Royal Flying Corps.
Flying machine with Major V Barrington-Kennet has fallen near Serre. Pilot dead. German Aviators. [29]

It is also known that he was buried with dignity by these same aviators in Miraumont Communal Cemetery, close to Albert.

The final lines of the Balliol College memorial to him read:

> BK with all his qualities of strength and courage and practical intelligence was a perfect soldier, one whose personality pervaded the Squadron. Soldiering must have been in his blood.

The following was written by an anonymous *Flight* columnist, 'The Dreamer', in May 1916:

> This week I read of Major V. A. Barrington-Kennett, previously reported missing, now unofficially reported killed. And I feel for his gallant father, Lieutenant-Colonel Barrington-Kennett, who by this death loses his third son in this war, leaving but one of four brothers fighting for their King. Poor "B-K," he was everybody's friend, and it grieves me that I shall never again see him stalking the plain at Salisbury, with a cheery word for all. Perhaps I, though humble and unknown, may yet be permitted to offer to his family my sincere condolences, and express the wish that at least the surviving brother may be spared to them.[30]

Finally we return to Victor's great friend, George Butterworth, who is perhaps best known for his song settings based on A E Housman's collection of poems from *A Shropshire Lad*. In a lasting tribute to Victor and perhaps the Barrington-Kennett family, written on the title page of the original manuscript of *Six Songs from a Shropshire Lad* (held by the British Library) is a dedication; '*To V.A.B.K.*'[31] This is such a poignant gesture to a close friend; a friendship cut so tragically short.

At the outbreak of the Great War, George Butterworth joined the army; he was mentioned in dispatches and awarded the Military Cross. Sadly he was killed in the Battle of the Somme in the early hours of 5 August 1916 and did not live to receive his MC or to fulfil the promise he showed as an outstanding British composer.

Major Victor Barrington-Kennett was awarded the 1914-15 Star, the British War Medal and the Victory Medal. Since he was mentioned in dispatches an oak leaf clasp is attached diagonally on the ribbon of the Victory Medal. He is buried in Miraumont Communal Cemetery in the village of Miraumont. The village is approximately eight miles north-east of the town of Albert in the Somme region of France. The grave reference is A.1.

~ **6** ~

Second Lieutenant Aubrey Barrington-Kennett

Oxfordshire and Buckinghamshire Light Infantry

Aubrey Hampden Barrington-Kennett was born on 8 September 1890 at Norrysbury, Cockfosters Road, East Barnet, the home of his mother's sister Catherine Annesley Malcolmson. However, the census shows that by 1891 Aubrey and his mother Ellinor had returned safely to the family home at 23 Sloane Gardens, Chelsea. When he was ten Aubrey returned to East Barnet to board at Ludgrove School where the headmaster, Arthur Tempest Dunn, was his cousin's husband.

After four years at Ludgrove, Aubrey moved to Radley College where he became a prefect and acted in the Latin Comedy *Rudens* (The Rope). The *Radleian* magazine of 23 November 1907[1] describes his performance:

> Mr Barrington-Kennett as Plesidippus had a slighter part than most of the heroes of Latin Comedy; he played it fairly but we should have liked it better if he had thought himself of more importance.

After Radley, Aubrey went up to University College Oxford and whilst there he joined the Oxford University Officers Training Corps (OTC). He became a Lance Sergeant in this unit and trained with the 2nd Battalion, Oxfordshire and Buckinghamshire Light Infantry at Aldershot for six weeks during the summer of 1912. On completion of his studies in December 1912 Aubrey left the OTC and, although he was nominated for an Army Commission, he declined and began a financial career with the Canadian Agency Ltd in London. (His brother, Victor, also spent some time with this Company in 1910 - it went into receivership in 1914). Like Victor, he soon came to regret this decision and on 7 February 1913 he completed an 'Application for Appointment to a Commission in the Special Reserve of Officers in the Oxfordshire and Buckinghamshire Light Infantry'[2] and persuaded his old adjutant at the University OTC to write a letter of support:[3]

> A boy called Barrington-Kennett, brother of the flying man, was nominated here last term for an Army Commission and suddenly chucked

it up, though he was fully qualified except for one group in his schools. He is now anxious to join the supplementary list of the Regiment he was going into, i.e., the 52nd [Oxfordshire and Buckinghamshire], but he has difficulty putting in his six months' training ... I find it pretty hard to get these fellows to come forward at all, and it appears that it is always the probationary training that keeps putting them off. At present I have two or three people nibbling at Commissions, but it is very hard to keep them to it. H M Wilson.

His application form for a commission in this regiment shows his permanent address as Tillington House, Petworth, his London address as 6 Princes Street, EC and his profession as 'Financial House of Business'. The form was completed in a fine hand and confidently signed. On 2 March 1913 Aubrey attended Queen Alexandra's Military Hospital in London for a medical examination.[4] He was twenty-one years old, nearly 6ft 1in in height and weighed 149lbs. His hearing was good and his teeth 'sufficient'. Clearly he was a tall, slim gentleman but the report does not say whether the 'teeth sufficient' referred to quantity or quality. On the same day he was commissioned as a 2nd Lieutenant in the Reserve of Officers of the Oxfordshire and Buckinghamshire Regiment. He completed his

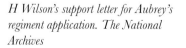

H Wilson's support letter for Aubrey's regiment application. The National Archives

Aubrey Barrington-Kennett in the uniform of the Oxfordshire and Buckinghamshire Light Infantry. Courtesy Radley College Archives

probationary training in late September 1913 and joined C Company of the 2nd Battalion soon after.

Aubrey was one of three young officers chosen to take the battalion colours to the regimental depot at Cowley, Oxfordshire on 5 August 1914 for safekeeping while the regiment was fighting on the Western Front. A week later, after being inspected by King George V, his battalion left Albuhera Barracks, Aldershot, and travelled by train to Southampton. At 8pm that evening the men embarked on the SS *Lake Michigan* for Boulogne and arrived in the early hours of the next morning.[5]

I certify the above answers to be correct, and I request that I may be appointed to the

Supplementary Special Reserve, Oxfordshire & Buckinghamshire L.I.

AH. Bavington Kennett.

(Usual signature of Candidate.)

Date February 7th 1913.

Signature of parent or guardian, if the Candidate is under 21 years of age.

Aubrey's signature in a fine hand. The National Archives

As part of the 5th Infantry Brigade, 2nd Division, the battalion immediately moved to the Western Front in Belgium to take part in the first British battle of the war at Mons. After hard fighting the British were eventually forced into 'The Retreat from Mons', which lasted for two weeks and took the army to the outskirts of Paris before the substantial counter-attack at the Battle of the Marne (5-9 September 1914).

As the German First and Second Armies began to retreat, the Allies hastily pursued them, making contact on the evening of 13 September close to the River Aisne. In dense fog that night most of the British Army crossed the river on pontoons or partially demolished bridges and assembled around the small towns of Bourg-et-Comin and Venizel. The 2nd Battalion Ox and Bucks Light Infantry crossed in the late afternoon on a pontoon bridge at Pont Arcy and by the evening of the following day the men had reached the liberated village of Soupir, close to Soissons in Picardy.

At noon on 16 September, C and D Companies were resting in a large cave when, around 5pm they were called forward to support front line troops. Just as C Company was emerging, a large German shell burst in their midst, killing three officers and eight men, but Aubrey survived unscathed. Three days later, the battalion moved into the front line trenches. First into the trenches at La Cour-de-Soupir farm were A and D Companies and although they spent a quiet first morning, in the early afternoon the German artillery opened up on the trenches and continued for six hours. B and C Companies were sheltering in the caves in reserve but they began to move towards the front line as the enemy were preparing to attack. They were shelled all the way from the caves to the farm and incurred several casualties including Aubrey, who was seriously wounded.[6] Lieutenant Colonel Davies' diary records:

A few were hit between the farm and the caves, and unfortunately Evelegh and Barrington-Kennett were among them. The former was killed outright. The latter, though badly hit, refused to allow the men to carry him to the cave in which the dressing-station had been established. When eventually brought in, he was very cheerful, though rather badly wounded in the neck, jaw and back. He was got away to hospital at night but the next day he died at Vieil Arcy.[7]

Captain G Blewitt noted in his diary for 19 September:

I was hit by a shrapnel bullet just below the eye at about 3pm, and Harden put on my first field dressing. By the time the show was over, my face was beginning to get painful, so I went back to the second cave, which was our hospital, to see Thurston, the doctor. The cave was a mass of wounded and horrible. Here I found poor Barrington-Kennett, terribly wounded, and I lay down beside him, as he preferred me to the orderly, and I did what I could for him. The Colonel came and saw us, and was very kind. At 11pm the horse ambulance came up, and we drove to Vieil Arcy'. 'September 20th – [Vieil Arcy] The doctor took off my first field dressing about 11.30am….Poor Barrington-Kennett died about 12.30pm after having his arm off.[8]

On Saturday 26 September Basil Barrington-Kennett, who was with the Royal Flying Corps at St Omer, heard that his brother was missing. Maurice Baring (a friend of Basil) wrote in his diary:

B.K had got news two days previously that his brother, in the Oxfordshire and Buckinghamshire Light Infantry, was missing and wounded, and wanted to go to an advance hospital to get news…I went with B.K. to Braine, Bourg and beyond. On the way we passed Sir Douglas Haig on horseback with his escort. He stopped us and asked where we were going. B.K. satisfied him. After a long and very roundabout drive we came to a small field hospital. B.K. went in and I waited outside. As I was waiting a shrapnel shell burst in the middle of the road we had just left. After a short interval a second shell burst in the field beyond the hospital, and then a third somewhat shorter. B.K. came out. I said laughing "we are being shelled." Then I saw he had just received news that his brother had been killed. He had been buried in the little cemetery a few yards off. We went to look for the grave and found it. His grave with some others was freshly dug; flowers on it and a neat wooden cross. B.K. saluted. I left him there alone two or three minutes by himself; then we drove away. A third shell burst on the road.[9]

Today 2nd Lieutenant Aubrey Hampden Barrington-Kennett lies at peace in Vailly British Cemetery, close to the small town of Vailly-sur-Aisne, on the north bank of the River Aisne and eight miles east of Soissons. The grave reference is II.E.8. The cemetery was made after the Armistice when graves were brought in from other burial grounds and from the battlefields. Most of those buried here died in September 1914 and many were originally interred at La Cour-de-Soupir.

2nd Lieutenant Aubrey Barrington-Kennett was awarded the 1914 Star with bronze clasp (this clasp indicates that not only did the recipient serve between 5 August 1914 and midnight on 22 November 1914, but that he had actually served under fire during this period), the British War medal and the Victory Medal.

Ellinor Barrington-Kennett wrote this poem, *In Remembrance*, commemorating her youngest son:[10]

The 'Cour de Soupirs' place of Sighs
Engraven on our heart it lies
For there our dear and youngest son
The wreath of laurel bravely won.

When the morning's rosy ray
Ushered in the new born day
Beyond the reach of mortal sight
His pure young spirit took its flight.

We laid him in the orchard's shade
And with the peasants' kindly aid
We decked his grave with flowers
Fresh waking in those morning hours.

The headstone for Second Lieutenant Aubrey H Barrington-Kennett in Vailly British Cemetery, France. © Author's collection

7

Private Albert Bailey G/17779

Royal Sussex Regiment

Albert Henry Bailey was born in the late spring of 1895 in Tangmere, near Chichester, to Henry and Charlotte Bailey and was one of three children. His mother died at the age of 41 in the summer of 1906 and his father remarried the following year. His new wife was Mary Elizabeth Sarah Haslett from Tillington and the family moved into Tillington Hill where Henry became a domestic gardener. Both of Mary's parents were dead: her father George had been a master baker and grocer with premises in Upperton, but he had died in the winter of 1886; her mother, who with Mary had continued to run the business, died in 1902. By 1911 Albert, aged fifteen, was a 'carpenter's assistant' living at home with his father, stepmother and sister Edith

From his Army Medal Roll we know that Albert enrolled in the Royal Sussex Regiment. Like most young recruits from Tillington he probably made his way to the Petworth Armoury to join D Company of the 4th Battalion. His Army Service Number was 2202 suggesting an enrolment date of late September to early October 1914. Although his early training would have been with the 4th, he transferred to the newly formed 2/4th when the senior battalion was posted to Gallipoli in July 1915. There is no record of why Albert did not sail for Gallipoli with his battalion, but since he joined a territorial battalion he was only committed to serving on the home front and not overseas.

Albert's medal roll. The National Archives

By the middle of 1916 voluntary recruitment had seriously declined and could not keep up with the desperate need for reinforcements. Conscription had been introduced in the spring for single men up to the age of forty-one, but by May it had been extended to include married men. This urgent need for more reinforcements also put pressure on officers of the territorial battalions to urge their men to sign the Imperial Service Obligation, agreeing to serve overseas. Private Albert Bailey probably signed this agreement during 1916, just before he was posted to the 12th Battalion Royal Sussex Regiment in the 39th Division.[1] The division had been fighting on the Western Front since March 1916, but since Albert did not join them until the early autumn of that year he was spared the horrors of the Battle of Boar's Head close to Richebourg L'Avoué.

This battle is worthy of note since it is little known outside the County of Sussex. It was fought on 30 June 1916 and has been called 'The Day Sussex Died'. The division had received orders to attack the German lines on the Boar's Head salient (so named because the line of trenches created resembled the head of a boar). This attack was planned to deflect German attention from the huge offensive about to take place on the Somme. The full-scale assault, led by the 12th and 13th Battalions Royal Sussex Regiment supported by the 11th of the same regiment, lasted less than five hours and was a disaster. The Germans had known for several days of the impending attack and many 'Southdowners' were cut down by machine-gun fire as they crossed open land. The 13th was nearly eliminated and the 12th suffered 429 casualties, almost fifty percent of the battalion. This futile attack left the regiment in urgent need of reinforcements, but it was not until early September that the 12th Battalion was restored to near full strength.

The records of a Private George Balkham[2] show that he embarked at Folkestone on 12 July 1916 and travelled via Boulogne to Etaples on the French Coast. Here he was trained in trench warfare and conditioned for the harsh, dangerous life at the front. On the first day of September he was posted to the 12th Battalion with the service number G/17792. Since Albert's 12th Battalion number was G/17779 he was most probably in the group that included Balkham. The medal rolls show that several men from the 2/4th Battalion had numbers close to G/17779, suggesting that a large group transferred to the 12th at the same time to provide much-needed reinforcements. Albert reached his new battalion sometime between 5 and 12 September when 300 reinforcements arrived in three drafts. At this time the 39th Division, including the 12th Battalion, had returned to action during the Battle of the Somme, attacking enemy positions close to the villages of Englebelmer and Auchonvilliers, north of Albert. The battalion, now including Albert, continued fighting on the Somme until 13 November when they moved via Doullens to Poperinghe in Belgium, arriving five days later. Here the men spent an extended training period until they were ordered closer to Ypres in early December. During the next eight months the men settled into an uneasy routine comprising front line duty, night-time trench maintenance and training or resting at one of several camps.

Although the British had held Ypres throughout the war, the German Army occupied much of the high ground south of the city. From these positions the enemy artillery had a good view of the Allied front lines and continually shelled them and the city. Before any advance through Belgium was possible these guns had to be silenced and so in early June a campaign was planned which became known as the Third Battle of Ypres—often referred to as Passchendaele. A precursor to this campaign was to eliminate the guns on the Messines Ridge. To do this the British had secretly been digging mines under the German positions and by 6 June 1917 twenty-one mines had been filled with a million tons of explosives. In a coordinated effort, on 7 June, all the mines were detonated together at exactly 3.10am. Many German troops were killed outright and others were dazed and stunned, allowing the British to take most of their objectives before nightfall.

The campaign proper began at 3.50am on 31 July when, after an intensive bombardment with some 3,000 guns, several divisions including the 39th attacked the German lines close to the village of Passchendaele. The three Sussex Battalions attacked together from positions close to Hill Top Farm only two miles from the centre of Ypres. In spite of heavy resistance and mounting casualties, the 12th secured their objectives and by 8am the 13th had captured the village of St Julien. The division, was relieved in early August and transported by train to a safe rest camp over the French border, fifteen miles from the front. In addition to rest, perhaps this break also provided time for Albert and others to reflect on the horrors now behind them and to be thankful that they had survived thus far. After a much-deserved break the men returned to the front on 12 August, but did not take part in the next two battles of the campaign (Langemarck and Menin Road).

By late August all three Sussex Battalions had been moved to the front lines south of the Menin Road in a sector called 'Tower Hamlets' in preparation for the next phase of the campaign, the Battle of Polygon Wood, due to start on 26 September. During the first three years of the war this whole area had been churned up by constant fighting and regular artillery fire. These bombardments had also destroyed most roads in the area making the movement of supplies to the front extremely difficult and dangerous. All trees had been destroyed by 1917, making Polygon Wood a wood in name only and without any protection. The objective of the offensive was to capture high ground on both sides of a stretch of the Menin Road lying to the south - an advance of some 1,500 yards.

The attack began at 5.50am on the misty morning of 26 September with the 11th and 13th Sussex leading the advance and the 12th in support. Under the cover of the artillery barrage the infantry made some progress, advancing through Tower Hamlets to the surrounding high ground. This limited success came at a tragically high cost as the enemy shelled the battalions throughout the day and met them with heavy machine-gun fire. The 12th Battalion was moved up to reinforce the attack and they too suffered badly. The men, however, were able to consolidate their gains and the battle ended the next day after several counter attacks were crushed by British artillery fire.

The 116th Brigade war diary records:[3] '1.20pm 26th Sept - Informed Division that all units had suffered heavy casualties, especially 11th R.S.R., but had gained objectives'.

In addition the 12th Battalion war diary also mentions the casualties for the period 23-27 September: 'officers: 2 wounded, other ranks: 48 killed, 117 wounded and 26 missing'. Private Albert Bailey, G/17779, was killed in the Battle of Polygon Wood on 26 September, most likely from machine-gun fire. He is buried in Tyne Cot Cemetery, six miles north east of Ypres and within the grounds of the Tyne Cot Memorial. The grave reference is XLIV. G. 37.

Private Bailey was entitled to the British War Medal and the Victory Medal.

Private Albert H Bailey's headstone, Tyne Cot Cemetery, Belgium. © Author's collection

8

Private Austin Bartlett G/1369

Royal Sussex Regiment

Austin George Henry Bartlett was born in Compton, Devon in 1895. In 1901 the family was living in Royal Field Artillery Barracks at Newport, Monmouthshire where his father, John Austin Bartlett, was a Sergeant Master Cook. He was posted to Bordon Camp in Hampshire and both Austin and his brother Kenneth desperately wanted to follow him into the Royal Field Artillery. It appears that the camp provided this opportunity, since young boys were being enlisted. Kenneth was the eldest and, on 1 April 1908, at the age of fourteen years and three months, he signed his papers for the Royal Field Artillery. Kenneth fought on the Western Front throughout the war reaching the rank of Warrant Officer Class 1 and was awarded the Good Conduct Medal and the Military Medal. He remained in service until early 1931 when he returned to civilian life.

Private Austin Bartlett. De Ruvigny Roll of Honour

Austin was also keen to join the army at an early age and on 19 May 1909, aged fourteen years and five months he enlisted in the Royal Horse and Field Artillery for twelve years. The previous day he had been examined by Captain Kiddle, an RAMC doctor and pronounced 'fit for the Army'. He was 5 feet 2¾ inches in height and weighed just 91lbs. His Army rank was listed as 'Boy'.[1] One year later he was discharged as medically unfit for further service. No details of his condition were given, but it could not have been too serious because a year later, now seventeen, he was a wagoner on a farm. The 1911 census also shows that the family was now living in Hawkley, near Liss in Hampshire. Austin's father had become an army pensioner and commercial traveller selling boots and clothing. His mother, Emily and sister Constance were both living at home looking after the house.

Austin Bartlett is listed on the Tillington Roll of Honour[2] for the fallen of the Great War, but there are no records of where he lived or any date of his residence in the parish. As the April 1911 census shows him working in Hawkley and he enlisted at Petworth in September 1914, he must have moved to Tillington between these dates.

Austin made his way to the Petworth Armoury and enlisted in the Royal Sussex Regiment. This would probably have been D Company, 4th Battalion but no records exist until after his training when he was posted to the 2nd Battalion as Private Austin Bartlett G/1369. This battalion formed part of the British Expeditionary Force and had been in France since August 1914. Austin's medal card[3] shows that he sailed for France on 11 January 1915. This was the same day that the 2nd left the trenches close to the railway embankment and canal in Cambrin, close to Bethune and moved a few miles north to the village of Cuinchy (or Guinchy) where they endured heavy shelling. Austin most probably reached his new unit on the afternoon of 13 January in a draft of 210 reinforcements. The battalion war diary records:

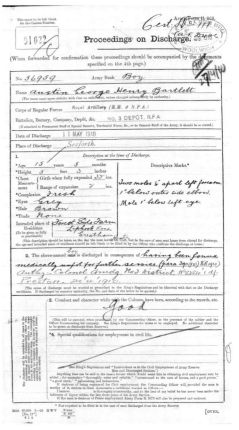

Austin's Army discharge paper. Ancestry.co.uk

A draft of 210 arrived at 2.10pm + Lt Gramshaw[e]. These went straight into the trenches when they arrived from Annequin where they had billeted the night before. All Kitchener's August recruits. They seemed to be a good lot.[4]

With the battalion closer to full strength it continued duty in and out of the trenches, usually being relieved by the 1st Battalion, Loyal North Lancashire Regiment, but on 21 January they moved to billets in Bethune for an extended rest period.

War diary for 23 January – Bethune
At 9.30am first company [A] went to bathe at an establishment started in Bethune by RAMC for washing each Bde [Brigade] as it comes out of the trenches. The men hand in their dirty underclothes and are given

a new set and also have their khaki ironed to kill any vermin that may have accumulated during a month of unwashed state. The men were enormously cheered up by their bathes - we got 2½ Coys done by 3.30 when clean underclothes ran out and we had to stop. [5]

Unfortunately the rest period ended abruptly when on 25 January the battalion awoke to the sound of heavy enemy artillery fire. They received orders to move at once to Cuinchy where the Germans were attacking. The 2nd Sussex was sent forward in late afternoon to reinforce the defending troops, and drove the enemy back, re-taking ground lost earlier in the day. For this decisive action the battalion received special congratulations from Brigadier General Westmacott, Commander of the 2nd Infantry Brigade.

The winter of 1914-15 was cold, wet and muddy and the ground was often hard with frost. The men lived mostly in the open, which left them vulnerable to conditions such as frostbite and trench foot. Austin was one of these men since on 3 February 1915 he was invalided home with frostbite. After recovering he returned to the Western Front in early October, probably passing through the base camp at Etaples where he was posted to the 9th Battalion, Royal Sussex Regiment, which was resting near Proven in Belgium. In November the battalion marched to new billets in Houlle close to St Omer, in France. Here they spent the whole of December well away from any front line, but early in the New Year the unit returned to Belgium and encamped near Poperinghe. The men went into front line trenches near Hooge on 11 February where at first, things were relatively quiet. Two days later the Germans started a heavy bombardment that lasted eight hours and caused much damage including thirty casualties. Austin was killed instantly by an enemy shell.[6]

The De Ruvigny Roll of Honour[7] provides a more personal account of Austin up to the time of his death. An officer wrote (to his parents):

> I am writing to you on behalf of Capt O'Beirne, the Commander of the Company to which Private A Bartlett belonged. He himself is suffering from a nervous breakdown after the strain of the last week, but he wanted me to tell you how he feels with you in your terrible grief, and how proud he was to have Private Bartlett in his company and Sergt F Barnard [also said]: He was killed - death being instantaneous - on 13 Feb by a shell. We were being subjected to a severe bombardment: Private Bartlett was killed between 12-2 in the afternoon.

Private Austin Bartlett G/1369 is buried close to Ypres in the Menin Road South Cemetery, grave reference I. G. 3. He was awarded the 1914-15 Star, the British War Medal and the Victory Medal. His back pay and war gratuity amounting to £10. 5s. 1d. were sent to Emily, his mother.

9

Corporal Percy Boxall 21502

Royal Flying Corps

The parish history of the Boxall family goes back at least to 1816 when Percy's grandfather was born. His namesake son, James, was born in Tillington in 1864. At age seventeen James was a bricklayer's labourer but over the next ten years he rose to become a bricklayer while living with his parents at Little Common, Tillington. In the year of the 1891 census he married Emma Knight (born in Shalford, Surrey in 1867) at All Hallows' Church on 4 October and they moved into their new home on the Midhurst Road, Tillington (probably Little Common). By 1901 they had a family of five children, including Percy Charles born in autumn 1893 and christened at All Hallows on 26 November 1893.

By 1911 James had prospered, setting up his own building company and moving the family to a larger house called 'Fir Grove', on the edge of Tillington. Apart from a splendid view of the South Downs, the property included several acres of land, ideal for a builder's yard. The census classes James as a builder, his eldest son James William (eighteen-years-old) as 'assisting in the business' and Percy (seventeen-years-old) as a carpenter. This was the beginning of the very successful and long-lasting Boxall Builders.

Percy Boxall in Tillington Church choir 1912.
Courtesy Tillington PCC

On 21 September 1914 Percy made his way to the Armoury at Petworth where Lord Leconfield was the honorary recruiting officer securing recruits for the Royal Sussex Regiment. Percy enlisted in the 4th (Reserve) Battalion, Royal Sussex Regiment. His attestation papers[1] show that this was part of the Territorial Force and he signed on for four years' service in the United Kingdom. He gave his occupation as 'carpenter joiner in father's employ'. It is strange that his attestation papers stated that he joined the reserve battalion, since at this time there was only one 4th Battalion and it was not until January 1915 that a second reserve battalion was formed.

The army career of Private Percy Boxall 4/2181 began at Horsham where on 22 October he signed the Imperial Service Obligation agreeing to serve overseas. On the last day of the month, together with several other men, he was posted to the senior (1/4th) battalion at Newhaven where it was part of the coastal defences in the event of a German invasion from the sea. Whilst at Horsham, Percy was clearly very pleased that football was a popular pastime during rest periods. Accordingly he wrote home to his parents on 29 September:

Dear D & M
I have received the box, thank you very much, the fruit is lovely. Do you mind sending me my football things viz boots, knickers, stockings, jersey (blue and white), and shin guards. We are having a football team.
Love Percy.[2]

Team games were promoted during training both to encourage the young soldiers to meet each other and more importantly to engender a sense of camaraderie—so vital for the horrors to come. Football seemed to be taken more seriously after the battalion's move to Newhaven, where there was a newly formed 4th Battalion Football League.[3] The league comprised eight teams, A to H, one from each Company (and hence recruitment area) and D Company (Petworth) no doubt expectantly awaited the arrival of Private Boxall's kit.

From the records it appears that the battalion was just able to finish the 1914-15 football season but, once it became clear that there was little chance of a coastal invasion, the battalion was taken into the 160th Infantry Brigade, 53rd (Welsh) Division, and on 24 April 1915 it moved to Cambridge and then Bedford for further training before being sent overseas. On the second day of July 1915 orders arrived to re-equip for service in the Mediterranean and two weeks later the battalion entrained for Devonport. Here, with the rest of the division, they boarded HMT *Ulysses* and set sail for Alexandria and then to Mudros, a port on the Greek island of Lemnos, for a landing at Suvla Bay, Gallipoli.

The British troops who landed at Suvla Bay on 6/7 August 1915 were poorly co-ordinated, lacked leadership, and achieved few of their military objectives in the high hills surrounding the bay. One objective, Scimitar Hill, had been taken but was quickly lost, taken again and lost for a second time. Battalions of the 53rd Division, including 'The Sussex' landed on C beach in the early hours of 9 August and later that morning, after three weeks at sea, the raw soldiers were thrown into the midst of yet another attempt on the hill. By this time, however, the scrub on the hillside was ablaze causing serious casualties and forcing a total withdrawal.

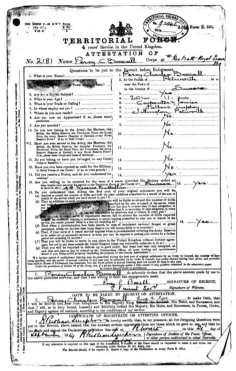

Percy's attestation paper for 4th Battalion Royal Sussex Regiment. Ancestry.co.uk

A postcard home from Percy. Courtesy Dave Lewis

In addition to the extreme terrain and the strength of the enemy, disease soon set in and quickly swept through the troops causing many deaths and proved to be as dangerous as the front line.

> Conditions on Gallipoli defy description. The terrain and close fighting did not allow for the dead to be buried. Flies and other vermin flourished in the heat, which caused epidemic sickness ... Of the 213,000 British casualties on Gallipoli, 145,000 were due to sickness; chief causes being dysentery, diarrhoea, and enteric fever.[4]

At the end of September Percy was one of many to contract dysentery and although he was initially admitted to the 19th General Hospital at Alexandria in Egypt, a month later it was decided that he should be returned to the UK. He was carried aboard the Hospital Ship HMHS *Asturias*, arriving home on 8 November where he continued hospital treatment.

HMHS *Asturias* had been requisitioned from the Royal Mail Steam Packet Company in August 1914 and became one of the largest hospital ships. Once called into war service, she was painted in hospital colours and refitted to carry swinging cot beds for 1,200 patients and was usually based in Southampton. In March 1917, *Asturias* was returning to Southampton after discharging patients at Avonmouth when she was attacked by a German submarine and struck by a torpedo that destroyed one of her propellers and the rudder, as well as flooding the engine room. Although she was sinking, the Captain managed to beach the ship off Salcombe, Devon.[5]

In January 1916 Percy returned to the Reserve Battalion Royal Sussex at Cambridge until 4 March. On that day he was technically discharged from the Territorial Force, at his own request, so that he could re-enlist in the regular army to join the Royal Flying Corps, which at that time was part of the regular army. His discharge papers read 'discharged in consequence of re-enlisting into RFC at Cambridge. Character: very good'.[6] The day after his discharge he enlisted, for the 'duration of the war' in the RFC. As a skilled carpenter he became 'a carpenter for rigger' at a pay rate of two shillings per day.

He was posted to RFC Central Flying School at Upavon, Wiltshire, where he must have found plenty of work adjusting and repairing the wooden framework of early aeroplanes regularly crashed by trainee RFC pilots. The main training aircraft was the Avro 504, a biplane with two cockpits to accommodate the instructor in the rear and the pupil in the front cockpit.

For the next eighteen months Percy enjoyed a relatively uneventful period, no doubt enjoying his work, making new friendships and proud of his promotion to Corporal. Tragically all this came to an end when on the morning of Wednesday 19 December 1917, when only twenty-four years old, he was killed on the airfield at Upavon. An inexperienced pilot of an Avro 504 lost control of his aircraft as he taxied and his left wing collided with the left wing of a Moraine aeroplane that was about to take off. Corporal Boxall was steadying the left wing of this plane (the right wing being steadied by another airman) as is usual for take off and he was crushed between the two wings, killing him almost instantly.

The details of this tragic accident were printed in the *Western Gazette*, Yeovil, on Friday 28 December 1917:[7]

FLYING FATALITY AT UPAVON - TWO MACHINES IN COLLISION
The Central Flying School, Upavon, was on Wednesday week the scene of a fatal accident.

Corporal Percy Charles Boxall, R.F.C. aged 24, was killed by the collision of two aeroplanes while on the ground. An inquest was held on the body at the Hospital, Central Flying School, by Mr F.A.P. Sylvester, the County Coroner for Mid-Wilts, on Thursday. Mr F.G. Hampton was elected foreman of the jury, and P.C. West, Upavon, acted as Coroner's officer.

Sergt Wilson R. Hoffmaster, RFC said that the accident occurred on the south tarmac. Witness was standing by the right wing of a Morraine aeroplane, which was about to be taken up for a flight. The engine was being tested before going up. Deceased was standing by the left hand plane. It is customary for those holding an aeroplane to watch the pilot who by lifting his hand gives the signal for "All clear", when the machine is immediately loosed. The first intimation witness had of the accident was seeing the pilot rise in his seat. There was a crash immediately afterwards on the deceased's side of the machine. Witness had not time to realise what was happening. He did not see the actual collision, but just saw deceased fall dead. Witness said that the force of the collision swung the Morraine right round, and he only had sufficient time to jump clear. Questioned by the Coroner, witness said that no-one else was seriously injured: one man was struck by splinters.

Second Lieut. Harry Wearne, R.F.C., General List, said he was the pilot of the Avro machine which ran into the Morraine. His machine was one in a line of machines which were being used for flying. It was next but one in the line to the Avro. He had been instructed to "taxi" out and go up for a flight. There was hardly any wind blowing at the time. Witness gave the signal for "All clear" and began to "taxi" out. He was ordered to go straight ahead, but after a few yards, his aeroplane unaccountably made a sudden swerve to the right, and before he could avoid the accident he crashed into the Morraine machine. The left wing of his machine struck the left wing of the Morraine, pinning deceased between the two. Witness did not see deceased struck. He himself was not hurt. In reply to the Coroner, witness said he thought that the machine got out of his control, and before he could do anything the accident had happened. He was an inexperienced airman and there were so many things to be done that before he could find the switch and stop the machine the crash had come. Witness thought probably the machine swerved round because the rudder was wrong. He had only made one solo flight before. Earlier in the day, on that occasion, he got off fairly well. The Coroner said that evidently witness had made an error of judgement. He said he should have attended to the steering of his machine.

Lieut. John Morecombe, R.F.C., said he was a flight instructor and had ordered the previous witness to make a flight. His instructions to him were to "taxi" out, see all clear, and get away. Questioned by the Coroner, witness said that when going out the engine should be alternatively switched on and off, and not kept full on. Witness started the aeroplane in the right direction for the pilot, but turned it off. Witness saw the crash, and noticed a man fall.

Capt. James Keenham, R.A.M.C., said deceased was dead when he arrived. The injuries were to the chest and head. There were no fractures. Death was instantaneous, and was caused by pressure and shock.

The Coroner exonerated the pilot from blame, and hoped that his future flying career would not be affected, and that he would be free from any further mishaps of the kind. No doubt he had made an error of judgement, but involuntary action connecting the brain with muscles is only acquired after long practice.

The jury returned a verdict of 'Accidental death', caused by being crushed between two aeroplanes.

Corporal Percy Boxall's body was returned to Tillington where he was buried in the cemetery beneath a stone cross, carved with the initials of the Royal Flying Corps. Later his parents were laid to rest alongside his grave.

Percy was awarded the 1914-15 Star, the British War Medal and the Victory Medal.

Percy's headstone in Tillington cemetery. © *Author's collection*

10

Private Arthur Bridger 92115

Nottingham and Derbyshire Regiment

Arthur Bridger was born in the parish of Tillington around 1 April 1891. The census of that year shows his parents - James, an agricultural labourer and Elizabeth - living at River with their children Charles, Annie and four day old Arthur. It must have been an exciting day for the family when, on Sunday 31 May 1891, the Reverend George Shaffen christened Arthur James in All Hallows' Church, Tillington. Ten years later the family was still living at River, daughter Lizzie had been born and Charles, now fourteen-years-old, was a labourer on a local market garden. Arthur was ten years old and presumably at school, although there are no records for him at Tillington School.

The 1911 census shows Arthur lodging with William Knight, the local baker and confectioner, in Lombard Street, Petworth. Both he and his friend, Horace Lucas, were employed as baker's assistants. (Horace went on to serve with the Norfolk Regiment; he was very seriously wounded and died in December 1915).

Kitchener's fourth army was formed in late 1914 and, in addition to soldiers, it needed men to keep them supplied with all the essentials of life as well as guns and ammunition. This was the role of the Army Service Corps (the Royal prefix was added in late 1918) and hence the recruiting sergeants were always on the lookout for cooks, bakers, caterers and so on. Using horse-drawn and motor

Lombard Street, Petworth. © The Francis Frith Collection

vehicles, railways and waterways, these unsung heroes performed prodigious feats of logistics and were one of the great strengths by which the war was won.

In early May 1915, no doubt encouraged by his job as a baker's assistant, Arthur travelled to Aldershot where he listened intently as a graphic and colourful role in the Service Corps was explained to him by a persuasive sergeant, at the end of which he eagerly enlisted and left the recruitment office as Private Arthur James Bridger S4/093362; the S stood for 'Supply' and the '4' for Kitchener's fourth new army. Tradesmen were enlisted into the Supply Section for their skills such as a clerk, baker or butcher, and given the number prefix 'SS'. Those not experienced but showing an interest in a trade were also enlisted with the prefix 'S'. We know that Arthur was a baker's assistant, but did this mean that he was learning the trade or that he delivered bread to the baker's customers? His early army service would suggest the latter. Only four months after joining the Corps, Arthur went to France where initially he was no doubt with a Field Bakery unit well behind the front lines. His Medal Index Card[1] states that Arthur was a driver, but this is not consistent with his S4 number prefix since most motor drivers in his unit had the prefix M or MT.

Perhaps Arthur revealed that he could drive a horse and wagon and was, without changing his service number, transferred to another unit that transported supplies closer to the front lines. We know from other soldier records that service numbers within the Army Service Corps were rarely changed when a soldier was moved or gained further qualifications within the corps.

The next record of Arthur shows that he was posted to the 11th Battalion, Nottingham and Derby Regiment (The Sherwood Foresters or the Men from the Greenwood), becoming Private 92115.[2] This service number suggests that he was transferred to the Regiment in July 1917. The circumstances for the change are not clear, but if he had been wounded and repatriated for a period of recuperation, on his return he would have passed through a base depot from where he could be transferred to any regiment. The 11th Battalion, Sherwood Foresters was involved in the opening day of the Somme offensive on 1 July 1916 and suffered such grievous losses that it was relieved the same night. The battalion continued to be engaged for the rest of the year but by early 1917 was in desperate need of reinforcements. It is, therefore, highly likely that Arthur was posted to the 11th Battalion in a contingent of reinforcements in July 1917. His medal roll shows that other soldiers from the Army Service Corps were drafted into the 11th Battalion at the same time. Among the officers of the battalion was Captain Edward Brittain.

In November 1917 Arthur moved with the battalion to Italy to assist the Italians facing the German/Austrian offensive. On 15 June 1918, the Austrian Army launched a surprise attack with a heavy bombardment on the British front line on San Sisto Ridge, north of Vincenza. Captain Brittain led his men in a counter-offensive and had just regained the lost positions when he was shot through the head by a sniper and died instantly.[3] Edward was the beloved brother of Vera Brittain and his death was the final tragedy in her *Testament of Youth*,[4] one of the most famous Great War memoirs. Vera died in 1970 and her will requested that her ashes be scattered on Edward's war grave in an Italian village near the ridge where he was killed.

Soon after Edward was killed Lieutenant Colonel Hudson led a counter-attack with the remaining men of the 11th Battalion, saving the situation and earning a Victoria Cross for outstanding bravery and leadership.[5]

The Sherwood Foresters returned to France in September 1918 where they joined the 74th Brigade in the 25th Division. At this time the division was being rebuilt after suffering huge losses during May and June and the 11th Battalion was one of several battalions drafted in to bring it up to strength.

During October 1918 the division fought in the Battles of Beaurevoir and Cambrai, the latter taking place in and around the city between 8 and 10 October. This battle was an overwhelming success with light casualties. The Sherwood Foresters, with the rest of the 25th Division, were relieved during the night of 11/12 October and rested at Prémont whilst being re-organised, reinforced and refitted. The men were, however, soon on the move again when, at 5.20am on a very misty October morning, the fourth army attacked on a ten-mile front south of Le Cateau. The aim was to reach the Sambre and Oise Canal, but progress was difficult and after two days only a few units had managed to advance five miles. The first and third armies were then brought into action north of Le Cateau and on 20 October they advanced two miles. A night attack with all three armies three days later was more successful, advancing six miles in two days and putting the British troops twenty miles beyond the Hindenburg Line.

The Sherwood Foresters played little part in the early action but were in position by 23 October, making their contribution to the six mile advance. During this operation the division liberated the village of Pommereuil and cleared the Bois L'Eveque, resting only when they reached the outskirts of Le Cateau. They advanced through the town along the Le Cateau to Basuel Road where they dug in for the night. The 11th Battalion war diary takes up the story:

> At 04.30 hours the Brigade moved forward to attack in the same formation as the previous day. A tank which was understood to be assisting in the attack did not materialise. Upon reaching the starting point heavy machine-gun fire was encountered. Shortly after the attack commenced the battalion came across a belt of barbed wire and when passing through this, heavy machine gun and sniper fire caused most of the casualties incurred in the day's fighting.[6]

The casualties on 24 October were four officers wounded, 15 other ranks killed, 55 wounded, and 8 missing. Private Arthur Bridger 92115, aged 27, was one of the fifteen killed. Arthur is buried in Pommereuil British Cemetery in the village of Pommereuil two miles east of Le Cateau: grave reference E.13. His back pay and war gratuity amounting to £27. 10s. 4d was sent to his father James in River.

Private Arthur James Bridger was awarded the 1914-15 Star, the British War Medal and the Victory Medal.

11

Private Thomas Bridgewater G/17765

Royal Sussex Regiment

In 1891 the Bridgewater family were living on the Upperton Road, Tillington, in what must have been a large house because already William and Fanny Bridgewater had six children and were also accommodating two lodgers. By 1901 the family had grown by another four children, including Thomas George, who was born early in 1897 and christened at All Hallows' Church on 28 March of that year.

Interestingly, Thomas was enrolled at the Tillington Village School at the early age of three years and eleven months on 22 October 1900. His admission record shows that he was born on 3 January 1897 and his admission number was 742. He walked down the Upperton Road every morning for ten years on his way to the village school and no doubt on occasion bought a few sweets at the shop next to the school. He left school on 23 December 1910, just eleven days before his fourteenth birthday. Thomas did not follow his father and brothers in becoming a farm labourer. Instead the 1911 census shows that he was employed as a house painter.

It is probable that sometime in late November 1914 Thomas, perhaps with several friends, was caught up in the excitement of the recruiting campaigns and towards the end of his seventeenth year he walked into Petworth and enlisted, initially for four years, in the Royal Sussex Regiment. He would have been posted to a territorial unit of this regiment and from his service number, 2988, it was mostly likely D Company of the 4th Battalion. He probably completed his initial training with the 1/4th Battalion at both Horsham and Newhaven. However, in late April 1915 the battalion moved to Cambridge to complete its training before sailing to Gallipoli, in July. At this time Thomas was still too young to go overseas, so was transferred to the 2/4th Reserve Battalion.

During 1916 the reserve battalion was stationed at Belhus Park Camp in Essex, where Thomas received a postcard, possibly from a girlfriend, telling him that she had arrived safely at Lewes. The postcard was addressed to: Pte T G Bridgewater No 2988, 2/4 Batt, Royal Sussex Regiment, C Company, Belhus Park Camp Aveley, Purfleet, Essex.[1]

On 28 July 1916 another soldier, Private Arthur Fitt, 4569 of E Company sent a postcard to his wife from the same camp confirming that 2/4th Battalion was still at Belhus Park Camp during the summer months. His service records[2] have survived and have been documented by his grandson, Peter Cox. From these records Peter found that Private Fitt left England, most likely with a large group of reinforcements, for France on 7 September 1916. Their first stop was the Etaples Training Camp, close to Boulogne, where many fresh troops were prepared for the horrors of the Western Front and life in the trenches. Later the

same month Private Fitt was given a new service number G/16024 and posted to the 13th Battalion, Royal Sussex Regiment, a battalion desperately in need of reinforcements following the terrible casualties suffered by the 11th, 12th and 13th Battalions during the Battle of Boar's Head at the end of June.

Postcard to Thomas giving his battalion and location.
Courtesy Charles Thompson

Unfortunately Thomas's records have not survived but his movements appear to mirror those of Arthur Fitt. Thomas was also posted to the 13th Battalion, with a new service number G/17765, which can be dated to September 1916. It is likely therefore, that he also left England with the same group of soldiers, trained for a short time at Etaples and then was posted to his new battalion on 19 September, reaching it the following day. The war diary records the arrival of the draft:

> Redan Ridge – 20. 9. 16. A draft of 201 other ranks reported for duty and were taken on the strength. This draft remained at transport lines Bertrancourt under Brigade orders. [3]

At this time the battalion was in the front line and it was not uncommon for reinforcements to be held with the transport until the battalion had been relieved. Here the newcomers could be brought up to date with the current situation facing their unit and shown the routes used to get to and from the front line. The 'transport' was a very busy and popular place with stores, mobile ovens, reserve ammunition dumps and often a tailor's shop. It was also a mobile farm with over 50 horses and mules together with unofficial dogs and cats. Medics would often send men needing a break back to the transport to enjoy the familiar company of animals. Newly arrived men, however, were soon moved into the battalion ranks:

Redan Ridge – 22. 9. 16. Draft of 201 men moved to Mailly-Maillet and were detailed for working parties.

Redan Ridge – 23. 9. 16. Draft joined the battalion. Artillery on both sides active.

In the afternoon a German mortar fell on a trench killing nine soldiers, eight of whom had just arrived with the draft. Thomas was not among them.

During the first part of October the battalion remained in Mailly-Maillet but on 15 October the 116th Brigade (all three Sussex Battalions, together with the 14th Hampshires) crossed the River Ancre making their way towards the formidable German stronghold called the 'Schwaben Redoubt' which was built on a ridge above Thiepval and now largely in British hands following continued attacks by several Allied divisions between July and early October 1916. 'Stuff Trench', however, remained the last German foothold in the redoubt and, with other battalions, the 13th was tasked with capturing it. Preparations for the attack began on 17 October and four days later everything was ready. From the 13th War Diary for that day:

> The Battalion proceeded to the right sub-section of the Redoubt Section preparatory to the attack on Stuff Trench which was to be made in conjunction with the 11th Batt Royal Sussex Regt. At 11am B and C Companies moved up from Schwaben Trench in artillery formation and on reaching Bainbridge trench extended in 3 separate lines on a frontage of approximately 250 yards … At 12.06pm the artillery commenced and our men advanced very close up to our artillery barrage and entered Stuff Trench in perfect line. In the main not much opposition was encountered except on the right flank … and here some opposition was met with but after some 40 minutes determined bombing this was overcome and the whole of Stuff Trench and the Communication Trench were in our hands. For the rest of the day the captured position was heavily shelled but no counter-attack was launched by the enemy.

Although the assault was over quite quickly, both sides sustained heavy casualties, particularly the 11th Battalion. The 13th War Diary records: 'Our casualties were not unduly heavy; officers wounded 3; other ranks killed 25, wounded 71, missing 30'.

Private Thomas Bridgewater, aged nineteen and having spent less than two months on the Western Front, was one of the twenty-five courageous men killed in this attack, which was part of the Battle of Ancre Heights, in turn part of the Battle of the Somme, a battle that symbolised the horrors of warfare. He now lies with friends from the battalion in the tranquil Grandcourt Road Cemetery, near the village of Grandcourt, some seven miles north east of

Albert in Picardy, and close to the old line of Stuff Trench. This small village cemetery is isolated in the middle of a field of cereals and is only accessed by crossing two fields with similar crops. Standing at his graveside one is poignantly reminded of the fields surrounding his home village of Tillington. The grave reference is B.5. Private Bridgewater was awarded the British War Medal and the Victory Medal.

12

Private William Bryder TF/260042

Royal Sussex Regiment

William Bryder was born in Tillington, to William and Alice Kate Bryder of Tillington Hill, in the winter of 1897. He was confirmed at All Hallows on Wednesday 27 November 1912. His father was born in Croydon, moved to Sussex and became a carpenter/joiner and undertaker in Tillington. The 1911 census shows William aged thirteen living at home with his parents but now having moved to Park Terrace, Tillington. On leaving school at the age of fourteen it is likely that William joined his father as an apprentice carpenter.

Unfortunately we know little of his wartime service as his record has not survived. In September 1914, however, when William was only seventeen-years-old and underage for the army, he managed to slip his way into the 1/4th Battalion, Royal Sussex, probably via the Petworth recruiting centre. Official policy was that a man had to be eighteen to sign up and nineteen to fight overseas but in the early twentieth century most of the population did not have birth certificates so it was easy to add a few months to one's age. As two shillings and sixpence (the equivalent of £6 today) was paid to the recruiting officer for each new soldier, a blind eye was no doubt often turned.

William became Private Bryder 2212 and was probably posted to Newhaven in late October 1914 where, in case of an invasion from the sea,

William Bryder in the uniform of the Royal Sussex Regiment. Courtesy Bill Bryder

the 1/4th Battalion was guarding key installations including the harbour.[1] The successful recruiting campaigns of late 1914 and 1915 meant that more training battalions were needed and one of these was the 2/4th Reserve Battalion, formed at Horsham in January 1915. When, in August, the senior battalion was mobilised and set sail for Gallipoli,[2] William was still under age to fight overseas and hence was posted to the home-based reserve battalion. A Christmas card to his parents revealed that he was still serving with the 4th Battalion in late 1916.[3]

In 1917 all territorial force soldiers were given new regimental numbers and William was allotted the number TF/260042. This is within a range of numbers allocated to the 5th Battalion of The Royal Sussex Regiment in the first weeks of 1917, rather than the 4th Battalion. Therefore we know that in the early weeks of 1917, the year he reached his nineteenth birthday, William was posted to the 5th Battalion (48th Division), which had been fighting in France since 1915.

The 5th Battalion war diary gives few clues to the movement of reinforcements during 1917 except to complain that they were too few:

31st August 1917, Canal Bank, Ypres
Reinforcements badly needed as effective working strength getting very low – 2 platoons having practically disappeared. [4]

William's stay with the 5th Battalion was a relatively short one, for in November 1917 the complete 48th Division moved to Italy. For some reason William did not travel with it but was posted to C Company of the 7th Battalion, Royal Sussex Regiment (12th Division), either at the end of a rest period near the pretty village of Veil Hesdin, Pas de Calais, or more likely towards the end of the unsuccessful Battle of Cambrai, in which the 7th played an important role. There is little detail of the movement of reinforcements in the battalion war diary, but an entry for 28 November 1917 suggests that 109 other ranks joined the unit to increase the battalion strength following a number of futile attacks after the main battle.[5]

From photographs of William in uniform, with the crossed flags insignia sewn onto his lower left sleeve, we know that at some point he became a signaller (a trade, not a rank) in his battalion. We cannot be sure when this was, but he may have been trained in signalling while with the 4th Battalion and was fully qualified by the time he joined the 5th.

The Royal Engineers were responsible for communications at the highest levels of command (Army Corps and Division) but in a battalion, signallers carried out these duties. William's duties would involve communicating between battalion headquarters, company and platoon commanders in the trenches. Although a much-prized job, it was also a highly dangerous one, since signallers had to make sure their telephone lines were maintained and repaired, even when enemy artillery was bombarding the battalion front lines.

In his diary, *A Signallers War*,[6] Sergeant Bernard Brookes comments that during training in August 1914:

> I had a stroke of luck … I had been appointed a Signaller for E Company [Queen's Westminster Rifles] … A Signaller does no digging, guards, fatigues or dirty work; although when the Battalion is resting he has cycling duty and other work connected with signaling … started to master the mysteries of Morse Code and Semaphore…. and with the aid of a map we had to find our way through certain lanes to a given point.
>
> On Sunday the 20th September I had leave to go home and fetch my cycle, having been informed that it would be purchased from me for military purposes, and left in my care. [to carry out his duties]. The next day I was offered by Army Officials the sum of £5 for my bicycle and I was quite willing to accept this amount.

In *Old Soldiers Never Die*[7], Private Frank Richards recalls his exploits as a Signaller with the Royal Welch Fusiliers. For some reason Frank had several times turned down the opportunity to become a signaller, but in July 1915 he was given no option and joined the battalion signallers:

> There were at this time eighteen signallers to a battalion, with a sergeant in charge; in the front line there were generally three signallers in each company and the remainder in Battalion Headquarters …. Signallers were also runners. Each station had its D3 telephone, which was a small portable instrument which could be used for speaking or sending Morse. We sent all our messages in Morse, which was quicker and more accurate than speaking them. The noise of battle and artillery fire close to the front line usually made voice communication impractical and hence Morse Code was mainly used. All companies and Battalion Headquarters were linked up [via telephone wires] …. In sectors where there was plenty of strafing, the lines would often get broken and many a good signaller went West in the act of repairing a broken wire … A signaller's life on the whole was far more pleasant than a rifle-and-bayonet man's.

Telephone wires usually ran through the communication trenches from battalion headquarters to the front line trenches, where signallers would send and receive messages and orders relating to how the battle was progressing. Unfortunately these lines would often be broken by artillery fire and it was the responsibility of signallers to repair them, whatever the danger. They also had to act as runners, carrying messages by hand through machine-gun fire and artillery bombardment. It is no surprise then that the life expectancy of a signaller was rather short.

After the somewhat futile Battle of Cambrai, in early December 1917, the 7th Battalion was relieved and moved by train, bus and marches to Cochendal - a rest area behind the front lines where the men could bathe, train and prepare for Christmas. With preparations well in hand the battalion hoped they would not be moved before the celebrations. Unfortunately, however, this was not to be since on 23 December the whole brigade was moved by route march to an area close to the village of Berguette, midway between Aire and Lillers. The Christmas fare - pigs, turkeys, geese, beer, fruit, etc, which had been purchased from canteen funds sometime earlier - was ordered to be thrown away before the move since the transport was only for regulation loads. Needless to say many of the provisions, including pigs, found their way to the new billets and the battalion spent a very happy 'holiday' with Christmas dinner being served in the small school of a nearby village. According to the battalion war diary, a Boxing Day route march was organised to work off the effects of the previous day's celebration. William sent his parents a Christmas card.[8]

The battalion spent the early part of 1918 in Doulieu where the men settled into a routine of front line duty and rest. At the beginning of March it left the area and moved into brigade reserve close to the railway station in the village of Sailly-sur-la-Lys in Nord Pas de Calais. Towards the end of the month the enemy became more active with increased artillery bombardments, including gas shells, suggesting that the German Command was planning some form of attack. Indeed they were, for on 21 March a major German offensive (Operation Michael) began and the battalion was immediately ordered to Steenbecque, to the east of Lille. Two days later the men were warned to leave all surplus stores and kit and prepare for an immediate move. It was clear that something big was looming and the following day they marched to Burbure, near Lilliers, where the brigade was concentrating its forces. After fifteen miles the men reached their destination and at 9pm the same day they boarded buses ready for a further move, though delays meant that the column of buses did not set off until close to midnight. As the column moved to the south of Arras, the appalling seriousness of the situation became clear as they met a defeated British Army. On 21 March the Germans had launched an attack on a front of forty miles, from Le Fère to Vimy, Nord Pas de Calais. This attack eventually succeeded and by late on 24 March when the 7th Battalion, as part of 36 Brigade, reached the battle area, the enemy was surging all over the countryside and chaos reigned. The men managed to reach their destination of Warloy about 9am the next day where they rested in a field. All too soon they moved on again and after passing to the east of Albert, 36 Brigade took up a position north of Aveluy to hold the crossing points over the River Ancre (C and D Companies in the front line, A and B Companies in support).

Soon after midday on 26 March enemy troops were spotted advancing down the slopes into the Ancre valley. By 11.30pm that night they had broken through on the left of the sector and by early the following morning they were attacking on the battalion's right. The war diary recounts:

> Aveluy Wood, 27/3/1918. About 9 am the enemy attacked on our right &
> the Bn on our right fell back. A Coy formed a defensive flank along the S
> edge of Aveluy Wood & later B Coy were also put in on the right flank to
> bridge a gap between D & A Coy. The Bn was now formed on 2 sides of a
> square – C & D facing E & A & B facing S. About 5 pm enemy attacked on
> the whole front & succeeded in breaking into the wood at the S. E. corner.
> A Coy retired slightly, killing a large number of the enemy. 2/Lt Rogers
> was taken prisoner but succeeded in escaping. D Coy retired to BN HQ
> which were at Quarry Post. The attack was held up at Bn HQ which were
> temporarily surrounded.

In *The British Campaign in France and Flanders, January to July 1918*, [9] by Sir
Arthur Conan Doyle, the author refers to the fighting around the battalion
headquarters on 27 March:

> The Germans, by a most determined advance, drove a wedge between
> the Berkshires and the Sussex [7th Battalion], and another between the
> Sussex and the Fusiliers, but in each case isolated bodies of men continued
> the desperate fight. The battle raged for a time round the battalion
> headquarters of the Sussex, where Colonel Impey, revolver in hand,
> turned the tide of fight like some leader of old. The losses were terrible,
> but the line shook itself clear of Germans and though they attacked again
> upon the morning of March 28, they were again beaten off.

Several enemy attacks were repelled by the 12th Division during this 'First
Battle of Arras', a battle which halted the German advance but one in which the
division suffered heavy losses. On 31 March the German offensive was paused
to allow the men two days rest. The shortage of reserve troops, ammunition
and equipment, however, made it impossible for them to continue the advance
and on the evening of 5 April the German Commander, General Ludendorff,
brought Operation Michael to an end. In one days fighting (27 March) the 7th
Battalion lost 23 of their number and tragically Private William Bryder of C
Company was one of these men.

Sir Arthur Conan Doyle paid a poignant tribute to the courage of the
12th Division during the desperate fighting around Arras when he said:

> Late that night [28th March] …. The whole of the 12th Division was
> now rested for a time, but they withdrew from their line in glory, for it is
> no exaggeration to say that they had fought the Germans to an absolute
> standstill. [10]

We can be sure that William showed great courage in his final hours and although he was never found, he is commemorated on the Pozières Memorial, close to the village of Pozières some four miles north-east of Albert in Picardy. The memorial reference is Panel 46 and 47.

William's inscription on the Thiepval Memorial, Belgium. © Author's collection

Private Bryder was awarded the British War Medal and the Victory Medal.

~ 13 ~

Private Harold Budd 164431

Canadian Infantry

When Harold Budd's father, John, married Lucy in February 1876 he was nineteen-years-old and working on his father's farm in Fittleworth. Some years later the couple left their home village when John became the miller at Lods Bridge Mill, Lodsworth. At this time they had two children, John Basil aged three and Edith Lucy who was just a few months old and sadly destined not to see her second birthday. By the time of the 1891 census John had changed his employment, becoming a farmer and surveyor of highways, and the family had grown larger with daughter, Hilda, aged five, and three-year-old Harold George. Home was now Malt House Farm, Selham. Interestingly, by 1901, John had reverted back to his old employment of 'Corn Miller' and returned to Lods Bridge Mill. At this time Harold was in his last year of school and no doubt wondering whether to join his father as a miller or look for something more exciting to do with his young life.

Lod's Mill, Lodsworth, Sussex. Unknown

We cannot be certain of Harold's decision but at some point before 1911 he did seek more excitement, or perhaps independence, and became a railway ticket collector, boarding with a signalman and his family at Railway Cottages,

SS Tunsian. © *Copyright expired*

Lyminster, Arundel. By 1913 life was becoming a little dull once again and so Harold decided to emigrate, to 'the land of opportunity'. On 21 March 1913 he boarded the SS *Tunisian* at Liverpool with ticket No 58860[1] and set sail for Halifax, Nova Scotia. We don't know why he decided to emigrate to Canada, but some seventy-five years earlier in 1835, under the Petworth Emigration Scheme, there was a passenger called Budd who sailed from Portsmouth on the 402-ton barque *Burrell* to Quebec[2] and another who sailed from the same port on 28 April 1836, arriving in Quebec on 5 June.[3] Hence Harold may have been joining family already living in Canada or perhaps he was caught up in the rush to emigrate there during the early part of the new century.

Canada had long been seen as the land of opportunity and between 1901 and 1911 the total population increased by nearly two million through immigration. Immigration peaked in 1913 with 400,870 people stating that they were coming to the country to farm. Although Harold's stated intention was to become a gardener he, like so many other immigrants, became a farm worker.

We know little of his employment in Canada but over the first two years Harold travelled the 820 miles from Halifax to Hamilton. It was now 1915 and on 27 September he relinquished his farming career and enlisted in the Canadian Army. According to his military papers Harold was already in the Volunteer Militia (2nd Dragoons, C Squadron) when he enlisted. On 4 October he was posted to the 84th Battalion, Canadian Expeditionary Force (CEF) as Private Harold Budd 164431. His medical examination revealed that he was five feet six inches tall with a ruddy complexion, blue eyes, fair hair and tattoos on each forearm. On his attestation form[4] he gave his town of birth as Petworth and his next of kin as living in Tillington. Strangely Harold gave his age as twenty-five and his date of birth as 28 December 1890, whereas he was actually twenty-seven years old.

With war casualties mounting, Canada was called upon to train and send more battalions to England as quickly as possible. The 84th Battalion, raised on 10 July 1915, was one of these units. The men of the battalion were initially transported to Halifax where, on 18 June 1916, the SS *Empress of Britain* awaited their arrival. A voyage of eleven days brought them safely to Liverpool where Harold was immediately transferred in a draft of 750 men to the 75th Battalion Canadian Infantry (Mississuaga) and transported to Bramshott in Hampshire (some fifteen miles from his home village of Tillington). On 13 July he made his military will, stating 'In the event of my death I give the whole of my property and effects to my Father Mr John Budd, South Lane, Tillington, Petworth, Sussex, England'.[5]

After eleven days training in the area, the 75th Infantry arose very early on 11 July and marched to Liphook in two sections to catch the 5.30am and 6.30am trains for Southampton. On arrival the men made their way to the embarkation sheds where they rested. At 5pm the same evening they boarded the steamship *Mona's Queen*, which weighed anchor for Le Havre around 8pm.[6] The battalion remained for one day at the port and then was transported to farm billets near Ypres in Belgium. After some training in how to deal with gas attack and trench warfare, sections of the battalion went into the front line in the Voormezeele sector just south of Ypres. For Harold and most of the 75th Infantry this was their first experience of warfare and soon they would come to know the utter misery of the trenches and the devastation felt at losing friends in battle. In the meantime the men left

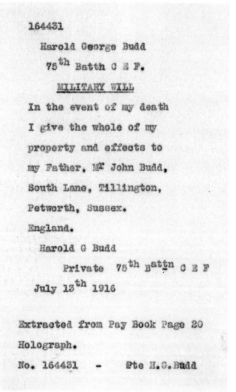

Harold's will written 13 July 1916. National Archives of Canada, Ottawa

Belgium and began several days of marching, via Hazebrouck and Arques, to the railway depot at Audruicq close to Calais. Here they entrained and in crowded carriages they jolted and bumped their way, via Calais and Boulogne, to Doullens arriving at 3am on 4 October. Sergeant L Mcleod of the 102nd Canadian Infantry on the same journey takes up the story:

Doullens is a fair sized town with tempting out-door cafés, but we were not destined to gain any enjoyment therefrom, marching direct from the station through the town, to Gézaincourt, where we were billeted for the night. Gézaincourt proved to be larger than the majority of villages, boasting an extensive hospital building. Hence we proceeded on Oct. 5th to Val de Maison where the night was spent under canvas. The following day's march brought us to Vadincourt, an apology for a hamlet lying on the hill above Contay where Canadian Corps Headquarters had been established. Vadencourt remains a damp and dismal memory of rain soaked shelters erected in a dripping wood on soggy soil.[7]

From Vadencourt the 75th Battalion, Canadian Infantry, made its way to Tar Hill, an area of raised ground west of Albert on the Bapaume Road, arriving on 10 October. For nearly four weeks the battalion moved in and out of the front line trenches with only short rest periods in billets in Albert and Bouzincourt.

As the autumn advanced the Somme became a sea of mud, causing great difficulties for the allies. The first snow fell on the night of 17/18 November, coinciding with the beginning of the final phase of the Battle of the Ancre, which itself was the last major Battle of the Somme before winter. Conditions on the morning of 18 November were dreadful with sleet and rain reducing visibility to nil. The war diary records:

> On the morning of the 18th at 6.10am a successful attack was made on DESIRE TRENCH by this Battalion, with the 54th on the left and the 50th on the right. The 50th Battalion on the right failed to capture their objective and consequently our Battalion was exposed to a heavy enfilade fire and continuous sniping from enemy trench on our right. We established a block in DESIRE TRENCH a few yards west of PYS ROAD and dug a new trench about 100 yards north of DESIRE TRENCH. This position was held by us until relieved at 5 am on the 20th Nov by the 102nd Battalion.

Although the Canadian troops succeeded in capturing Desire Trench in the German support line, there was little cause for celebration because in total they suffered 29,029 casualties for some four miles of mud. The 75th Battalion lost 'two officers killed, 55 other ranks killed, 40 missing and 142 wounded'. However, the men did gain major battle experience that would serve them well when the Battle of Vimy Ridge began on 9 April 1917. After several days of marching the battalion reached Estrée Cauchy on 20 December 1916 and over the next few days it saw action in the trenches, losing two men and four wounded. They were relieved on Christmas Eve but the war diary makes no mention of how Christmas itself was spent. Further losses were recorded when they returned to the front line trenches at the beginning of 1917. On 8 January the men were relieved and moved back to divisional reserve at Camblain L'Abbé on the west of Vimy.

On 6 January, whilst still in the front line, Harold was taken from the trenches and admitted to 18 Casualty Clearing Station Lapugnoy,[8] some fifteen miles north, dangerously ill with lobar pneumonia. It had probably started earlier as influenza, which was common amongst the troops particularly during winter. The weather, close quarters, malnourishment, and the stresses of combat all encouraged influenza. In many cases weakened lungs were further infected with a deadly bacteria causing lobar or bronchopneumonia, a major cause of death in young men admitted to base hospitals. Harold's medical records[9] show that on 15 January he seemed to improve a little, but unfortunately this was not sustained and he died on 17 January 1917 in the care of a dedicated nursing staff. Field Marshal Haigh had written in his diary of 23 August 1915[10] of the Lapugnoy facility:

> It arrived from England six weeks ago and is most complete in every way. Some 20 or 30 large Indian tents are arranged with stretchers for the accommodation of 4 or 500 wounded. There is room in an adjoining meadow for more tents so that 800 wounded could be taken in. The ambulance trains are 'stabled' at Lapugnoy Station so that stretchers can be carried straight from the tents & put into the train.

Private Harold Budd was laid to rest in the Lapugnoy Military Cemetery close to No 18 Casualty Clearing Station. The cemetery lies on the outskirts of the village of Lapugnoy, some four miles west of Bethune. The grave reference is II. F. 5. Private Budd is also commemorated in the First World War Book of Remembrance, page 209, held in the Memorial Chamber of the Peace Tower in Ottawa, Canada. He was awarded the British War Medal and the Victory Medal.

~ 14 ~

Private William Butt G/1694

Royal Sussex Regiment

Jane Quennell was born in Woolbeding, Sussex in 1852 and by 1861 she was living with her parents, two sisters and two brothers at Sickleham in Tillington. Jane and her younger sister, Ann, were scholars at Tillington School. It is probable that during her school days Jane met Henry Butt, who was only one year older. By the age of ten, Henry had left school and in 1861 was a farm labourer living with his parents in Upperton Street, Tillington. Jane was still at school. At some time over the next few years Henry and Jane became sweethearts and in the late summer of 1874 they were married at All Hallows' Church by Curate James Puttick.

By 1881 the couple were living at Hill Top Cottage, Tillington with their two children, Edward and Henry. Their third - William - was born in early spring 1883 and christened at All Hallows' Church on 25 March. When he reached the age of four or five he would have most likely attended Tillington School, a short walk from his home. At the time of the 1901 census William was eighteen-years-old, single and living at home, making his way as a domestic gardener. Ten years later he was still single and still living at home, but had changed his employment for now he was a bricklayer's labourer.

Perhaps with a sense of patriotism and the promise of pay substantially better than that of a labourer, William decided that it was time to join the army. Around 7 September 1914, at the age of thirty-one, he travelled to Chichester to enlist in the 2nd Battalion, Royal Sussex Regiment. This battalion had already sailed for France in the late evening of 12 August 1914[1] and therefore it is likely that Private William Butt G/1694 was trained with the 3rd (Reserve) Battalion based at Dover. In preparation for moving to France the senior battalion stopped taking in new recruits in early August, instead these men were posted to the new training battalion. The 2nd Battalion war diary for 4 August states: '101 men ordered to 3rd Royal Sussex Regt at Dover … 3 officers and 15 NCO's were ordered to Depot as instructors to new unit formed there'. Some nine months later, on 18 May 1915, with his training behind him William was posted to France where he probably spent one or two days at a base camp on the French coast before being posted to the 2nd Battalion.

At the time William joined his battalion it was still recovering from heavy losses sustained on Sunday 9 May during the bloody one-day Battle of Aubers Ridge. On that day the battalion was ordered to dislodge the Germans and drive them back from their lines opposite Richebourg L'Avoué. At 3.30am the attack began on a front 400 yards wide, across open fields, but quickly ran into trouble as the German machine guns opened up and the men hastily retired and dug in as best they could. At 7.30pm the remnants of the shocked and shattered 2nd Battalion made its way to billets nearby. When the roll call was answered there were 562 casualties, more than half the battalion, and most men killed that day have no known graves.

The men rested on 10 May but the following day they marched to Oblinghem near Bethune to be joined by a much-needed draft of reinforcements. William was not in this draft but, with 270 other reinforcements, he reached the battalion at the village of Cambrin, close to Bethune, on 22 May.[2] For the rest of the summer the battalion had a relatively quiet time, spending only short periods at the front.

This all changed on 25 September, when the devastating Battle of Loos began. This was the largest offensive mounted in 1915 and the first time the British used poison gas. Although some minor gains were made, including the town of Loos, it was at the cost of some 50,000 Allied casualties.

At 1.50am the 2nd Battalion moved into the wet, muddy front line trenches close to the mining town of Hulloch, to the north of Loos. Their orders were to support the attacking battalions as soon as they had broken through the enemy lines. The attack began at 6.30am on another grey wet, fateful day for the battalion.

The 2nd Battalion war diary for 25 September reads:

Near Hulluch … At 6.30am the assaulting Battns advanced and the Royal Sussex immediately pushed on to our front line trench … the wind had veered round and had carried some of the gas back over our Front Trench causing a good deal of confusion amongst the troops…My Company Commanders then on their own initiative at once advanced and pushed on to the Assault Battalion thus becoming part of the Assaulting Line at a very early stage of the attack. This advance was pushed right up to the German wire which was not cut and at this stage all our officers and men who had reached or got close to the wire were either killed or wounded. The Ryl Sussex Machine Gun Section which had advanced with the Battalion endeavoured to reach the German Line but were annihilated about 50 yards in front of Lone Tree [A well known isolated cherry tree which bloomed on the battlefield during spring 1915].

It was mid-afternoon, after two attempts by another battalion, before the Germans were forced out of their trenches. At 3.15pm the Commanding

Officer of the 2nd Battalion, Royal Sussex Regiment, gathered together his remaining men, some seventy in all, and after the Germans surrendered they quickly moved into the vacated trenches. This small group of weary men had little time to settle before they were ordered to move on to Chalk Pit and occupy trenches along the Lens to La Bassée Road. This line was held until the battalion was relieved on 26 September and two days later they were in Loos.

On this fateful Saturday in September the 2nd Battalion suffered 481 casualties, including 181 killed, of whom two-thirds have no known graves. Private William Butt G/1694 was part of this courageous assault and tragically lost his life at the age of thirty-two years fighting for his King and Country. His body was not found but he is remembered, along with many others from the 2nd Battalion, Royal Sussex Regiment, on the Loos Memorial, located about a mile west of the village of Loos-en-Gohelle in the Pas de Calais. The Memorial reference is Panel 69 to 73.

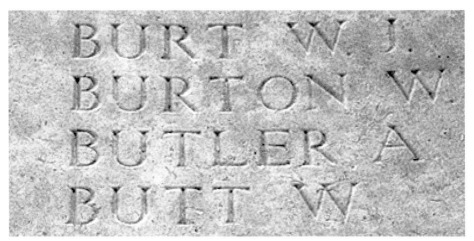

William Butt's inscription on the Loos Memorial. © Author's collection

Private Butt was awarded the 1914-15 Star, the British War Medal and the Victory Medal.

Lance Corporal Charles Judge from Tillington was also killed in this battle on the same day, but his body was recovered.

~ 15 ~

Private Thomas Daniels G/53052

Royal Fusiliers

Thomas was the youngest of five children born to Daniel and Ann (née Bridgewater) Daniels on 31 January 1898 and was christened in All Hallows' Church two weeks later. At the time of the 1901 census the family was living at New Cottages in Petworth, but by 1911 Daniel and Ann and their two youngest boys, Thomas and Jesse, had returned to Tillington taking up residence at 521 Monument Lodge.

At the age of four years and eight months Thomas, together with his brother, became pupils at Tillington School with admission numbers 813 and 812 respectively.[1] Thomas attended school for ten years, leaving two days after his fourteenth birthday on 2 February 1912. It is likely that he either joined his father as a farm labourer or joined Jesse, who by this time had left school to become an assistant gardener.

Thomas reached the age of eighteen on the last day of January 1916, one month before compulsory conscription was introduced. There is no clear evidence whether he voluntarily enlisted in the army, or was conscripted. From details written on his army will, we know that he underwent basic training with the 25th Training Reserve Battalion. As this battalion was not designated the 25th until September 1916 it seems that Thomas joined after this date.

Conscription overwhelmed the regimental training system and hence Training Reserve Battalions were created to instruct the huge numbers being called

Thomas Daniels in the uniform of the Royal Fusiliers. Courtesy of Bill Bryder

up. Men in these battalions were not affiliated to any regiment during their basic infantry training, but had an army number and, once trained, each was drafted into a named regiment in need of reinforcements. Private Daniel's number was TR/9/1226.

Thomas made a will dated 21 February 1917, suggesting that he was coming to the end of his training and preparing to serve overseas. With a group of reinforcements he was initially sent to a base depot on the French Coast for further training and to ready him for the horrors of trench warfare. His medal roll[2] shows that on 2 March he was posted to the 1st Battalion, Royal Fusiliers, but two weeks later Private Thomas Daniels GS/53052 was transferred to the 2nd Battalion of the same regiment, part of 86th Brigade in the 29th Division. The probable reason for this was that the 2nd had suffered more losses in March than the 1st Battalion and hence had a greater need of reinforcements.

After serving on Gallipoli the 2nd Battalion moved to the Western Front in March 1916,[3] so when Thomas joined them the men were experienced and battle-hardened from the peninsula and a year fighting in the trenches of northern France and Belgium. With other reinforcements, he caught up with the battalion either on 19 March (draft of 121) or 20 March (draft of 106). By the latter date the men had just arrived in Araines, a small town on the Somme some twelve miles from Abbeville. The battalion regularly moved around the area but saw little action until 20 May 1917 when they moved into the front line at Monchy-Le Preux, south east of Arras. After a long, bloody battle for the village the battalion was finally relieved ten days later and returned to Arras to bathe and rest. With only two days of relaxation the men were once again on the move; after a short march they 'enjoyed' a cramped bumpy train journey to Lanches. The battalion, with the rest of the division, now prepared for the next battle that was to prove one of the most horrific of the war.

The Third Battle of Ypres dragged on from the last day of July until 10 November and was conducted in a relatively small area to the north-west of Ypres.

The Story of the 29th Division provides more detail of the conditions endured by the men at this time:

> The cramped theatre with its slimy canals, beeks, [small streams] sloughs [swamps], bogs, and inundations; its shelled duck-board tracks, its isolated outposts, its incessant shelling and incessant rain, its mists and fogs, its corpses and its pestilential, miasmic odours, outdid anything that even the Somme or Arras could boast.[4]

During the three months of the Third Battle of Ypres, there were in fact several battles and the 29th Division took part in three of these; The Battle of Langemarck – 16 August, The Battle of Broodseinde – 4 October and The Battle of Poelcapelle – 9 October. For the last of these battles the 86th Infantry

Brigade was commanded by newly arrived Brigadier-General G R H (Ronnie) Cheape, MC. He fought with great distinction in this battle and throughout the rest of the war. In *The Story of the 29th Division* the Brigadier was described as:

> A young man, a Fife laird and an adept at the wild sports of the Highlands. He was strong and sinewy, clear-eyed and hawk-nosed and incapable of fatigue ... Most important of all, he was a fighting man, and although he was only now introduced into the 29th, he knew that it was a hard-hitting, resolute unit … In a word, he was just the man for the 86th, and they were just the men for him.[5]

Under Brigadier General Cheape's command, the men of the brigade showed great courage in battle and Thomas survived the first two encounters with the enemy, but tragically he was killed in the Battle of Poelcapelle on 9 October 1917.

Although this battle involved several army divisions, the main objective for the 29th Division was to push the Allied front line forward 1,650 yards on the right and 2,500 yards on the left towards Houthulst Forest, north-west of Poelcapelle village. The 1st Lancashire Fusiliers and the 2nd Royal Fusiliers from the 86th Brigade led the attack. The night before zero hour rain poured down in torrents, filling all the potholes with water and making conditions absolutely atrocious. The advance was to be made in three stages, with time to consolidate between each intermediate objective. The rain stopped at midnight and the attack began at 5:20am. In reaching the first objective, Olga Farm, German machine guns claimed many casualties in the Lancashires, so two companies of the 2nd Battalion Royal Fusiliers were moved up to strengthen the line and, with the surviving troops, they advanced on Condé House by rushes from shell-hole to shell-hole. It was quickly taken, but fire from two German fortified positions stopped any further advance. Although the enemy began a strong counter-attack, they were engaged by rifle and machine-gun fire slowing their advance. At 8:55am heavy shelling from British artillery smashed the German attack and the final objective was reached at 10am. Private Thomas Daniels lost his life during the second or final advance, probably cut down by German machine-gun fire. The division history gives more detail:

> It was a desperate day's work. The two fusilier battalions had shown themselves supreme in attack and defence, and their valour is epitomised in the feats which won for each battalion a V.C. The eighteenth V.C. of the war was won by Sergeant Molyneux of the 2nd Battalion Royal Fusiliers.[6]

The *London Gazette* Citation for his Victoria Cross reads:

> During an attack, which was held up by machine-gun fire, which caused

many casualties, Sergeant Molyneux instantly organised a bombing party to clear the trench in front of a house. Many of the enemy were killed and a machine gun was captured. Having cleared this obstacle, he immediately jumped out of the trench and called for some one to follow him, and rushed for the house. By the time the men arrived he was in the thick of a hand-to-hand fight; this only lasted a short time, and the enemy surrendered, and in addition to the dead and wounded, between twenty and thirty prisoners were taken.[7]

No doubt all the men showed courage in attacking the enemy under such terrible conditions and many paid with their lives. Casualties were high in all battalions; forty-six men from the 2nd Royal Fusiliers were recorded as missing, never to be found, and many others were wounded. Total casualties for the 29th Division were 1,112. Private Thomas Daniels GS/53052 does not have a marked grave but he is commemorated on the Tyne Cot Memorial (memorial reference is Panel 28 to 30 and 162 to 162A and 163A – Royal Fusilier panels), together with forty-five comrades. This memorial to the missing commemorates 34,887 names of men from the United Kingdom and New Zealand Forces who died between 16 August and 10 November 1917 and have no known graves. It is located on the ridge reached by the Commonwealth Forces on 4 October 1917 during the Battle of Broodseinde, a battle in which Thomas had taken part.

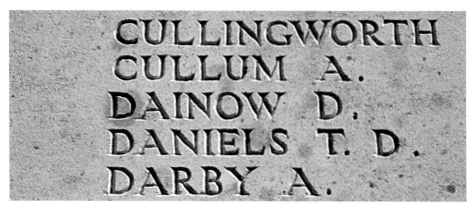

The inscription for T D Daniels on the Tyne Cot Memorial, Belgium. © Author's collection

General Sir Hubert Gough, Officer Commanding the Fifth Army, of which the 29th Division formed part, wrote movingly on the 14 October:

During the Third Battle of Ypres the 29th Division have set a fine example. Their work in preparing for the battle has been uniformly excellent, their minor operations have been successful, and during the general engagements of the 16th August, the 4th and 9th of October, they have still further enhanced their great reputation. Please convey to all ranks my deep appreciation and gratitude for all they have accomplished since their arrival in June in what was then the Ypres Salient.[8]

Thomas's will stated:

> In the event of my death all my belongings goes to my mother Mrs [Ann] Daniels, New Lodges, Tillington Road, Petworth, Sussex. But in the case of death occurring to her first my eldest sister shall share amongst the family. Mrs W Bryder, 3 Park Terrace, Tillington, Petworth, Sussex. But my watch which I gained from school I should like my sister Carrie to have.
>   Signature Pte T D Daniels, 25th T R Batt. Feb 21st 1917.

Thomas's will dated 21 February 1917.
Soldiers' wills Probatesearch.service.gov.uk.

In addition to Thomas's belongings his mother was entitled to his outstanding pay of £3. 11s. 4d. and a £3. 10s. 0d. war gratuity payment. These sums were paid on 15 June 1918 and 21 November 1919 respectively.

Private Daniels was awarded the British War Medal and the Victory Medal.

16

Lance Sergeant William Duck TF/320155

Royal Sussex Regiment

William Duck was born at the beginning of October 1894 and was christened a few days later on 4 October by the Reverend George Shaffen at All Hallows' Church. His parents, Herbert and Emily, lived at Grittenham Farm, on the outskirts of Tillington, and young William was born in the farmhouse. Whilst no records have been found it is likely that from the age of five William attended Tillington School and probably bought sweets from the shop next-door run for many years by Mrs Emma White. By the 1911 census he was sixteen, had left school and was working on his father's farm.

Being a farmer's son William would have had daily contact with powerful, graceful work-horses and no doubt quickly developed a love for them. At the outbreak of war he was predictably keen to join a cavalry regiment; for William this was the Sussex Yeomanry. He joined C Squadron of the 1/1st Sussex Yeomanry sometime between early August and early September 1914 and became Trooper William Duck 1857.

Before 1914 the Sussex Yeomanry was a part-time, mounted unit of the Territorial Force with headquarters in Brighton and with squadron stations at Hove, Lewes, Chichester and Hastings. Men joining the unit often provided their own horses and no doubt William did just that. If so he would have been in good company for on 4 August 1914 Siegfried Sassoon walked into the drill hall at Lewes and, refusing any rank, enlisted as a trooper in the Sussex Yeomanry.[1] By the time the regiment had moved to their new quarters near Canterbury, Trooper Sassoon also found himself in C Squadron together with his beloved hunting horse 'Cockbird'. Unfortunately a few days later he had to leave his horse with an officer because it was unable to carry a trooper's heavy equipment.[2] Soon after the regiment arrived at Canterbury the Yeomanry was split into those willing to serve overseas, the 1/1st Sussex Yeomanry, and those men who wished to remain behind, the 2/1st Sussex Yeomanry.[3] Troopers Duck and Sassoon remained with the former unit. Colonel Lord Leconfield had been associated with the Sussex Yeomanry for many years and readily agreed to be second in command of the 2/1st Territorial Training unit.

The Yeomanry was accommodated on three farms on the outskirts of

Canterbury and during the late summer of 1914 the men were billeted in barns, sheds and even shacks made of branches and straw, while the horses enjoyed the fine-weather grazing in the open fields. The men did, however, train hard, both at the regimental riding school where they honed their riding skills and at the rifle range on the golf links at Sandwich. Unfortunately, with the approach of winter this agreeable training gave way to a more important means of exercise when most troopers were consigned to assist a local contractor in the building of sturdy wooden huts and stabling.[4]

The History of the Regiment[5] makes little mention of training during the first half of 1915, but recalls a Horse Show and Sports in May and cricket matches on the Canterbury ground throughout the summer months. Sadly the yeomanry said goodbye to Siegfried Sassoon on 28 May when he left to take up a commission in the Royal Welch Fusiliers.[6]

Emotions must have been high when, at the end of August 1915, the 1/1st Yeomanry was 'dismounted' and overnight the men lost their horses becoming foot-soldiers with little understanding of what this involved. A short period of infantryman training followed including bayonet practice, trench digging and bomb throwing. This training period, during which William was promoted to Corporal, came to an abrupt end when embarkation orders came through. It must have been a new experience for the unit when in the dreary early dawn of 21 September the men marched through the streets of Canterbury to the railway station where they boarded a train for Liverpool. Three days later, along with several thousand soldiers from other dismounted yeomanry units, the Sussex men boarded the mighty RMS *Olympic*, sister ship to the *Titanic* and *Britannic*. Later that day the ship, painted in dazzle camouflage of several colours, eased out of the River Mersey bound for the small port of Mudros

RMS *Olympic*. Ⓒ *Copyright expired*

on the Greek island of Lemnos.[7] The eventful voyage saw the ship steaming across the Bay of Biscay where conditions were so awful that ninety-five percent of the men were very sick. No doubt everyone was relieved when the ship passed through the Straits of Gibraltar and into the calmer waters of the Mediterranean. RMS *Olympic* reached Mudros harbour on the on 4 October where the Sussex Yeomanry was transferred to the SS *Sarnia*, an old British ferry more familiar with the Southampton-Le Havre crossing. This crowded little boat transported the yeomanry to W beach (Lancashire Landing) at Cape Helles, on the southern tip of the Gallipoli peninsula. The men disembarked across some very rickety planking and on to the beach where they were issued with rations and marched some miles along the beach to Gully Ravine, which was to become their home for several weeks and was close to the front line trenches. For the past month these ex-cavalry men had either been training to become infantrymen or had been at sea, but on 8 October 1915 they found themselves, under orders of the 42nd (East Lancashire) Division, preparing to go into the front line trenches to face a fearsome, well-trained enemy that had already caused large Allied casualties. The men made their way to the trenches at Border Barricade and Crawley Crater, but on arrival found that conditions were extremely grim and unhygienic. It was no wonder that dysentery quickly became a greater threat than the enemy and many men were lost to casualty stations on the beach or hospitals further afield.

During their time on Gallipoli the yeomanry were in action in the area surrounding Border Barricade, but by mid-November severe, early winter storms exhausted the men and they were struggling to survive. By December the strength of the unit was fast being depleted by dysentery, but the men began to rally as rumours circulated that they were to be evacuated. On Christmas Eve the unit, now down to only half its full complement, moved close to the beach where it was held in reserve. On 29 December the order to move came through and the men excitedly readied their kit to be transported down to the beach. No sooner had this been done than the order was cancelled and the men spent a night without their kit or food. The evacuation, however, began the next day and by early evening the men were aboard the SS *Princess Alberta* bound for Lemnos where they camped three miles from Mudros harbour. The men expected a short stay but remained on the island for over a month occupied with parades, tug-of-war competitions and marathons. Finally on 2 February 1916 they boarded HMT *Caledonian* bound for Alexandria in Egypt.[8]

The division was moved to the Suez Canal Zone where the yeomanry was absorbed into the 3rd Dismounted Brigade and put to work on the canal defences. In March 1917 the last of several reorganisations saw the Sussex Yeomanry become the 16th Battalion Royal Sussex Regiment in the 230th Infantry Brigade, 74th Division.[9] Also around this time a new six-figure system of numbering men of all TF units was introduced, so William, until now Corporal Duck 1857, became Corporal Duck TF/320155. No sooner had the new division been formed than it went into battle in Palestine at the Second Battle of Gaza in mid-April 1917. Later in the same year they were also involved in the Third Battle and in the capture and defence of Jerusalem. In March 1918, after fighting in the Battle of Tell'Asur the division was warned that it would soon be moving to France to strengthen the British Force. William was now a Lance Sergeant and duly sailed with the division from Alexandria, arriving in Marseilles on 7 May. From here the division travelled by train to northern France and was settled near Abbeville by mid-May.

The battalion's first major action on French soil was at the Battle of Bapaume, part of the Second Battle of the Somme, (31 August - 3 September 1918). The men went on to fight in the Battle of Epehy on 18 September and were only rested at the beginning of October. The written history for this period records:

> The continuous fighting and movement of the past six weeks, coupled with a complete lack of reinforcements to date, had reduced the battalion to a skeleton. None were now left but the real stickers, whom nothing could kill and nothing could daunt.[10]

On 11 October the battalion was in a position just to the south-west of Lille and the men were preparing for a general attack. This was, however, postponed and instead the battalion was ordered to carry out a raid the following day on a small wood, in front of the larger La Haie Wood, in which there were two concrete 'pill boxes' occupied by the enemy and a major obstacle to any advance. Unfortunately heavy rain and a powerful machine-gun defence combined to force a British retreat. This strength-sapping disappointment was tempered to some degree with the news that the battalion was to be relieved at once. Unfortunately a few hours before the relief was due a postponement order came through and the original attack previously planned for that day was to take place after all. The battalion history reads:

> At last the stage was set for the same old scene and we started crawling forward towards the railway line. The two right companies got over with little opposition and established themselves on the far side. The left company whose total strength was one weak platoon [typically 30/40 men], worked up to the edge of the wood with the pill boxes, the scene of our abortive raid and during this operation lost an invaluable N.C.O. in Sergt. Duck, who was killed while advancing on the wood with a patrol. This N.C.O. had been with us ever since the Gallipoli days and had proved his great worth time after time. Finally the line was established and the Battalion was at last relieved.[11]

Lance Sergeant William Duck TF/320155 was killed in the early hours of 14

October 1918. The battalion rested for forty-eight hours before they received orders to move. They marched through the small French villages of Fournes, Santes and on to Flequieres where they billeted for the night before continuing through more villages to Camphin where they stayed until 24 October. These villages are all close to Lille and everywhere the people came running out to welcome the liberating troops. Street banners were in abundance: 'Glory to our Liberators' and 'We thank you British Soldiers' they read. Perhaps most appreciated were the warm embraces from the ladies, and the mysterious appearance of bottles of wine that for so long had been hidden from the Germans.

William Duck had fought gallantly in Gallipoli, Egypt, Palestine and France and inspired the men under him. In another two days he would have enjoyed the welcome shown by so many French villagers and returned to Tillington with stories to fill a library. Alas this was not to be, but he did not die in vain; he died a hero fighting for freedom and history records the deep gratitude shown by the people throughout the world for all those like him who made the ultimate sacrifice.

Lance Sergeant Duck now rests in Aubers Ridge British Cemetery close to the village of Aubers, some six miles south of Armentières in northern France. The grave reference is VI. B. 18. His back pay and war gratuity amounted to £43.7s. 2d, and this was sent to his father Herbert in Tillington.

Lance Sergeant Duck was awarded the 1914-15 Star, the British War Medal and the Victory Medal.

17

Corporal Joseph Dummer 32216

Royal Field Artillery

Ancestors of the Dummer family have lived within the parish since at least the mid-eighteenth century and much longer in the close vicinity. Descendants still live in the community and the beautiful 'Dummer's Cottage' (once two cottages where two sisters lived all their lives) dates from around 1735 and is testament to the longevity of a hardworking, well-loved family.

Edward Dummer was born in Easebourne in 1836 and according to the 1871 census he was married to Sarah with a family of three sons and four daughters; all lived in a cottage on Netherlands Farm where Edward was a shepherd. By 1881 the family had four more children, including Joseph, and, perhaps needing more accommodation, they had moved to South Dean in the southern west corner of the Parish. Edward was still working as a shepherd and, as South Dean is not too far from Netherlands Farm, it is likely that he was still tending their flock.

Joseph was born in autumn 1875 to Edward and Sarah and was christened in All Hallows' Church on 26 September. Although there are no school records for him, each morning Joseph would probably walk the two miles across open fields to Tillington School, returning home in the afternoon filled with a little more knowledge. With the rudimentary education of a village school there was little choice of work for boys as they reached their fourteenth birthdays and many, including the Dummer boys, became agricultural labourers.

Although Joseph was a farm worker it is clear that he wanted more excitement and perhaps a better standard of living, for during his seventeenth year he took the first steps in his military career, enlisting as a volunteer in the 3rd Battalion Royal Sussex Militia at Chichester Barracks. No doubt his aim was to become a regular soldier for at the age of seventeen years and seven months, on 5 April 1893 at Chichester, he enlisted for a short service (five years with the Colours and seven years in the Reserve) in the 12th (Prince of Wales Royal) Lancers[1] and became Trooper J Dummer, 3666. His medical examination states that he was fit for service and shows that he was 5ft 8¾in tall, weighing 150lbs, with a ruddy complexion, brown eyes, and red hair. The record also notes that he had been tattooed with a heart, anchor, crossed swords and the word

'Mizpah', probably all on his right forearm. The latter tattoo is interesting since Mizpah is Hebrew meaning 'The Lord watch between me and thee when we are apart one from another'. Perhaps Joseph had this done just before he enlisted with thoughts of his mother and the family.

After joining the 12th Lancers he was initially stationed in Manchester and then moved to regimental barracks—either in Hounslow or Aldershot. As a farm labourer he was used to working with horses and as a trooper in the Cavalry he was with them every day. Perhaps it was no surprise to his family, therefore, when he told them that he had begun training as a shoeing smith (the military term for a farrier). Joseph completed his training and was appointed Shoeing Smith Dummer, in C Squadron, on 20 August 1896. Two years later he successfully completed a

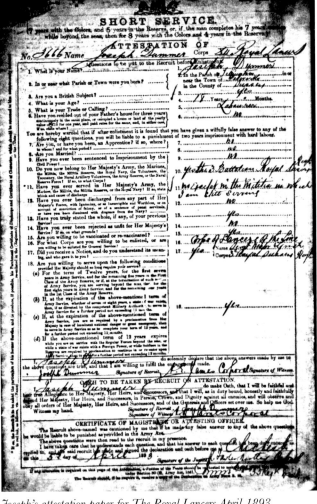

Joseph's attestation paper for The Royal Lancers April 1893. The National Archives

Veterinary Course at Aldershot and was now ready to play his full part in whatever the Lancers were called upon to do.

The appointment brought an increase in pay and he was able to avoid several tiresome duties and parades often associated with the life of a soldier. Napoleon once said that 'an army moves on its stomach, but the cavalry moves on its hooves', and it was the responsibility of shoeing smiths to keep the horses moving. Each cavalry squadron would have a shoeing smith for running repairs who would carry equipment and spare shoes. If a horse lost a shoe in battle then the smith, under fire, would replace it. Training would have prepared Joseph for the many dangerous situations in which he might find himself as he fought with the regiment.

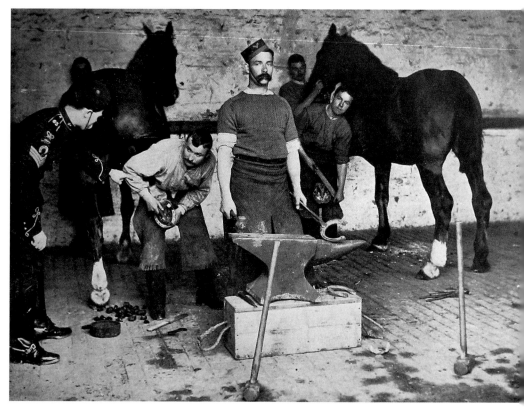

Shoeing smiths at work during the Boer War. Ⓒ *Copyright expired*

He did not have to wait long for on 11 October 1899 the Boer War broke out in South Africa and British troops were quickly mobilised, including the 12th Royal Lancers. They travelled to Tilbury under gloomy autumn skies and the following day, 23 October, embarked from Victoria Docks on the *City of Vienna* and the *Mohawk.* Joseph's C Squadron was on the *Mohawk;* according to the regimental history[2] the voyage was uncomfortable and the food unpleasant but the ship docked in Cape Town harbour without incident after twenty-six days.

> *London Times*, 23 October 1899:
> Amongst the troops embarked in the City of Vienna were the 12th
> Lancers consisting of 15 officers, one warrant officer and 310 men, 295
> horses, 1 gun and 3 vehicles. The troops for the Mohawk comprised 11
> officers, 248 men and 206 horses of the 12th Lancers.

After some patrolling and skirmishing in the latter part of the year, the turn of the century saw the regiment gaining honours in several battles including the Relief of Kimberley, Paardeberg, Dreifontein and Diamond Hill.

In late December 1899 Lord Frederick Roberts arrived in South Africa to take overall command of the British Forces after several embarrassing defeats. His first task was to relieve the diamond-mining town of Kimberley, which had been under siege by the Boers since early October. It was Lord Roberts's plan to relieve the town with a cavalry raid that would include the 12th Lancers. By 15 February 1900 the cavalry was resting on the north bank of the River Modder within reach of Kimberley. Unfortunately the onward route passed through a shallow valley lined with hills on both sides and held by the Boers. Sir John French, in charge of the cavalry, made a bold decision to send his entire command on a charge through the valley to the pass at the far end. After a five-mile gallop the cavalry division reached the pass, quickly defeated the Boers protecting it and opened the road to Kimberley. The correspondent of the *Daily News* wrote:

> Such a sight has not before been witnessed by this generation ... there was no faltering, regiment after regiment swept by at an easy gallop, the 8th and 16th Lancers, Householders, 12th Lancers, 10th Hussars and a squadron of Inniskillings followed each other in open formation.[3]

Kimberley was relieved at 6.30pm the same day (15 February) as the Boer Forces abandoned their lines and retreated. That evening the 12th Lancers bivouacked near a market garden and, although exhausted, they had the strength to open a barrel of brandy sent out to them by Cecil Rhodes who had been in the besieged town.

The retreating Boers made their way to the Modder River where they rested. With the 12th Lancers in the lead, French left Kimberley with orders to intercept them as quickly as possible. It was 2am on 17 February when the cavalry caught up with them but, instead of attacking the smaller British force, the Boers decided to dig in along the banks of the river close to Paardeberg Drift, thus allowing the British to pin them down and await the arrival of infantry reinforcements. Several units of Canadian Infantry arrived and were immediately ordered to make a frontal attack on the Boer trenches. With the failure of these assaults the strategy was changed from attack to siege and, several days later, on the night of 26/27 February, the Boer Commander realised that his position was hopeless and surrendered.

Referring to the action at Paardeberg, Sir John Frederick in his *History of the War in South Africa 1899-1902*[4] stated:

> The action, having regard both to the skill and audacity displayed by General French and to the immediate strategic results thereby obtained, must be reckoned amongst the great achievements of British Cavalry in War.

Following the Paardeberg siege, the British captured Driefontein and Bloemfontein, the capital of the Orange Free State. The latter city fell on 13 March 1900 and here the army rested. 'After five weeks in clothes in which they stood up the 12th were issued a complete change, their underclothes being, most wisely, burnt immediately'.[5]

At the end of April 1900 it was time to move north to take Pretoria, the capital of the Transvaal. The column moved quickly, clearing the enemy from towns and villages along the route and serious resistance was only encountered near the Boer stronghold of Johannesburg. The arrival of reinforcements, however, greatly increased the British fire-power and by 30 May, under cover of darkness, the Boers fled from the city. British forces entered Johannesburg the next day but stayed only long enough to organise a protecting force before pushing straight on to Pretoria which they surrounded in early June; soon the cavalry rode triumphantly into the capital. For a short time the war seemed to be over but then news came through that the Boers had re-grouped on a chain of hills, including Diamond Hill, to the east of Pretoria. With little rest the British moved against the Boer forces and by 12 June had successfully dislodged them.

With their forces greatly depleted and dispersed, the Boers turned to guerrilla warfare tactics including sabotage, raids and ambushes, for the remainder of the conflict. The 12th Lancers found themselves repeatedly chasing incidents from which the Boers had long since fled. This sporadic resistance continued; railways were sabotaged, supply columns ambushed, and even a squadron of the Lancers was attacked. Such actions continued into the first half of 1901 and the men spent long hours in the saddle, fruitlessly searching for Boer gangs. By this time Joseph had received two good-conduct pay rises and on 29 November 1901 he was promoted to Corporal, giving him another increase in pay.

At the dawn of 1902 the Lancers moved south to deal with an apparent threat to Cape Town. This, however, did not materialise and the regiment spent the early months clearing further pockets of resistance. The last of the Boers surrendered in May 1902 and the Treaty of Vereeniging ended the war that month.

With the Boer conflict over, the Lancers were posted to India for eight years, returning to Potschefstroom, South Africa in 1911. During this time Joseph completed his eight years 'with the Colours', so in early February 1903 he was transferred to the Reserve and probably returned to England. Clearly unhappy with this move Joseph no doubt pestered the regimental office, until in early May of the same year he was allowed to rejoin the 'Colours' - but only as a private - and posted back to South Africa. We know that Joseph returned to his Regiment because he is listed in the 1911 census 'Overseas Military' for Potschefstroom.[6] Whilst stationed here his good work and conduct led to his regaining the rank of corporal. It was perhaps with mixed emotions that the men left this beautiful city in December 1913 when they were ordered home to England. Two squadrons were posted to Norwich and the third, including Joseph, to Weedon in Northamptonshire. A year later Joseph, having served an incredible twenty-one years in the regiment, was discharged at Weedon on 4 April 1914.

His discharge papers show that he was thirty-nine years old, 5ft 10in in height with a ruddy complexion, brown eyes and red hair.

His character awarded in accordance with King's Regulations reads:

> A very good reliable hard working man, sober and honest. An excellent farrier and a real good man. He did very well in the South African war where he was in my Troop all the time. His military character was summarised as "exemplary".[7]

After his discharge Joseph may have returned briefly to his family home in Upperton, but a regular soldier of Joseph's calibre was not going to retire gracefully from military service and, now aged forty, he volunteered to serve again in the Great War. He was living in Melton Mowbray and on 15 June 1915 he travelled to Leicester where he enrolled as a shoeing smith with the 176th (CLXXVI) Brigade, Royal Field Artillery (RFA). He was promoted to Corporal Shoeing Smith Dummer 32216 on 11 July 1915 which interestingly was the third time he had been promoted to this rank during his military career. The brigade left Southampton on the night of 8 January 1916 and arrived at Le Havre the next day. On 3 February the 176th Brigade was reorganised as the 8th London Brigade RFA with the 47th Division. This division was in general headquarters reserve during February, training (in the snow) south of St Omer in the Bomy area. In early March it was moved further south to an area close to Vimy.

On 11 March Joseph was admitted to the 5th London Field Ambulance in France suffering from rheumatoid arthritis in his wrist. From the field ambulance he was admitted to the 6th Stationary Hospital at Rouen and returned to England on 14 April having served ninety-eight days in France. He was treated at hospitals in London and came under the administration of 5C Reserve Brigade RFA. Joseph was recommended for discharge as no longer physically fit by the 2nd London General Hospital on 21 September 1916. He left the army for the second time on 5 October with a character reference that read: 'steady, sober and hardworking'.

As a result of cold, muddy winters, poor food and regular gas attacks many soldiers fighting in the Great War contracted tuberculosis. Although there is no mention of this in army medical records for Joseph, his death certificate states that he contracted acute pulmonary tuberculosis soon after leaving the army and within three months he died at the home of his sister Anne in Upperton aged forty-one years. He never married and is buried in Tillington cemetery beneath a Commonwealth War Graves headstone.

*Joseph's Commonwealth War Graves headstone in Tillington
Cemetery. © Author's collection*

Corporal Dummer was awarded the Queen's South Africa Medal with
battle clasps for Wittebergen, Diamond Hill, Johannesburg, Paardeberg and
Relief of Kimberley, the King's South Africa Medal with 1901 & 1902 clasps.
He was also entitled to the British War Medal and Victory Medal for his time
in the Royal Field Artillery.

19 Cheyne Gardens, Chelsea 2016. © Author's collection

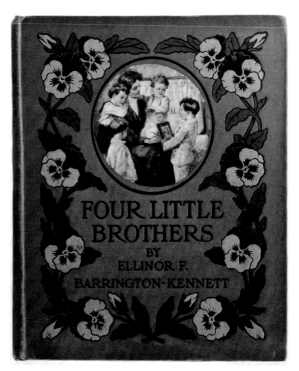

Four Little Brothers *cover by Ellinor Barrington-Kennett.*
© *Author's collection*

Violet Barrington-Kennett's bicycle before restoration. Courtesy Chris Gingell

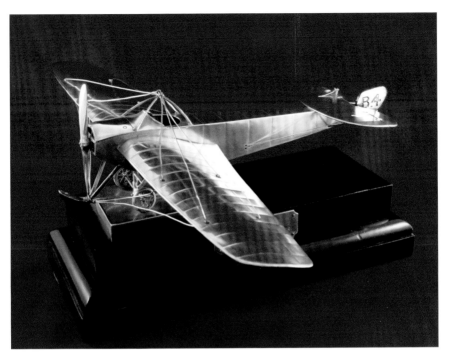

A silver model of the Nieuport B4: wedding present to Basil from his colleagues in the RFC.
© *Author's collection*

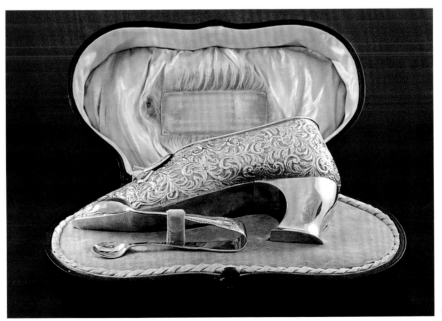

A silver sugar bowl: wedding present to Basil from 'Col' Samuel Cody. © *Author's collection*

2nd Lt. Aubrey Hampden Barrington-Kennett.

GREAT UNCLE OF MIKE & NICK DUDER
21st September 1914.

My dear Colonel Barrington Kennett,

You will long before this letter arrives have had the sad news of your poor boy's death.

I thought you would like to hear from me something about him. It was just an unlucky shell that caught him. We are in a place that is liable to be shelled at any time, and it was after shelling had begun that he was moving from one part of the position to another when he got wounded by splinters chiefly in the jaw and neck.

He was very plucky about it, would not allow the two men with him to carry him to a safe place, but in order to save them from being hit ordered them each under cover and remained in the open himself till the brunt of the shelling was over. This was a very brave act, especially as he must have been suffering from the shock of his wounds. The men offered to carry him in but he would not let them.

When he was brought in he was very cheerful. He kept wonderfully cool over it and was in quite good spirits.

We got him away in an ambulance the same evening, and everyone hoped he would make a good recovery, but yesterday to our great sorrow we heard he had died of his wounds.

I cannot tell you what a loss he was both personally and as a soldier. He had done so well all through the hard times we had, always cheerful, and everyone liked him.

We shall miss him very much, and remember him always. You may indeed be proud of the way he died. It was a very fine thing indeed to refuse assistance himself, and to save the men with him, and the way he bore his wounds made everyone admire him. You will be glad to know that I do not think he suffered great pain. It was I think chiefly shock and discomfort.

Whatever he felt, he bore it marvellously well.

Yours very sincerely,

H. B. DAVIES.

Copy letter received
2nd October 1914 from :
   Lt-Col. H. B. Davies,
      Commanding
         Oxfordshire & Buckinghamshire Light Infantry,
           (52nd Light Infantry).

True copy. B.K.

Letter received by Colonel Barrington-Kennett on he death of his youngest son, Aubrey. Courtesy Nick Duder.

Victor Barrington-Kennett's headstone in Miraumont Communal Cemetery.
© *Author's collection*

Watercolour of HMHS Asturias. The picture of HMHS Asturias is reproduced with the permission of Mike Greaves ASGFA and The Maritime Archaeology Trust's HLF Forgotten Wrecks of The First World War Project.

Grandcourt Road Cemetery: Thomas Bridgewater. © Author's collection

Christmas Card from William Bryder to his parents, date unknown. © *Author's collection*

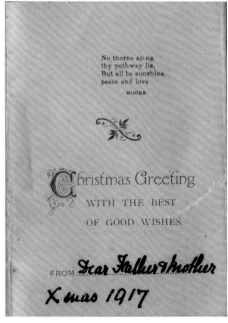

Christmas card from William Bryder to his parents 1917. © *Author's collection*

William Bryder's Memorial Plaque (Dead Man's Penny). © Author's collection

Pozieres British Cemetery: William Bryder. © Author's collection

18

Private Charles Edwicker 33344

East Surrey Regiment

On Christmas Day 1875 Henry Edwicker married Charlotte Collins at Hove near Brighton and by 1881 the couple were living in Upperton where Henry was a domestic gardener (probably on the Pitshill Estate). They had two children, Robert and Alice, but between 1887 and 1890 two more children, Frank and Rose, were born. In 1890 the family moved to Rectory Cottage, Selham where their daughter Bessie was born that year. Henry was no longer a gardener but had become a coachman/domestic servant (probably working for the Vicar of Selham).

Over the next nine years Henry and Charlotte had four more children - Sarah, Herbert, Arthur and Charles - and by 1901 the family had made a further move to Dye House, Duncton Common where father was once again employed as a gardener. In 1909 the family returned to Upperton for a short period before yet another move to Petworth. The 1911 census shows the family living in Grove Street, Petworth, where Henry was still a gardener.

Charles Henry Edwicker was born in Selham. Interestingly the Civil Registration shows that his birth was registered in the last quarter of 1898, but according to the baptism records for Selham Church, the Reverend S M Campbell christened him on 14 August 1898. His school record gives his date of birth as 14 July 1898.

Entry for Charles Edwicker in the Register of Baptisms for Selham Church. WSRO, Chichester

Charles began his school life when he was enrolled at Duncton School on 9 September 1901 (school number 445) aged just three years and two months. Some four months after his eleventh birthday he and his family moved to Upperton and on 8 November 1909 he entered Tillington School (Admission No. 132), only to leave seven months later when the family moved to Petworth. Although at this time Charles was only twelve years old there are no school records for him in Petworth.

Rather late into the war, at the age of nineteen, Charles joined the army. He enlisted at Chichester probably in the 4th Reserve Battalion of the Royal Sussex Regiment and his service number suggests a joining date of March 1917. After training, and at this late stage in the war, there would have been no choice of regiment and Private Charles Edwicker was posted to the 8th Battalion, East Surrey Regiment (18th Division) where he was allocated the service number 33344. This posting would have been part of an intake to reinforce the battalion which was fighting on the Western Front.

The division had embarked for France in late July 1915[1] and had taken part in several significant battles during 1916. The following year, in early May, the battalion fought bravely during the Battle of Cherisy after which the men were rewarded with an extended rest period. In early July they moved via Dickebusch in Belgium to a new camp at Chateau Segard close to Ypres and awaited further orders.

In earlier fighting, Allied Forces had pushed a bulge, known as a 'salient', into the German front line to the east of Ypres. It was Field Marshal Sir Douglas Haigh's plan to break out from the confines of this salient (Ypres Salient), advance through the German lines and at the same time free the Belgium coast. This was to be a major offensive (Third Battle of Ypres) involving the second and fifth armies with many divisions, including several from Australia and New Zealand. After several weeks of planning and preparation everything was ready.

At 3.50am on 31 July, as the sun was beginning to clear away the early morning mist, one thousand British guns began their awesome barrage on Glencorse Wood. From the beginning the battle went tragically wrong and by the afternoon of the same day it was clear that the attempt had failed. Ceaseless rain from 31 July to 4 August delayed a second, more powerful assault that eventually began on the night of 9 August. Unfortunately the enemy knew what was coming and responded with a devastating artillery barrage and machine-gun fire. Again the attack failed but this time casualties were very heavy, largely from German shellfire. The battalion was slowly relieved but it was not completed until after dawn on 11 August. A short stay at Dickebusch camp was followed by a welcome train journey to West Wippenhoek and then on to billets at Zegerscappel, within striking distance of the front line at Poelcappelle.

So it was that on 16 August Private Edwicker and 54 other reinforcements arrived to strengthen the 8th Battalion. Little did they know what the men had been through during the first months of 1917, nor could they imagine the courage that would be needed in the coming months to equal that of their new battle-worn comrades.

The 18th Division did not take part in the continuing offensive, which included the Battle of Langemarck, the Battle of the Menin Road and the Battle of Poelcappelle. Instead, for the first few weeks after his arrival, Private Edwicker and the rest of the battalion were undergoing training in the use of rifle grenades and laying signalling wires. Thankfully all this hard work was regularly punctuated with sports and social activities including a brigade boxing tournament, numerous football matches and day trips to the seaside on the French coast close to Dunkirk. This life of training and rest came to an end on 9 October when the battalion moved to 'Dirty Bucket Camp' just west of Ypres in preparation to re-join the latter stages of the offensive.

In spite of the appalling conditions and the suffering of so many men, and ignoring warnings by meteorologists that the torrential downpour of 8 October would continue, Haigh sanctioned the next attack to take Passchendaele beginning on 12 October. The 8th Battalion war diary records that on the evening of the 10 October:

> The Battalion moved forward ... by motor lorries ... ammunition and bombs were drawn from Hurst Park, after which the battalion proceeded to the front line and took up its battle positions.

The First Battle of Passchendaele began with a British barrage at 5.20am on the dark wet, muddy morning of 12 October. According to the men, the barrage was much too light to do any real damage to the enemy guns. Hence as soon as the battalion began to advance they were met with great force, both with artillery and machine guns. There was mud everywhere and men quickly became exhausted as they tried to move forward. In addition the artillery guns sank into the mud, lowering the muzzles and shortening their range.

The 8th East Surreys were severely punished when they tried to attack enemy machine-gun posts, making little progress, and by the afternoon they had been pushed back to their own start line. Before the end of the day there were 13,000 Allied casualties, including Private Charles Edwicker 33344 who was seriously wounded during this furious battle. He was taken to the nearest forward medical station just behind the British front line. From here he was carried by horse-drawn field ambulance to the 47th Casualty Clearing Station at Dozinghem just outside the town of Poperinge, some ten miles west of Ypres. No doubt he received the best medical treatment that the time and conditions allowed, but nevertheless Charles died of his wounds at the age of nineteen on 14 October 1917 after only two months in Flanders. He was buried in the nearby Dozinghem Military Cemetery, where he lies today with over 3,000 other soldiers who also gave their lives.

Dozinghem Military Cemetery is located to the north-west of Poperinge, close to Leper (Ypres). The grave reference is XF.2. The back pay owing to Charles and his war gratuity amounted to £5. 13s. 5d, which was sent to his father Henry.

Private Charles Edwicker was awarded the British War Medal and the Victory Medal.

19

Bombadier Wilfred Everley 73491

Royal Field Artillery

In 1891 Arthur and Harriett Everley were living with their five children in the parish of Wellow near Bath. Arthur was a thatcher and, by 1898, they had moved to 30 Bugley Street, Warminster; their sixth child, Wilfred Victor, was born on 13 March that year. The family moved on again, because the four-year-old Wilfred joined Penton Mewsey Church of England School[1] on 17 November 1902; it was close to Andover and some thirty-five miles from Warminster. Arthur was no doubt following available work as three weeks later they left their home again and a further year on they were living in Exton, twelve miles from Petersfield. Wilfred joined Exton and Corhampton Endowed School[2] on 7 March 1904. His admission number was 858 and his last school was given as Andover, which provides a clue to where the family spent most of 1903. This is further substantiated by the 1911 census which shows their son Leslie was born at Penton, Andover in 1903. By early 1905 the family had established a new home in Cheriton, where Wilfred settled into School Lane End Board/Council School until March 1906.[3]

No more is known of Wilfred until 1911 when, aged thirteen, he was living at home a few miles from Cheriton and, like two of his brothers, he was a domestic gardener. Some time between 1911 and mid-1913 Wilfred left home and made his way to Surbiton in Surrey where he became a milkman with H R Brown, dairy farmer at Ditton Hill Farm.

Wilfred's brother George had been in the army since 1902 and surely told exciting stories about the adventures of army life. Wilfred would no doubt recall these stories as he went about his daily work - until 19 August 1913 when he decided it was time for his own adventure. He made his way to a Kingston recruitment centre and enlisted in the Royal Field Artillery (Regular Army). He gave his age as eighteen years and five months. It was in fact fifteen years six months, but nevertheless he became Gunner Everley 73491 and was posted to the 134th Battery, 32nd Brigade, 4th Divison. His medical records show that Wilfred was 5ft 9in tall, weighed 140lbs and had brown eyes, brown hair, and a fresh complexion.[4]

Training began immediately, probably at Woolwich, with PT

Royal Field Artillery loading an 18 pounder gun. Ⓒ *Copyright expired*

exercises and drill to strengthen the new recruits. The Gunners would then begin their training on the field guns. The Royal Field Artillery was usually equipped with 18-pounder field guns which were drawn by a team of six horses and had a crew of ten men, six of whom operated it in action. There was a driver on one side of each pair and the gunners each had a number. No1 was in charge giving the orders; No2 worked the range finding drum and operated the breech mechanism; No3 fired the gun whilst No4 and No5 worked alternately as loaders. While No5 was loading a shell, No4 would be picking another one and setting the fuses with the assistance of No6. Each member of the gun team would have been trained, at least partially, on all the positions to keep the gun firing in the event of injury.

During early August 1914 the 32nd Brigade was stationed at Woolwich but on 18 August it was ordered to Harrow where the 4th Division was concentrating in preparation for an overseas move. On 22 August the brigade boarded trains bound for Southampton and at 2pm that day the men embarked on the SS *Thespis* bound for Boulogne. They arrived around mid-day on the following day and travelled by rail to Bohain; next day they marched to Briastre close to Le Cateau where, travel weary, they assembled with other divisional field artillery batteries.[5]

As the 4th Division was leaving Harrow for Southampton, the small British Expeditionary Force (BEF) which had crossed to France between 9 and 15 August was, by 21 August, advancing westwards towards Mons in Belgium. At the same time the large German Army was moving through Southern Belgium towards them. On 23 August, en masse, the Germans attacked (The Battle of Mons), forcing the BEF to retire southwards. The following day, with mounting casualties, the whole BEF began an ordered retirement from the area around Mons. This was also the day that the 4th Division, including the 32nd Brigade, arrived to the west of Le Cateau to cover the withdrawal of the II Corps. They were ordered to stand and fight and soon the men of the 32nd Brigade saw their first action in support of the 11th Infantry Brigade close to the village of Ligny. The 134th Battery, including Wilfred who had been promoted to acting bombardier, took up a position astride the road just south west of the village and began firing on German artillery and infantry positions.

It was nearing 7am when the German onslaught began. They possessed vastly superior weaponry and, despite a vigorous artillery duel, the outcome could be in no doubt. Around 4pm the 32nd Brigade was ordered to retire and by 4.45pm the entire 4th Division was retreating. The brigade together with the 12th Infantry Brigade became the rear guard as the retirement continued and by 2 September the division had reached Dammartin, only some thirty miles from Paris.

After a march of nearly 150 miles in eleven days the German advance was halted on the evening of 5 September and the 32nd Brigade was ordered to march at once to join the cavalry division at Marmont and prepare for a counter attack. At this time the brigade war diary became more positive and began to talk of readiness and of advancing:

6th September-7.00am - Advanced with the 4th Cav Bde to Gastins … 11.30am – Bde moved forward with 4th Cavalry. Bde to position of readiness just sw of Champmoulin. 134th Bty coming into action in observation just north of second u in Beaulieu. 6.45pm – Advanced to Jouy le Chalet and bivouacked there at 8.30pm.

The Battle of the Marne began on 6 September when the enemy advance was halted and a week later the exhausted German troops had been driven back almost forty miles to the River Aisne. Here they dug in on the high ground of the Chemin des Dames ridge on the north bank of the river and the horrors of trench warfare became a reality. By mid-September the 32nd Brigade had crossed the Aisne River and was advancing towards Laon, regularly encountering enemy artillery and infantry. The men continued marching northwards and by early November they had reached Flanders in a sector on the French/Belgian border close to Armentières. They remained here until the spring of 1915 when they moved to a position north-east of Ypres and fought in the Second Battle of Ypres.

In July the 4th Division was one of the first British formations to move down to the Somme where it took over the line in front of the German fortress village of Beaumont Hamel. The division remained here until the following year when they took part in the opening day of the Battle of the Somme on 1 July 1916. For several days prior to the battle the 32nd Brigade had been shelling the wire defences of the German trenches on the Redan Ridge and on 30 June it was reported that the wire was passable everywhere. The proposed line of attack ran for nearly fourteen miles from Maricourt in the south, northward to Serre, a few miles from Beaumont Hamel. The division infantry attacked the lines from the Serre Road to the Redan Ridge. Tragically, and unknown to the British, the German defences had survived the week-long bombardment and, as the advancing infantry moved down the exposed shallow slopes of the ridge, the enemy cross-fire cut into the advancing columns of men, killing or wounding most of them before they even reached no-man's land.

The Allied troops in the southern sector fared somewhat better but still only a few objectives were taken and it soon became apparent that the day had been a disaster with an unprecedented number of casualties. The 4th Division lost 6,000 men but overall casualties for the first day of the Somme were ten times this figure.

After such heavy losses the division was moved up to Belgium for a rest and to be resupplied with reinforcements drafted from England. Once replenished the division returned to the Somme in time to fight in the Battle of Le Transloy Ridge which began on 1 October 1916. Although the battle ended seventeen days later the British troops continued to advance supported by artillery, including that of the 32nd Brigade. By now conditions were appalling with continuous rain for several days and, partly because of this, attacks on a number of German trenches were unsuccessful. 'Rainy and Dewdrop' trenches (between the villages of Le Transloy and Lesboeufs) were eventually taken on 28 October. There is no entry in the brigade war diary for 30 October, the day on which Wilfred was killed. From earlier entries, however, it is likely that he was either killed by a German shell or long-range machine-gun fire. He was only eighteen years old and according to army regulations should not have been fighting overseas.

Bombardier Everley is buried in The Guards Cemetery, Lesboeufs, ten miles north of Albert and only a few miles from Le Transloy. The grave reference is VIII. T. 3.

He was awarded the 1914 Star with clasp, the British War Medal and the Victory Medal. The clasp to the 1914 Star bears the words '5th Aug – 22nd Nov 1914, and was granted only to soldiers who had been under close enemy fire between these dates. Its purpose was to distinguish those who had not been in action from those who had been in the early battles. The clasp is stitched directly on to the ribbon of the 1914 Star.

Wilfred Everley's death was recorded in the Minutes of the Easter Vestry Meeting on 12 April 1917[6] at All Hallows' Church and his name is inscribed on the Great War brass memorial plates within the church. The Tillington Roll of Honour states that Wilfred Everley was a resident of Tillington. Although no evidence has been found of his time in the parish his parents may have stayed in the village for short time between 1913 and 1916, perhaps while his father was thatching local cottages. The Commonwealth Graves Commission details for Wilfred give his parents as Mr and Mrs Arthur Everley, of Ditton, Surrey. Interestingly Ditton is close to where Wilfred became a milkman shortly before joining the army in 1913.

20

Lance Corporal John Grice P/4354

Military Police

John William Grice was born in the late autumn of 1885 at Barkby in Leicestershire. In 1901 at the age of fifteen years he was living with his parents, John and Ann, in Vicarage Lane, Barkby where he was a 'domestic groom', probably for the local vicar, the Reverend Charles Clark. Ten years later he had left home and was living in Combe Cottage Gardens, Combe, near Kingston-on-Thames where he was employed as gardener foreman. Early in 1913, at the age of twenty-eight, he married Gertrude S Goode in Leicestershire and the couple set up home at 55 Hardy Road, Wimbledon, Surrey.

In mid-October 1915 Lord Derby was appointed Director of Recruiting for the New Armies of the Great War. A few days later he introduced the Derby Scheme to raise more men from the four million eligible males who had not, so far, volunteered. Men aged eighteen to forty were informed that, under the scheme, they could enlist with an obligation to come forward at a later date if called upon to do so. It is likely that John enlisted under this scheme but, as a married man, he would not have been among the first to be called up. The inevitable letter, however, arrived sometime in the late winter 1916 - much too soon for the young couple.

John enlisted in the Queens (Royal West Surrey) Regiment (service number G/15126) around March 1916. There were only two battalions of the regiment in the UK at this time, the 10th and 11th Battalions, and John joined one of these. Both left for France in May of that year, but John did not go with them. Instead he was posted to, or volunteered to join, the Corps of Military Police (Foot Branch) - probably at their Depot in Aldershot. His service number was changed to P/4354 and after training he probably spent a year in England patrolling the streets of towns and cities where troops were stationed.

It was, however, overseas that the Military Police quickly became indispensible. They were used to control traffic and for the first time demonstrated their ability to bring order out of chaos in the battlefield. To maintain order they also developed new methods for handling stragglers, prisoners-of-war, the recovery of weapons and many other tasks.

John was posted to Egypt on 11 January 1917 and at some point was promoted to Lance Corporal. There is no information on his military service in Egypt but in 1918 whilst serving there, at the age of thirty-three, he died and his death certificate records the cause of death as heart disease.

It has not been possible to find any evidence of John Grice living in Tillington. In fact in 1913 he was living with his wife, Gertrude, in Wimbledon; he did, however, join the Queens (West Surrey) Regiment in Petworth rather than the more obvious recruiting centre at Guildford. The Annual Vestry Minutes of All Hallows' Church recorded the deaths of all the parish soldiers throughout the war years, yet fails to mention John's death in 1918. The mystery is compounded because his name is recorded in the village church on a Great War Memorial tablet and his Commonwealth War Graves Commission entry gives his next of kin as his wife, still living in Wimbledon.

L/C John Grice was awarded the British War Medal and the Victory Medal. He is buried in the Port Said War Memorial Cemetery. Grave reference B.10.

21

Trooper George Hills 3388

The Life Guards

George Hills was born in River in the Parish of Tillington in the summer of 1893. His parents, William and Emma, ran a market garden and had lived in River at least since 1881. By 1911 George was seventeen-years-old, still living at home as a domestic gardener, most probably on his parents' smallholding. We do not know why in October 1914 he was in Exeter but he enlisted there in the 1st Life Guards, a Cavalry Regiment of the Regular Army (7th Cavalry Brigade, 3rd Cavalry Division).[1] By this time the Guards had left their temporary base at Ludgershall in Wiltshire and were billeted in Flanders close to Ypres. Although the 1st Guards began the war as a Cavalry Regiment they were soon dismounted and on the Western Front they functioned as an infantry unit.

Trooper Hills 3388 completed his training with the Reserve Guards, based at their Hyde Park Barracks in London, and on 3 December 1915[2] he was posted to the senior Regiment which was now billeted in an area close to Ebblinghem, between St Omer and Hazebrouck in northern France. He most probably went to the British Army base at Etaples, on the French coast, for trench warfare training before joining his unit. Although there is no record in the Guards war diary of any reinforcements he must have been part of an unrecorded draft of men reaching the regiment around mid-December 1915. By this time the men had moved to Rumilly just south of Cambrai, where they were settled into winter quarters close to regimental headquarters.

From October to December it appears that there was little action to note since the war diary records either 'nothing to report' or 'a further digging party sent to …,' often some distance away since the men travelled by motorbus. On one occasion they were sent to dig trenches in Zillebeke, a small village close to Ypres some 75 miles from their base. It is difficult to understand why men closer to the village could not be made available. The entry for Christmas Day reads: 'Nothing to report Christmas greetings exchanged between the King and Commander in Chief published'.[3]

We know that George was killed in action on 11 January 1916, but there is nothing in the war diary to suggest where or how. It reads:

January 3rd Rumilly – Personnel for the trenches left by train.

January 4th-20th – Nothing to report.

This latter comment is a little misleading since according to the private diary of Trooper F Eames of the 2nd Life Guards (same Brigade as the 1st):

January 4th marched to LaBourse billeted in a house close to a coal mine no convenience for cooking etc.

January 9th went into front line about two miles in front of Vermelles myself and other Bombers occupied sap in front of front line, firing trenches got a bit lively the second night … Lost 7 or 8 during the day with trench mortars.[4]

The second night would be 10/11 January. It is likely that George was with the brigade in the trenches close to Vermelles and was killed there by a mortar bomb on 11 January 1916.

Trooper Hills is buried in the British Cemetery at Vermelles and was awarded the 1914-15 Star, the British War Medal and the Victory Medal.

22

Lance Corproal Charles Judge S/2292

Royal Sussex Regiment

Charles Edward Judge was born in Boxmoor, Hertfordshire in 1898 to parents Edward and Kathleen. In 1911 the family was living in Back Lane, St Marybourne, near Andover, Hants. The census shows father Edward to be of private means. For a short period between 1912 and 1914 Charles was a resident of Tillington and in August 1914 he enlisted in the 3rd (Special Reserve) Battalion, Royal Sussex Regiment at Chichester with the service number LSR2292. This was a training unit based in Dover and then Newhaven. After training with the 3rd Battalion Charles was mobilised and posted to the 2nd Battalion, Royal Sussex Regiment which at the time was serving in France. His service number was changed to S/2292 and he arrived in France on 1 May 1915 with a party of reinforcements, most likely reaching his new battalion near Bethune on 11 May. The battalion war diary for this date reads: 'Draft of 120 NCO's and men joined'.[1]

The battalion spent a relatively quiet summer in the Bethune, Vermelles, Cambrin area, either training or in the trenches, both support and front line. During this period Charles was promoted to Lance Corporal. The unit was close to Hulluch when the Battle of Loos began on 25 September. They were the supporting battalion for the attack on the German line. At 1.50am they took up a position in the support line ready to move forward as the front line advanced. The attack began at 6.30am with a British artillery barrage and gas shells. Unfortunately the wind changed, blowing smoke and gas back towards the Allied lines. In the confusion the 2nd Battalion became part of the assaulting line pushing right up to the German wire; this had not been cut and all the officers and men who reached the wire were either killed or wounded by machine-gun or rifle fire. Later in the day the enemy in the front line surrendered and the remaining men of the 2nd Battalion pushed on to 'Chalk Pit' where they entrenched close to the Lens-La Bassee Road. Charles was killed in this attack. He was just seventeen-years-old. On this same day Sergeant Harry Wells of the 2nd Battalion was awarded a posthumous Victoria Cross for conspicuous bravery during the battle. There were nearly 200 battalion casualties many of whom have no known graves.

Lance Corporal Judge is buried in Dud Corner Cemetery, which is located about one mile west of the village of Loos-en-Gohelle in the Pas de Calais. The grave reference is VI. H. 10.

He was awarded the 1914-15 Star, the British War Medal and the Victory Medal.

The Great War records for Soldiers' Effects show that his back-pay of £3. 13s. 4d and war gratuity of £4 were sent to his father Edward.[2]

23

Private George Peacock 8186

Loyal North Lancashire Regiment

Wwilliam Peacock and his wife Fanny lived with their seven children in a cottage – now long-demolished - between the Horse Guards Inn and Hill Top in Tillington. Fanny and all her children were born here but William found his way to the village from Petworth. He was a bricklayer and his two eldest sons Harry and William were labourers in the building trade. No doubt when George was born in late autumn 1884 his father assumed that he too would follow in his brothers' footsteps. This assumption proved correct, at least for a time, for the 1901 census shows that sixteen-year-old George Peacock was a bricklayer, but by this time his parents had moved away from Hill Top and he was lodging with James and Jane Dummer a few doors away. Perhaps, whilst laying bricks early in 1902, George began to yearn for a more exciting life because in late 1902/03 soon after his eighteenth birthday he enlisted in the 2nd Battalion, The Loyal North Lancashire Regiment (LNLR) probably for twelve years (seven years with the colours and five in the reserves).[1] At the time of the 1911 census George was with his regiment at Ghorpuri Barracks at Poona in India in his final year before being posted home to the reserves.[2] It is likely that in 1914 he was mobilised from the reserves and posted to the 1st Battalion, LNLR, as 8186 Private George Peacock.

In early 1914 the battalion, destined to form part of the British Expeditionary Force with the 2nd Brigade 1st Division, was stationed at Aldershot where the men were busy training for war. They did not have to wait long, for on 12 August 1,007 new soldiers marched to Farnborough railway station and boarded two trains for Southampton. The following day all soldiers were embarked on the SS *Agapenor* but within minutes of leaving the dock the ship ran into a lighter, injuring one man and knocking a big hole in the side of the lighter. No real damage was done to the troop ship and it eventually left the Solent just before midnight, arriving at Le Havre the next morning.[3]

The French residents gave the men a hearty welcome as they marched through the town. A second lieutenant wrote in his diary:

We got a great reception on our way through the town; all the French damsels want to shake hands with us, and many are pulled into the ranks by the excited men. The men sing all the way up to camp, eliciting remarks from the French: "ils sont tres gais", etc. [4]

The following evening the battalion travelled by train via Paris to Cambrai where they spent the night and the next morning marched happily to Esquéhéries where they settled into two comfortable barns on a dairy farm. Again the lieutenant recalls:

> One man went up to the French Madame and wanted to buy some potatoes. After a great deal of talking in pigeon English he got the good lady to understand him; she replied, "N'ai pas", and the man understanding her to say the French for potatoes, promptly replied, 'Aye that's 'em give me some of those "N'aipas".

On the 21st of August the battalion started its march towards Belgium, covering sixteen miles on the first day. The next day the men reached Avesnes where they expected to stay the night, but early in the evening they were told to fall in and marched off urgently collecting ammunition from open boxes strewn along the roadside. This all came to nothing and after a long trek the battalion was billeted in a small village close to the Belgian border and the narrator continues:

> 'My Company is billeted in a barn, and are packed like sardines; however, we have had such a long march that we are thankful to get down. A very kind lady gave us some coffee, bread and jam, and I then turned in and sleep on a bundle of straw in a pig-stye. The smell is not of the sweetest, but I pass a good three hours sleep'.[5]

The battalion crossed the border in the early hours of 23 August and began moving towards Mons, where everyone expected to be fighting within the next few days. The men were even told that there would be a 'bloody battle on the morrow' and were given a hasty meal of bully and biscuit. At daybreak they got ready for the order to attack but instead they were told to retire about half a mile and thus began the famous retreat. The LNLR continued retreating at great speed until on 2 September they crossed the River Marne just before the engineers blew up the bridge. The retreat stopped and with renewed spirit the British Army began to move forward again, now forcing the Germans to retreat.

On 13 September this retreat halted and the enemy turned to fight. So began the Battle of the Aisne and on the following day the battalion, with others, attacked a factory near Troyon. Although successful, the enemy almost immediately counter-attacked in great strength, forcing the battalion to retire in haste. Over five hundred men were killed, wounded or missing in this, the battalion's first major action, and the counter-attack was so intense that it was not possible to retrieve the wounded. On 16 September the battalion began to deepen their shallow trenches, a timely action since in the afternoon the enemy attacked again but this time they were repulsed with the bayonet. It was on this day that the horrific trench warfare began.

In early October 1914 British troops on the Aisne were systematically replaced by elements of the French Army. The 1st Battalion The Loyal North Lancashire Regiment did not leave until 16 October and several long marches and two welcome train journeys later it had returned to Belgium where the men went into billets some two miles north of Ypres. This strategically important town was the last major obstacle preventing the German Army reaching the channel ports of Calais and Boulogne and thereby cutting off all Allied supply lines. It was a town that had to be held at all costs.

Throughout the third week in October the Germans sought desperately to break through to Ypres in an area close to the village of Langemarck. On 21 October the LNLR was billeted for the night in the town of Boegsinghe, north of Ypres. In the afternoon of the following day 'quick orders' were received to march to St Jean on the north-east outskirts of the city to support the 6th Brigade. The men had just settled into their billets when at 2.30am everyone was awakened with the news that they must immediately march to Pilkem a few miles away. Imagine the colourful language when, on arrival, Captain Allen broke the news that the battalion had been ordered to attack the advancing Germans. He wrote in the war diary:

23. 10. 1914
Orders were given to attack on left of the main road and towards the Inn near Bixschoote. The attack commenced early in the morning C [Company] on the left of the road and A on their left advanced by sections under Maj Burrows, D & B supported. The attack was driven home and about 11am we were about 300 yards just SE of Steenstraat. The shell fire and rifle fire were very heavy and we lost rather a lot. At 2pm the Germans began to slip out of their trenches. Our left was swung around and with the Rifles [A company] and a few S Staffords we charged the trenches and enfiladed them with the maxims [machine guns] under Lt Henderson. We captured the trenches and about 150-200 prisoners who surrendered. About 3pm we were shelled out of these trenches by our own artillery but by 3.30pm we regained the trenches and held them all night … The Battalion worked wonderfully well. I believe we lost about 5 officers and 150 men.[6]

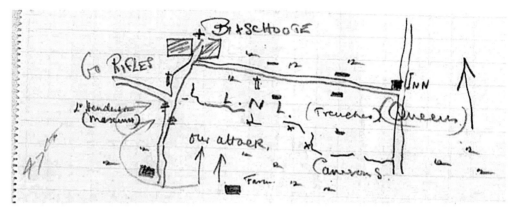

Map of attack sketched in the LNLR war diary. The National Archives

Soon after this 'Battle of Langemarck' the battalion received this message from the Brigadier General in command of the 2nd Brigade:

> The Brigadier General congratulates the 1/LN Lancs Regt - Northamptonshire Regt - and the 2nd KRRC, but desires specially to commend the fine soldier-like spirit of the 1st L N Lancs Regt which, advancing steadily under heavy shell and rifle fire, and aided by its machine guns, formed-up within a comparatively short distance of the enemy's trenches. Fixing bayonets, the battalion then charged, carried the trenches and occupied them, and to them must be allotted the majority of the prisoners captured. The Brigadier General congratulates himself on having in his Brigade, a Battalion which, after marching the whole of the night without food or rest was able to maintain its splendid record by determination and self-sacrifice displayed in this action.[7]

On the 25 October the men billeted overnight in Ypres and on the following day they marched towards Gheluvelt spending the night in trenches in a wood just off the Menin Road. Two days later the battalion was ordered to advance to support two other regiments in difficulty in what was known as the First Battle of Ypres. The advance was perilous with continuous shelling and machine-gun fire along the route and, although they did reach the attacking regiments, the pressure was too great and soon they all had to retire. In this move the units became mixed up and there were numerous casualties; many of the wounded had to be left before the safety of the original trenches was reached. Next morning under heavy shell fire the battalion attempted to reach the village of Gheluvelt. The second lieutenant continues:

> I reach the main road of Gheluvelt and there come to a standstill. It is quite impossible to advance any further on account of the terrific shelling. You cannot see parts of the village for the smoke and dust coming from

144

the bursting shells. Also bullets seem to come from all directions...it is impossible to advance through what is in front of us with the few men we have got. These men are dropping like flies around us, so we withdraw again to our trenches. This little movement which lasted about half an hour, has cost us dear...We are ordered to retire ... We are not strong enough to counter attack yet, so have to abandon all our wounded.

Probably wounded and left behind, George was captured by an advancing German unit on 30 October during the First Battle of Ypres. The records of the International Red Cross[8] in Geneva confirm this date and show that he was transported to a prisoner of war camp in pine woods just outside the town of Güstrow in Mecklenburg, Northern Germany. This camp was some 450 miles from Ypres and reaching it required at least a three-day train journey. This would have been harrowing; men were crowded into cattle wagons so densely that often they could only stand, at many stations food and water were refused and there was no treatment for the wounded.

Gustrow Prisoner of War camp during the Great War. Ⓒ *Copyright expired*

Sergeant Thomas Painting of the Kings Royal Rifles, a regiment which fought alongside the LNLR, was also taken prisoner around the same time and described his capture and arrival at Güstrow camp:[9]

We were marched to Wervik, given dry bread and coffee and billeted in the local church for the night. Next morning we marched, under escort, to

145

Lille and put in dungeons for the night. The following day at the railway station we were put into cattle trucks, 66 captives crowded into each truck so that we had to stand. We travelled for three days and finally arrived at Güstrow in Mecklenburg. And it was in a snowstorm. The tent that I was put into it was a huge tent, holding about five or six hundred people. There was a street through it, and on each side of the street there was a pen – six foot six in length – and straw was on the wet ground. And you were allowed two foot six in sleeping space, and that was your accommodation. Lie down in the straw on the damp ground and a thin blanket which you could hold up and see through it.

The winter of 1914-15 was particularly harsh in mainland Europe with snow and biting cold. Although wooden huts were built during 1915 the first prisoner intake had to endure this weather with only the shelter of inadequate, leaky tents and thin blankets. Lack of adequate food was also of great concern. Prisoners were not able to take their first bath until February 1915. It is no wonder that under these conditions many soldiers died of starvation and disease in the early months of captivity.

It was in early November 1914 that George, probably still suffering from his wounds, was thrust into these conditions. His Red Cross records show that he soon succumbed to pneumonia and, although he was transferred to the Güstrow camp hospital, drugs were extremely scarce and on 29 December 1914 George died. He was initially buried in the camp cemetery in a single grave No 47. In 1923, however, it was decided that the graves of Commonwealth servicemen who had died throughout Germany should be brought together in four permanent cemeteries. Hamburg Cemetery was one of these and burials from 120 burial grounds were brought here. George now lies peacefully in this immaculate cemetery. The grave reference is III. D. 10.

Private George Peacock qualified for the 1914 Star with clasp indicating that he served with his regiment in France and Belgium between 5 August and midnight of 22/23 November. The majority of recipients of the 'Mons Star' were officers and men of the regular British army who formed the British Expeditionary Force (the 'Old Contemptibles') and took part in the Retreat from Mons. This medal was awarded to 365,622 soldiers. Private Peacock was also entitled to the British War and Victory medals.

~ 24 ~

Gunner William Pellet 21834

Royal Garrison Artillery

William Pellett was born in Duncton early in 1874, the second son of Joseph and Charlotte Pellett. He was christened at Holy Trinity Church, Duncton on 15 February 1874. The 1881 census shows the family living in Littleton Cottages at Barlavington, near Petworth. By early 1891 the family (now with six children) had moved to Little Bognor, near Fittleworth where seventeen-year-old William and his father were both agricultural labourers. Unfortunately in the summer of 1891 his father died at the age of 54 and in 1901 his mother was living in Cross Lane, Petworth with her eldest son Henry James, two daughters and a grandson. Ten years later she had moved to Upperton where she was living with only her twelve-year-old grandson, Arthur. There is no record for William in the 1901 census and it is not until 1911 that we find him again. At the age of 37, and unmarried, William was serving as a Gunner with the 14th Company, Royal Garrison Artillery at their barracks in Shoeburyness, Essex.[1] (The company had been the resident unit at this garrison since 1903, manning the artillery batteries as part of the east coast defences. In the autumn of 1914, however, it left Shoeburyness equipped with three-inch anti-aircraft guns to provide air defence cover for the powder factories at Purfleet and Waltham Abbey).[2] William's absence from the 1901 census suggests that he may have been overseas - perhaps during the Boer war with an army unit before returning to join the 14th Company.

Between 1911 and 1914 William was probably released from the army, perhaps having served his time, but at the outbreak of the Great War he quickly enlisted again. In August 1914, at the age of 40, he travelled to Chichester and joined the 47th Siege Battery, Royal Garrison Artillery becoming Gunner Pellett 21834. On 26 November 1915 the battery was mobilised and sailed from Southampton to Bolougne.[3] On arriving in France at 1am the following morning, the men immediately marched to the nearby St Martin's Rest Camp. After resting for a few days the battery set off on a four-day march to Hazebrouck some 50 miles from Boulogne. Their arrival was delayed some hours because they managed to put one of their heavy guns into a ditch.

Siege batteries of the Royal Garrison Artillery were usually deployed some distance behind the front line and were usually armed with six-inch or eight-inch heavy howitzers that could deliver high explosive shells over long distances. Their major targets were enemy artillery, ammunition dumps, roads and railways.

An 8-inch howitzer ready to fire. © *Copyright expired*

By 8 December the battery was close to the front lines south-east of Vlamertinghe in Belgium. It was here that, according to the war diary, 'the Batt first opened fire at 3pm 8th Dec 1915 … In the week ending 12 12 15 the Batt fired 250 rounds. Ranges ranging from 7500 to 9800 yards'. A further entry for New Year's Eve reports:

> The New Year was ushered in by a series of rounds from 47 Battery on Sterling Castle [an enemy stronghold] this having been arranged by 50th Div[ision].

The 47th Siege Battery remained in the Vlamertinghe area until mid-June firing some 250 rounds per week at enemy targets. Their time in Belgium seems to have been spent in training and rehearsals for a much bigger and bloodier battle to come. In fact the Battle of the Somme, fought on both sides of the northern reaches of the river, was to be the largest battle fought during the Great War and perhaps the bloodiest battle in history with around one million Allied soldiers either killed or wounded.

On the night of 14 June the battery began removing their guns, which on the next day were transported by rail to Longueau, a town in Picardy situated close to the River Somme. The men left the train and marched a further twenty miles to Bray-sur-Somme. Soon after arriving there the war diary reports: 'Battery attached to 14th HAG (Heavy Artillery Group) with

4th Army'. Although the great battle was not scheduled to begin until 1 July a devastating preliminary bombardment was planned. For this, shells equivalent to one million pounds of explosive had to be carried up to the guns over long strength-sapping miles by innumerable infantry working parties. The barrage, which was to last six days, began on Saturday 24 June with the deafening roar of 3,000 British and French guns. The field guns were positioned some 1,000 yards from the German lines, attempting to cut the barbed wire protecting the trenches. The heavy howitzers of the siege batteries were positioned a further mile to the rear, tasked with demolishing the enemy trenches and fortifications including concrete machine-gun posts.

In spite of a heavy thunderstorm on 23 June, the men of the 47th battery and their four howitzers were ready to play their part, firing 780 shells most days in the direction of the village of Fricourt, a noted German stronghold close to Albert and two miles from the River Somme.

As the barrage reached its final stages, thousands of British troops were leaving billets, barns and tents in the villages and countryside for miles behind the Allied lines. This exodus grudgingly made its way to the assembly trenches before taking part in a battle that came to symbolise the abject horrors of war.

The first day of July was a fine, warm summer's day but that was the only good thing about this particular Saturday. The battle began at 7.30am when nearly 750,000 men (mainly British) climbed out of their trenches ready to attack the German lines along a front of nearly fourteen miles. What these men could not know was that the endless days of bombardment had done little to silence the enemy, so as they advanced across the flat, open expanse that was no-man's land, they were cut down in their thousands by machine-gun and rifle fire.

The 47th Battery was supporting the infantry divisions of XV Corps advancing towards Fricourt. They shelled targets close to and in the village causing severe damage, which led to its capture by the 17th Division the following day.

On 9 July the guns were moved close to Mametz where they continued shelling enemy trenches. By the end of July the battery had fired 8,459 rounds since the beginning of the battle. As the horrific fighting continued, the eight-inch howitzers' firepower was at first concentrated on Delville Wood, then for a prolonged period on the area around Ginchy, a German-held village that was eventually captured on the evening of 9 September. Towards the end of September the weather broke, giving way to almost continuous rain through the first days of October. Under these conditions moving the guns to yet another new position must have been difficult and to keep them firing day after day almost impossible. Nevertheless in the first ten days of October the battery fired a daily average of fifty-two rounds on to an area around and including the stronghold village of Ligny-Thilloy in support of troops attacking a low ridge lying close to Le Transloy. The Battle of Le Transloy was a desperate effort, in mud and freezing conditions, to gain some high ground from which to begin a new campaign in 1917. The battle began on 1 October but, with the exception of the capture of a small village, little further progress was made and, with the approach of winter, no more major offensives were carried out.

During the Somme offensive, after reporting the number of rounds fired, the war diary of the 47th Brigade often commented 'no hostile artillery fire on Battery'. On 6 October, however, casualties from a hostile shell were mentioned:

> 6am - 18 rounds were fired on Thilloy village 3.15pm - 42 rounds were fired on Thilloy village. Casualties from hostile shell 1243 Gnr Aitken G S [killed]: 1394 Acting Bombadier Bishop WS [wounded]: 1055 Gnr Coates F H [wounded]: 43701 Gnr Page A [wounded]: 21834 Gnr Pellett W [wounded].

It was unusual for other ranks to be mentioned in a war diary when they were killed or wounded, but in this case it provides accurate information on the location and circumstances of William's wounding. Clearly his wounds were life threatening because he was quickly passed through various levels of first-aid posts and hospitals until finally, after a journey of nearly 100 miles, he reached the major hospital at Etaples close to Boulogne and the English Channel. Tragically he died there of his wounds on 13 October 1916 aged 42.

During the Great War the area around Etaples, some seventeen miles south of Boulogne, was crowded with transit and training camps for thousands of reinforcing troops from England and with hospitals that could deal with 22,000 sick and wounded soldiers. Many were shipped home for further treatment or discharge but, with so many injured men being brought to the hospitals from all parts of northern France, a large cemetery was an inevitable necessity. William is buried, along with nearly 11,000 Commonwealth soldiers, in the Etaples Military Cemetery. The grave reference is VII. E. 4.

On his death William was owed £43. 1s. 9d pay and a £12. 10s war gratuity. His pay was divided between his mother, his brother and his six sisters. Each received £5. 5s. 3d. The war gratuity was only paid on 11 November 1919 and went to William's sister Daisy Ann.

War Gratuity details for William Pellett. Ancestry.co.uk

Gunner William Pellett 21834 qualified for the 1914-15 Star, the British War Medal and the Victory Medal.

25

Private Egbert (Reg) Pratt 30334

Machine Gun Corps (Infantry)

In 1881 John and Jane Pratt were market gardeners, with a substantial number of fruit trees at River, near Tillington. They had six acres of land and employed two men, one of whom was their twenty-five-year-old son, George who had married Ellen Money on 9 February 1878 at All Hallows' Church, Tillington. The couple moved into a house at River, probably on land owned by father John and in 1880 welcomed their first daughter, Elsie. Over the next seventeen years their family grew with Edgar (1883), Eber (1889), Egbert Reginald (1895) and Ethel (1897). All the children were born at River and clearly George and Ellen had decided that all their children's names should begin with the letter E, though Egbert was always known as 'Reg' by family and friends.

By 1911 it appears that the market garden had largely been taken over by the eldest sons, Edgar and Eber, whilst their father, George, concentrated on his cows. The census for that year describes him as a farmer and his son Egbert a 'Farmer's Son Working on Farm' and his two daughters are 'Farmer's Daughter Dairy Work'.

By the middle of 1915 the number of young men enlisting for the army was falling and new recruits did not keep pace with the terrible losses in France and Belgium. In an attempt to increase enlistment Lord Derby was appointed Director-General of Recruiting and he initiated

Private Reg Pratt in the uniform of the Royal Sussex Regiment. Courtesy Pratt family

'The Derby Scheme' for raising the numbers. Men aged eighteen to forty were informed that under the scheme they could continue to enlist voluntarily or attest with an obligation to come if called upon later.

It is believed that Reg may have volunteered or attested with obligation under this scheme. In January 1916 at Chichester he joined the 14th (Reserve) Battalion, Royal Sussex Regiment and given the number SD/5303.

Reg seems to have been a regular letter writer; in 1916 he wrote at least twenty-seven to his family. These letters, now in safe keeping with the family, provide an everyday account of his life whilst training and on the Western Front. They also give a wonderful impression of the Sussex dialect.

The letters begin on 23 January 1916, the day he travelled to Chichester to join the 14th (Reserve) Battalion, Royal Sussex Regiment. He says:

> all the artillery was closed; there was the Cavalry open. I did not want to go in that and the Engineers was only open for trades so I thought it was no good trying for that. Nearly all the chaps have been put in the 14th Sussex today.[1]

On that day he was issued with 'the karkie and all the whole kit' so parceled up his civilian clothes and sent them home via Selham Station. The next day the battalion set off for new quarters in Northampton. In C Company Reg found himself billeted in Currie Road, Kingsthorpe Hollow, which was close to the town but some fifteen minutes walk from the battalion mess.

> The living is very good, the dinner might be a bit better. I misses some things what I used to have at home. Will you send a pair of my gloves and watch and a few apples if they are not all gone. [5 February 1916].[2]

A year of warfare on the Western Front proved that, to be fully effective, machine guns must be used in larger units and crewed by specially trained men. To achieve this, the Machine Gun Corps (MGC) was formed in October 1915 with Infantry, Cavalry and Motor branches. A depot and training centre was established at Belton Park near Grantham, in Lincolnshire, together with a base depot at Camiers in France.

In early March 1916 Reg transferred from the 14th Battalion, Royal Sussex Regiment to the Infantry Section of the Machine Gun Corps at Belton Park, becoming Private E R Pratt, 30334. Men were selected from their battalions to undertake the six-week course at the machine-gun school on the basis of their marksmanship, intelligence or mechanical ability. Sharp shooters in the battalions could fire fifteen rifle rounds a minute whereas a machine gun could fire at least 300 rounds in the same time. A few lines from a soldier's story shown in the Belton House MGC Commemorative Exhibition of 2015, suggests that the selection process might, on occasion, be less formal:

Machine Gun Corps training base at Belton Park, Grantham. Courtesy Bill Fulton, MGC Old Comarades Association

We were put on parade one Saturday morning in early 1916, which was unusual and the next thing I know the Sergeant's running up and down the line with the Red Cap picking out people's names. Afterwards I asked the Sergeant what it was all about, "What's this?" I ask. "You're going to the Suicide Squad [nickname of MGC] on Monday", he replies. "You're off to Grantham".[3]

Although there is no mention of the reasons for his move in his letters, on 16 April 1916 Reg writes that he has arrived at Belton Park Camp and is settled into Hut C 3, H Line.

It [Belton Park] is a long way from the town, I went down last night, had a ride down in a motor from outside the park gates. Where we are camped, we did not know where to go the other night when we got back as it is a big park and a lot of huts scattered about, when we did find the right hut there was no beds for us it was all filled up so we had to lay on the floor 4 or 5 of us and have the kit bags for a pillow and make the best use of the overcoats. So next morning some of us was moved to the next hut No C3 … All they that never had a bed had to go to the store room and get the caseings and go to the hut where they keeps the straw and fill them up, then you had 3 blankets each then we had our beds.[4]

The address at the head of his letters shows that he was in 181st Company and just starting his training. By this time the old Maxims had been replaced

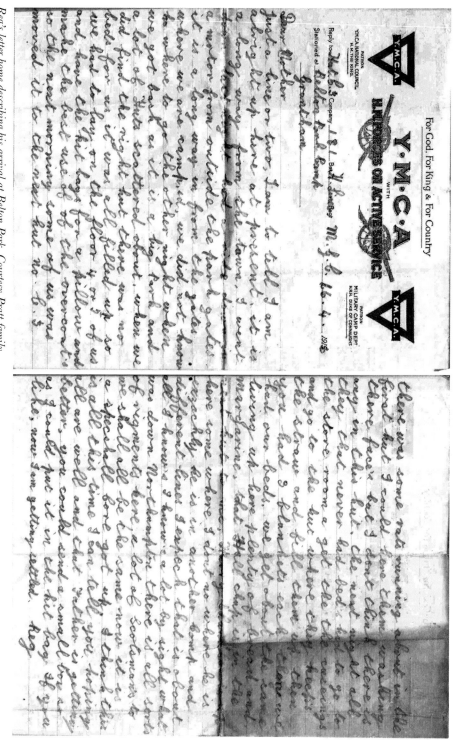

Reg's letter home describing his arrival at Belton Park. Courtesy Pratt family

by Vickers machine guns that were faster, water-cooled and fired from a tripod. A machine-gun crew usually consisted of six men. The first man carried the tripod and fired the gun, the second carried the gun and fed the ammunition, whilst the third and fourth men carried the ammunition, water for the cooling chamber and spare parts. The fifth man acted as a scout and the last man conducted the range finding. All the men in the team, however, were trained to take any position should someone be killed or injured. The most effective machine-gun positions were to the side of the advancing enemy troops with a number of guns overlapping their field of fire. This enfilading fire greatly increased the destructive power of the weapon. On 10 June Reg wrote to his sister Violet saying:

> We were warned for overseas yesterday. I think we shall move from here next Friday or perhaps before ... We had one night and a day in the [training] trenches this week. I had a job to keep awake all night, it don't do for you to go asleep. I see plenty of star shells go up, from what was supposed to be the enemy's trenches, they just light the place up nearly as light as the sun shining for a few seconds.[5]

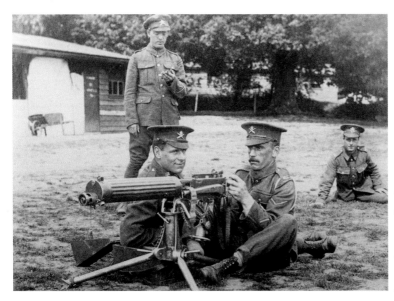

Training on Maxim machine guns at Belton Park. Courtesy Bill Fulton, MGC Old Comarades Association

On 13 June he wrote to his mother:

> We are going out on Friday I don't know where we are going not yet, I am certain it is overseas somewhere, they changed the number of the Coy [Company] today as you see on the address.[6]

The number was changed from 181st to the 123rd Company, Machine Gun Corps as they prepared for service overseas. The 123rd Machine Gun Company joined 123rd Brigade, 41st Division and whilst most of the division moved to

France in the first week of May 1916, the 123rd MGC did not set off until Saturday 17 June, joining the Brigade on 20 June.

The men journeyed from Grantham to Southampton by train arriving at 1.05pm. In the evening of the same day they boarded the SS *Caesara* whilst their equipment was loaded on to the SS *Bellerophon*. They sailed on the 5.30pm tide and arrived at Le Havre at 4.30am the following day. Later in the day they disembarked and marched to a rest camp for the night. In the early afternoon of 20 June the 123rd Company travelled by train to Steenwerck in northern France and after a short march joined the 41st Division at Le Bizet, close to the Belgian border.[7]

The 123rd Company spent July and the first two weeks of August in the trenches close Le Bizet and was frequently shelled by enemy artillery. There was, however, little activity during their stay in the front lines and on 16 August the company was relieved. After a short stay in billets the men were moved to Ergnies, a village close to the River Somme, in Picardy, some twelve miles south-east of Abbeville. In September and October the company fought in the Battles of Flers-Courcelette and Le Transloy Ridge. The former battle was part of the larger Battle of the Somme and is notable for being the first in which tanks were used.

In a letter home on 9 September Reg complains that he has a problem with lice and asks for some powder to be sent out:

> I have caught some of them small animals. I was not troubled with any all the time I was in the trenches. If you sends me some more of that powder it might drive them away.[8]

Unfortunately, however, it did not work and in a letter of 4 November to his sister Violet, Reg asks for an alternative treatment.

> I am in the trenches at present, there is a lot of rats about, they will get at all the food if you don't hang it up out of their way. That vermin powder that Mother sent don't seem much good, Harrison's Pomade is good stuff they say. I shall not be sorry when I can get rid of them things, if you get clean clothes on, it is just as bad in a day or two, the only thing to do is to kill all you can see.[9]

Meanwhile in late October 1916 the company moved to Belgium where it spent the next eight months 'holding the line' in an area (St Eloi Sector) close to Ypres. During this period the 123rd Company was in the front line, in reserve or resting close-by. The company war diary records that on 13 December twelve men were attached to the 1st Canadian Tunnelling Company also active in the St Eloi Sector. We know that Reg was one of these men because in his letter of 14 December he tells his mother:

I am on a tunneling job for a fortnight so I shall just spend xmas in the trenches. I was going to send you all some pretty xmas cards, but I shall not be able to now. [10]

No reason is given why the men assisted the Canadians and there is no mention of their arrival in the tunnellers' war diary. On 4 December, however, their diary records

Dear Violet   4th Nov 1916
Just a few lines to let you know I am still alright. I received your letter alright and Edgar's on the 1st Nov. We get a lot of rain at times now there is plenty of mud to. I expect you are getting plenty of wet wether now. 123rd M. G. Coy. B. E. F. France. I am in the trenches at present, there is a lot of rats about they will get at all the food if you dont hang it up out of their way. That vermin powder that Mother sent dont seem much good, Harrisson's homade is good stuff they say I shall not be sorry when I can get rid of them things

Reg's letter to his sister Violet telling of conditions in the trenches. Courtesy Pratt family

'Enemy shelling in the afternoon, direct hit on Buss House, killed machine gunners'.[11] Hence the twelve men of the 123rd could have been sent to provide temporary cover for these lost men. It is not certain when Reg returned but it was probably on 28 December, just in time to celebrate 'Christmas Day' on the 30 December with the rest of the Company when it returned from front line duty. The war diary for this date records:

> Christmas dinner was given to the Company, as on the 25th they were trench troops. The GOC of 123rd Infantry Brigade visited the Company during dinner, and drank the health of the Company, upon which, 3 hearty cheers were given to him.

Intensely cold conditions welcomed in the New Year and the men of the 123rd MGC soon found themselves back in the front line trenches they had occupied in late December. After five days they were briefly relieved, enabling them to strip down and service their machine guns. No doubt they were justly proud when on inspection the guns were all pronounced very serviceable and well cared for. On 14 January the company returned to the trenches and this was to be Reg's last duty for his King and Country for on 17 January 1917 he was killed. The war diary records:

> A large amount of indirect fire was carried out during the month, the Company gradually increasing the total to 10,000 round a night. The fire was carried out every night and during foggy weather, was on enemy dumps, dugouts, roads etc, throughout the month during tours in the trenches. The Company seemed to have got completely the upper hand

of enemy machine guns in the St Eloi Sector …. During the month 2 O.R. killed and 3 wounded.

There are no details of Reg's death but tragically he was one of only two company soldiers killed during that month.

Private Egbert 'Reg' Pratt was laid to rest in the Dickebusch New Military Cemetery some three miles south-west of Ypres, grave reference L35. He lies with over six hundred others who made the ultimate sacrifice. On his gravestone is inscribed 'Splendid he passed into the light, which nevermore shall fade' - from the hymn 'O Valiant Hearts'.

A book of remembrance for the MGC is held in St Wulfram's Church, Grantham and contains the names of all soldiers from the Corps, including an entry for Reg, who were killed in the Great War.

Private Pratt was entitled to the British War Medal and the Victory Medal.

Loos Memorial; William Butt. © Author's collection

William Duck's Headstone in Aubers Ridge British Cemetery. © Author's collection

Medal card and medal group (digitally recreated) for Joseph Dummer. © *Author's collection*

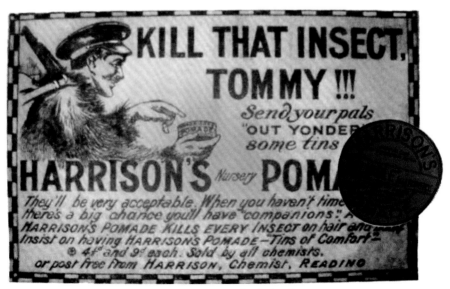

Harrison's Pomade WW1 product label. Courtesy Geoff Carefoot

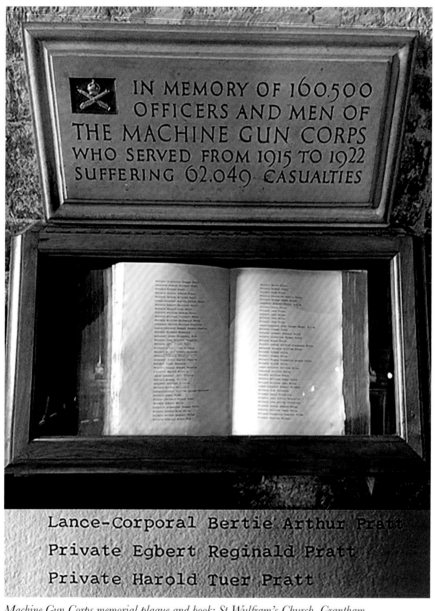

Machine Gun Corps memorial plaque and book: St Wulfram's Church, Grantham.
© Author's collection

The Great War Memorial at All Hallows' Church, Tillington. © Author's collection

The magnificent lectern presented to All Hallows' Church in memory of Victor Barrington-Kennett. © Author's collection

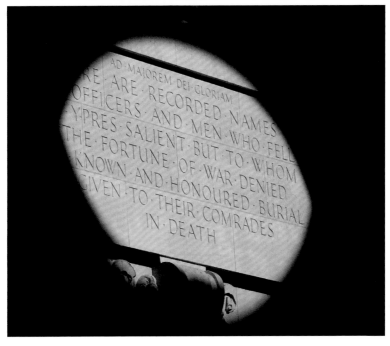

Sunlight falling poignantly on a Menin Gate Plaque. © Author's collection

A soldier of the Great War – known unto God. © *Author's collection*

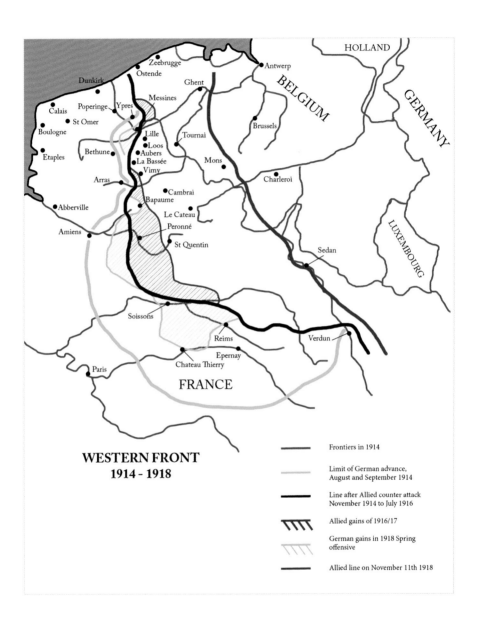

WESTERN FRONT
1914 - 1918

	Frontiers in 1914
	Limit of German advance, August and September 1914
	Line after Allied counter attack November 1914 to July 1916
	Allied gains of 1916/17
	German gains in 1918 Spring offensive
	Allied line on November 11th 1918

26

Private Frederick Scutt G/17557

Royal Sussex Regiment

Frederick Scutt was born at Newick, Sussex, on 10 June 1898 where his parents John and Emma had five other children and father was a dairyman. It appears that the family moved within Sussex several times since Frederick spent time at schools in Mundham and Donnington, both villages just south of Chichester. For two years from 1904 he was a pupil (admission No 592) at Donnington Church School, but by 1906 the family was on the move again, no doubt related to father's search for work. By 1911 they were living at 'Bigenon' Farm Cottage, Petworth.

Towards the end of November 1914 Frederick - at the age of sixteen - walked through the door of the Petworth Armoury. After some time standing in line, preparing his story, he stepped before the recruiting sergeant, perhaps telling him that although he looked very young he was in fact eighteen-years-old. No doubt turning a blind eye, the sergeant enlisted Frederick into D Company, 4th Battalion Royal Sussex Regiment whereupon he became Private Scutt 2283. The 4th Battalion was part of the territorial force and initially men served only on the home front until they signed the Imperial Service Obligation, agreeing to serve overseas. Most recruits signed during their training period and on 17 July 1915 the battalion set sail from Devonport on HMT *Ulysses* destined for Gallipoli.

Although Frederick managed to squeeze his way into the army he was below the legal age to fight overseas, which was nineteen. Consequently when the 4th Battalion left England with the Mediterranean Expeditionary Force he was transferred to the 2/4th Battalion, which remained part of the territorial force throughout the war. From his medal roll[1] we know that at some point, still under age, Frederick was encouraged to sign the Imperial Service Obligation. Having done so he was soon on his way to the Western Front via the British army base at Etaples near Boulogne on the French coast. After further training, possibly in mid-July 1916, he was assigned to the 5th Battalion Royal Sussex Regiment and given a new service number G/17557, but before he could transfer he was further re-assigned to the 13th Battalion of the same regiment (later he was to be posted to the 2nd and then to the 7th Battalion, Royal Sussex Regiment). This unit suffered terrible casualties on 30 June during a fruitless attack on the enemy at a position called Boar's Head near Richebourg l'Avoué and hence was in urgent need of reinforcements. Along with 108 other men Frederick caught up with his new battalion on 26 July close to Le Touret during a period of relief. The draft of new men bathed in the village before moving into the front line at Festubert on 28 July.[2]

During the rest of 1916 the battalion fought in the Battle of the Somme including the smaller battles of Thiepaval Ridge, Ancre Heights and the Ancre. By this time it was mid-November and in deteriorating weather fighting came to a temporary halt. On 17 November 'Lowther's Lambs were moved to Poperinghe in Belgium where they enjoyed some well-deserved rest and recreation. The New Year brought heavy snow falls and the battalions were forced to seek better shelter in the Ramparts of Ypres, a convent and a school. After extended periods of intensive training the men returned to Poperinghe at the end of June, fully prepared for the coming Ypres Offensive. From August to November 1917 all three battalions played a part in the major battles of this operation.

The winter was spent in billets close to Steenvorde where the men, often in thick snow, were occupied with yet more training, musketry practice and sports activities. In late January 1918 they returned to the battlefields of the Somme and to some of the worst fighting they had experienced.

The war diary for the 13th Battalion shows that in March 1918 they were caught up in the German 'Spring Offensive' (a massive, surprise German attack along fifty miles of the Western Front south of Arras, attempting to end the war before the Americans could participate fully). The offensive began on 21 March and it was on the next day near the hamlet of Sainte Emilie, fifteen miles north-west of St Quentin, that the 13th experienced the full force of the German attack. The result was almost complete annihilation of A Company and half of B Company before there was a general retreat. On 23 March the 13th Battalion attempted to make a stand against the fast-advancing enemy, but once again they were overwhelmed, forcing a hasty withdrawal through the town of Péronne. They suffered further heavy casualties and the unit was now so depleted that the remnants were incorporated into a 'composite battalion' with men from other battalions in a similar state.

After a period of rest the composite battalion made its way, by route march and train, to Ottawa Camp close to the safe area of Vlamertinghe in Belgium. Here the battalion was made up to strength with thirteen officers and 368 men from the 13th Gloucesters and given the name No 2 Battalion of the 39th Division. Unfortunately there are no records for Frederick's military service but this may well have been the 2nd Battalion referred to on his medal roll. If so, he served with them until 23 May 1918 when the battalion was further reduced in strength and forty-four men and one officer were returned to the army base at Etaples for posting to other units. This may have resulted in Frederick being posted to the 7th Battalion Royal Sussex Regiment.

All we know for certain is that he was with B Company of the 7th Battalion in September 1918.[3] During August the battalion had courageously delivered a good share of a fifteen-mile advance and some 1,000 prisoners. The battalion was strengthen in early September with a draft of 250 reinforcements and thirteen officers joining as the exhausted men rested close to Péronne.

The next major battle (The Battle of Epehy) was planned for 18 September and in preparation the 7th Sussex had moved up and assembled in front of the village of Epehy some ten miles north-east of Péronne.

The attack against the Hindenburg Line (Germany's heavily fortified last line of defence on the Western Front) began just before dawn on a very wet, dark morning that made it hard going for the infantry. Unfortunately dawn brought no respite and a heavy mist was exacerbated by smoke from the British artillery barrage. The success of the operation depended heavily on the early capture of Epehy, but the mist caused the troops to lose direction and their progress was soon unexpectedly halted by a strong barbed-wire barrier. As the men attempted to cut the wire they were killed or wounded by heavy machine-gun fire from enemy positions in the village, resulting in an appalling number of casualties including Frederick from B Company. The village was not taken until 7.45pm on the evening of 18 September by which time all but two of the battalion officers were casualties as were 200 other ranks. The war ended just two months later.

Private Frederick Scutt is buried with many of his friends from B Company in the peaceful cemetery at Epehy Wood Farm. He was awarded the British War Medal and the Victory medal.

The Medal Roll showing Frederick Scutt's movements between battalions. The National Archives

27

Private Charles Stoner G/3812

Royal Sussex Regiment

In early 1887, at the age of twenty-seven, William Stoner of Tillington married Eliza Chandler from Lurgashall. They set up home in Petworth at Brinksole, Limbo(w), Petworth where William was a copse labourer. Very soon daughter Agnes was born (1887), followed by Elizabeth (1889) and Florence (1891). In 1893 they had their first son, William, and later Charles (1895), Frederick (1899) and Dorothy (1903) were born. The 1901 census shows that sometime between 1893 and 1896 the family moved to Upperton where William became a domestic gardener. Charles Henry Stoner was christened in All Hallows' Church on 29 September 1895. After leaving Tillington School at the age of fourteen he became a farm labourer and by 1911 the family had returned to Petworth and was living in Lowheath Cottage (just off what is now the A283 west of Petworth).

At the outbreak of war in 1914 it was clear that many more soldiers would be needed to defeat the German army and, although Lord Kitchener's recruiting campaign began well it was perhaps not until news reached our shores of the British retreat following the Battle of Mons on 23 August, that enlistment suddenly improved and by September 500,000 men had volunteered.

The 2nd Battalion, Royal Sussex Regiment (in the 1st Division, 2nd Infantry Brigade) fought in the Battle of Mons and Charles may have read of this in the local papers. Shortly after his nineteenth birthday, between 24 and 26 September 1914 Charles travelled to Chichester to enlist in the Royal Sussex Regiment. The 2nd Battalion was fighting in France and therefore it is likely that Charles was posted to the 3rd (Reserve) Battalion which had been formed in August 1914 at Chichester specifically to train recruits for overseas battalions. Before he joined, the battalion had moved to Dover and in May 1915 they moved again to Newhaven for duty as the town Garrison.[1]

After his training Private Charles Stoner G/3812 was posted to the 2nd Battalion, Royal Sussex Regiment in France. He left England on 20 October 1915 to join the battalion, which was resting at Lillers, eight miles north-west of Bethune. On 25 October it received reinforcements of eight signallers and nineteen machine gunners and on 29 October eighteen other ranks arrived.[2]

It is likely that Charles was one of these but his function is not known.

All new reinforcements were encouraged to make a will before they headed to the front line. The wills, which laid out how soldiers' estates should be administered if they were killed in battle, were kept in a pocket service book tucked into their uniform. Charles made such a will on 30 October 1915, providing more evidence that he had joined the regiment only a few days earlier. It is also interesting to note that below his signature Charles had written his regiment as the 3rd Royal Sussex. This was perhaps a further indication that he had only just arrived.

The battalion was rested until 14 November and the war diary reports how they spent their time during this rest period:

The will written by Charles Stoner on 30 October 1915. Soldiers' wills Probatesearch. service.gov.uk

> Battalion in rest billets. A scale of parades was carried out daily including, running drill, physical exercises, drill and Musketery, Sergt Major's Parades. Regimental concerts were also held in the Theatre, Lillers.

On 14 November the battalion travelled by train to Hulluch and remained in reserve until 3 December when they moved up to the front line trenches at Loos for a short period. Nine days later they were relieved and moved back to Hulluch where they took over the front line 'in the vicinity of the quarries'. After two days the battalion was relieved and conveyed by motor bus to billets at Noeux les Mines some six miles west of Hulluch, where they rested for several days. The war diary entry for late December 1915 records:

> Dec 22nd - Battalion moved to support trenches in section B1.
> Dec 26th - Battalion moved up to firing line in section B1.

No mention of Christmas Day was made until the entry for 3 January 1916:

> On 3rd Jan Christmas Day was celebrated in billets, the 25th December

being spent in the trenches, and consequently but little celebration could take place, but however we made good on the 3rd.

For the first five months of 1916 the battalion was variously in support trenches, front line trenches or resting in the area around Loos and Lillers. The rest periods were punctuated with football matches and concerts. For 30/31 January the war diary records:

> In the 1st round of the 2nd Brigade Football Tournament, the Bn [Battalion] was successful in its match against the Northamptonshire Regiment winning by 5 goals to nil.

On the 2 February the commentary was continued:

> Regimental team took part in Brigade Final Football Competition, the result was a draw after extra time.

It seems that there was a replay on 6 February and this time the battalion won by a narrow margin of 1-0 and well-earned medals were distributed by Brigadier-General Thullier of the Royal Engineers.

A treat awaited the men on 28 March when the hot water baths at Fosse No 2 de Noeux (a pit head) awaited them. Most bathing was completed before the end of the month, which was fortunate since on 31 March the enemy shelled the baths and mine works with long-range guns, and bathing had to be cancelled.

Close to the hamlet of Les Brebis lay the now famous 'Double Crassier', two parallel 100ft-high spoil heaps from the surrounding mining operations which in June 1916 were very much in German hands. A plan was hatched by the 2nd Battalion Royal Sussex and the 2nd Kings Royal Rifles to attack these heaps on the night of 30 June. The attack started badly when an enemy artillery bombardment began ten minutes before zero hour at 9.10pm. In addition, the German wire defences had not been completely cut by the Allied artillery during the day and it was impossible to find a way through. The Germans brought up a second machine gun between the two crassiers and opened fire on the attacking troops at a range of thirty yards. It soon became clear that the attack had failed and the men were withdrawn to their original position.

The battalion left the Pas de Calais region on 6 July when the men marched six miles to Lillers where they boarded trains bound for the battlefields of the Somme. On arrival they marched a further eight miles to Flesselles before falling into their beds at billets in a number of local barns, in the early hours of the next day. Several more days marching brought the battalion close to Albert. On 10 July the troops, in fighting order, marched through the town to nearby Becourt Wood where the men bivouacked for several days in pouring rain amongst the trees.

During the following three months the battalion fought bravely in actions including the latter stages of the Battle of Albert (1-13 July), the Battle of Bazentin (14-17 July), the Battle of Pozieres (23 July) and the Battle of Flers-Courcelette. (15-22 September). On 19 September the battalion was ordered to return to Becourt Wood where once again the men bivouacked for several days in extremely wet conditions, made worse by the heavy enemy shelling. In the afternoon of 25 September the battalion left the wood and moved into support trenches in front of High Wood. At 5pm on the following afternoon orders were received:

> …..that the battalion would attack the German line 900 yds in front of PRUE TRENCH. This necessitated a relief of the 50th Division who were holding the line from which we were to attack. The attack was launched at 11pm, but was unsuccessful.

> Sept 27th At 2pm … the battalion again attacked the German position, B Coy led the assault with A Coy in close support. The battalion advanced steadily and in splendid order, in spite of much hostile artillery fire, and easily secured its objective … Our casualties during the advance were slight and the captured position was consolidated before dark…Our

British infantrymen at the Battle of Morval. Ⓒ *Copyright expired*

casualties in both attacks were other ranks killed 21, wounded 99, missing 36 (2nd Battalion war diary).

Charles was one of the thirty-six missing after this battle (Battle of Morval) and he is remembered on the Thiepval Memorial off the main Bapaume-to-Albert road. The panel reference is Pier and Face 7C.

Private Charles Stoner was killed just one day short of a year after his older brother William had been killed at Loos. The Register of Soldiers' Effects shows that his Estate was owed £4. 5s. 6d back pay and a war gratuity of £8. 10s. 0d. This money was passed to his mother, Eliza.[3]

Private Stoner was awarded the 1914-15 Star, the British War Medal and the Victory Medal.

28

Lance Sergeant William Stoner 11178

Coldstream Guards

W illiam George Stoner was born in the summer of 1893 to parents William and Eliza. His birth must have been accompanied by great joy for this was their first son and one can imagine his three young sisters anxious to play with him. His early life and that of his younger brother Charles have been described in the previous chapter.

The 1911 census shows that the family had returned to Petworth but the 19-year-old William had left home and was boarding with Emily Mason, a widow and innkeeper, at nearby Lowheath where he was employed as a brewery carman (driver of horse-drawn transport vehicle).

William, like his brother Charles, was no doubt enthused by Lord Kitchener's recruiting campaign and travelled to Chichester to enlist in the Coldstream Guards. His service number, 11178, suggests that he joined for wartime service during the first week in September 1914. It is likely that he trained at Windsor with the 5th Reserve Battalion, Coldstream Guards before being posted to the 1st Battalion of the same regiment.

William's Medal Index Card[1] shows that he entered the war on the Western Front in France on 24 February 1915 after approximately six months' training. By this time the 1st Battalion had been in France with the British Expeditionary Force since 14 August 1914 and had fought in the Battles of Mons, Marne, Ypres (First) and the winter campaign

The Medal Card for Charles showing his date of entry into France.
Ancestry.co.uk

of 1914-15.[2] For three weeks in February 1915 the battalion was resting and training near Ecquedecques, Pas-de-Calais. On 27 February they marched to overnight billets ten miles west to Hinges and late in the day William and 249 other reinforcements caught up with them. The following day the refreshed battalion continued their march to Richbourg L'Avoué where they went into Brigade Reserve. Here William gained his first short experience in the front line trenches when the battalion relieved the Black Watch. Two days later they were themselves relieved and went into billets at Le Touret.

During periods out of the trenches the 1st Battalion Coldstream Guards kept up their morale by making their own entertainment. On 6 June 1915 the war diary records the men enjoying what must have been a rare treat, a visit to the swimming baths in Bethune. There were several regiments billeted around Bethune at this time providing the opportunity for some inter-regimental sports, including a boxing match and horse show. The 1st Battalion, Coldstream Guards won prizes in both, including the prize for the best turned out horse.

On 25 August after marching to new billets in Lumbres, the 1st Battalion heard that they had been transferred from the 1st (Guards) Brigade in the 1st Division to the 2nd Brigade in the same division and some of the men were not too pleased with this apparent downgrade. Without emotion the war diary for 25 August records:

> The Col heard that he had got our new brigade. The Bn is now to form part of the 2nd Guards Brigade. Some are rather annoyed and think this is unfair. Our billets here are good.

As summer gave way to autumn the battalion was enjoying an extended quiet period still in billets at Lumbres. They occupied their time with drills, a boxing match against the 2nd Battalion Irish Guards and countless parades. All this, however, ended on 19 September when 'all leave was stopped and everyone on leave ordered to rejoin by (Thursday) 23rd'.[3] On the 22nd the men, 'sorry to leave Lumbres after a month there', marched to Delette and the next day continued in pouring rain to Therouanne, ten miles to the south-east of Lumbres, where they joined the rest of the brigade. The battalion did not move the following day but no doubt there was an air of expectancy amongst the men. Late in the evening the General Officer Commanding the XI Corps briefed all the battalion commanders, adding to the rumours that something big was in the offing. They did not have long to wait: on 25 September the first genuinely large-scale British offensive action began. The small town of Loos-en-Gohelle lies just north of the mining town of Lens in the industrial north-east of France. In 1915 the surrounding flat area was studded with pit heads, slag heaps and all manner of miners' dwellings. It was in this difficult terrain that the Battle of Loos was fought.

The plan was that seventeen infantry divisions of the French 10th Army

'Tower Bridge' and the village of Loos 1915. Courtesy Paul Reed.

and six British 1st Army Divisions should attack the German Sixth Army on a front of some twenty miles running from Arras to La Bassée. Reserve troops, including the guards division, some of which were fresh from England, were held some distance behind the front lines ready to come forward to consolidate any gains. The heavy bombardment over a period of four days before the attack meant that the enemy was both unsurprised and fully prepared.

The 1st Coldstream Guards were not involved in the fighting on the first day but during the evening of 26 September all three brigades of the guards division were moved to the front close to Le Rutoire Farm, where at 3am the next morning they relieved exhausted men of 21st and 24th Divisions. The battalion war diary for the same day reports that the 2nd Guards Brigade (including 1st Battalion Coldstream Guards) was ordered to:

> … attack the Wood & Chalk Pit in support of the 2nd Irish Guards at 4 pm. The Irish Guards attained objective but retired. No1 and No 2 Coy attacked and captured [Chalk Pit] Wood & Chalk Pit and dug themselves in on the far side. This position was made good and consolidated. Many wounded men who had been out since 25th brought in. Wood & Chalk Pit made a very prominent salient which rendered it a difficult position to hold.

The Irish Guards included Lieutenant John Kipling, son of Rudyard Kipling. On 27 September he was reported injured during their attack on Chalk Pit. A shell blast had apparently seriously injured him but in the continuing fighting his body was never recovered. His parents travelled to France in a vain attempt to find their son. They searched field hospitals and talked to his comrades and on 7 October a notice was published in *The Times* newspaper confirming the only known facts: 'wounded and missing', six weeks after his eighteenth birthday. In his grief Rudyard Kipling wrote his evocative poem *My Boy Jack* which, although is about a generic sailor (or Jack Tar), expresses the emotion of a father whose son has been lost. 'Have you news of my boy Jack? … Has anyone else had word of him?'

In 1919 the Commonwealth War Graves Commission believed that they had found the body of John Kipling lying in an unmarked grave. In the 1990s his body was re-buried with military honours in St Mary's Advanced Dressing Station Cemetery close to where John was found.

The Coldstream Guards held the Chalk Pits through the night and at 3.45 pm the next day, 28 September, they were ordered to attack a colliery head and workings known as Puits 14 bis. As soon as they advanced they were exposed to extremely heavy, sweeping machine-gun fire from the enemy position in a nearby wood. Although some men reached the objective it was impossible to hold and they fell back to the Chalk Pit. Lance Sergeant William Stoner, aged twenty three, was killed in this action and his body was never found. The war diary reads:

> At 3.45pm ordered to attack Puit 14 bis and establish line on railway with 2 companies, No 1 & 2 coys advanced with their left on the Lens – La Basse road. They were met almost before they got out of the trenches by terrific machine gun fire which enfiladed them from 3 sides [chiefly from Bois Victor Hugo]. They were absolutely mown down. 2 officers with 8 men reached the objective which they found not held by enemy but only enfiladed by yet another machine gun. Lt Riley & two men got back. The men behaved simply splendidly as not only were they subjected to this enormous enfilade machine gun fire but also to a most terrific bombardment by 8" shells and shrapnel and every kind of heavy gun fire which was most accurate.

In his book '*The Battle of Loos*',[4] Philip Warner noted that after 27 September:

> … two guards brigades were released to the reserve. However, this did not stop the 2nd Guards Brigade [now at about half strength] being used on the 28th to try to push the British Line further forward at Puits 14 bis, just north of Loos. The Coldstream [Guards] were almost exterminated in the attack.

No further territorial gains were made and the end of the Battle of Loos was finally declared on 8 October 1915.

Lance Sergeant Stoner is commemorated on the Loos Memorial that forms the back and sides of the Dud Corner Cemetery. It is located one mile west of the village of Loos-en-Gohelle in Pas de Calais. The Memorial reference is Panel 7 and 8.

Lance Sergeant Stoner was awarded the 1914-15 Star, the British War Medal and the Victory Medal.

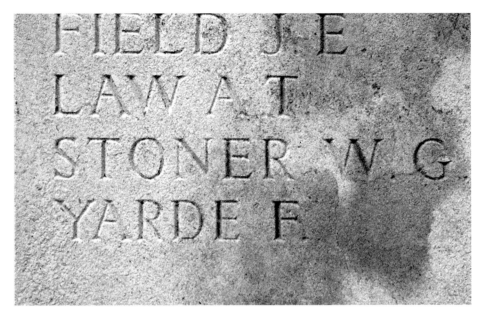

The inscription for Lance Sergeant W G Stoner on the Loos Memorial, France.
© Author's collection

29

Private George Summersell TF/200811

Royal Sussex Regiment

It is somewhat surprising that there should be any confusion with the birth date of a child, but in the case of George Frederick Summersell there are two possibilities. The National Register of Births records that he was born in the first quarter of 1897, whereas his father's army record clearly states that he was born on 24 December 1896. There is, however, a little more consensus on the date of his christening. The baptism records of St Mary's Church, Petworth show that he was christened on 3 April 1897 and this was officiated by Curate J W Watson.

George's parents John and Elizabeth Mary (née Blake) were married on 17 December 1887 in the small Saxon church of St Olave in North Street, Chichester. By this time John had been in the army for ten years, having enlisted in 43rd Brigade/107th Regiment of Foot at Chichester on 3 December 1877. In 1881 this unit officially became the Royal Sussex Regiment and the following year fought in Egypt. Within two years John had returned to England and, until he was discharged in 1906, he spent the rest of his service at home. The 1891 census shows Elizabeth living alone in the Barracks at New Broyle Road, Chichester, but perhaps John and the two children were away visiting relatives at the time. There is no trace of the family in the 1901 census, but we know that Colour Sergeant John Summersell was awarded the Long Service and Good Conduct medals and that he was discharged from the 2nd battalion Royal Sussex Regiment at Worthing on 3 December 1906. He stated that he had secured employment as a school attendance officer and that he would be living in Petworth.

The 1911 census finds a much-enlarged family living in Upperton where father John is described as an army pensioner and school attendance officer; he and his wife now have ten children and Elizabeth's widowed mother is living with them. George Frederick was fourteen-years-old and a baker's assistant and his elder brother, John William, had been in a part time battalion of the Royal Sussex Regiment since he was a fourteen-year-old.

John William's military record[1] shows that on 21 November 1908, aged seventeen, he enlisted for four years in the 4th Battalion of the same regiment at the Petworth recruiting centre and was given the service number 616. His medical examination at the time records that he was 5ft 5in tall, with good vision and good physical development and that he was passed fit for the Territorial Force. He attended annual training camps including Arundel, Newhaven and Hassocks. On 4 March 1912 he 're-engaged for four years' and in the same year was promoted to Lance Corporal. No doubt his father was very proud when he learnt of his son's advancement, but unfortunately he did not live to see John's further promotion. In autumn 1914 John was posted to the 2nd/4th Battalion and was later promoted to Acting Sergeant. The 2nd/4th did not go to war but became a training battalion for new recruits, preparing them to reinforce the senior 1/4th Battalion fighting overseas. It appears that Sergeant Summersell either became tired of training new recruits or was seeking new challenges for on 18 June 1916, after seven years and twenty-one days' service, John William was discharged from the Army 'in consequence of re-enlistment into the Royal Flying Corps'.[2]

Wasting no time John William travelled to Farnborough where, on 19 June 1916, he enlisted for the 'duration of war' in the RFC and was given the service number 26085. His civilian trade was given as 'plumber for acetylene welder' and so on enlistment he became air mechanic second class (2/AM), but by early spring of 1918 he had been promoted to 1/AM. His RFC records show that his trade classification was a 'fitter (Motor Transport)'. By this time the RFC had become the Royal Air Force and after an extended period in the UK, John William was posted to France to join No 2 Aircraft Depot in Candas, some twenty miles north of Amiens. Here men worked day and night to maintain aircraft and to salvage, repair or reconstruct crashed or damaged planes in order to maintain the fighting strength. On 3 August 1918 John William was transferred to No 1 Aircraft Depot at St Omer and then spent a short period with No 70 Squadron at Fienvillers before returning, to 2/AD in early October.

John William transferred to the RAF Reserve on 5 May 1919 and was finally discharged on 4 April 1920. He had married Edith Carn in the autumn of 1919 in Petworth and died aged 82 in 1973, in the Chichester area.

George perhaps encouraged by his brother's tales of army life, was by 1914 persuaded to join up. With the promise of excitement and adventure, he found his way to the drill hall in Petworth in November and, like many of his contemporaries, enlisted in D Company, 4th Battalion, Royal Sussex Regiment, emerging as Private G Summersell 4/2985 (changed to TF/200811 in 1917 when all TF soldiers were given new six digit numbers). After training with this unit, George remained with the 4th Battalion Royal Sussex.

On 24 April 1915 the battalion was posted to the 160th Brigade, 53rd (Welsh) Division in Cambridge and in May it moved to Bedford. As soon as training was completed the battalion received orders to re-equip for service in the Mediterranean and on 16 July it left Bedford aboard two trains bound for Devonport.[3] The next day the 1/4th Battalion embarked on HMT *Ulysses* to

SS Ulysses. Ⓒ *Copyright expired*

join the Mediterranean Expeditionary Force which, travelling via Alexandria and Port Said, steamed for Mudros Bay, a small port on the Greek island of Lemnos. From Mudros the *Ulysses* sailed for Suvla bay on the Gallipoli peninsula, arriving on 7 August. The 1/4th Battalion Royal Sussex Regiment entered the Great War on the evening of 8 August, two days after the landings began. They were to provide reinforcements for the original brigade landings that were so disastrous because of the blackness of night, the low tides for the landing crafts and the accuracy of Ottoman snipers. After landing, the 4th Battalion also experienced heavy enemy artillery fire as they tried to move from the beach into the hills. After a change of command the front was reorganised and reinforced with further troops from Greece and Egypt, but when this 'new army' failed to win the major battle at Scimitar Hill all British troops were evacuated in December 1915.

The battalion remained in action on the Gallipoli Peninsula until 13 December 1915, when it sailed aboard the SS *Elkahira* to Mudros Bay and on to Alexandria in Egypt. At the end of January 1916 the battalion's strength was given as nineteen Officers and 316 Other Ranks. It took the next five months to restore its numbers to thirty-nine officers and 887 other ranks and replace the losses of the Gallipoli action.

After a prolonged period of training in Egypt the battalion returned into action against Turkish forces in Palestine, initially in the area of Gaza, and on 9 April 1917 it participated in second battle of Gaza followed later by the third battle on 6 November. The British forces pressed the Turkish defenders north towards Jerusalem, which was captured on 9 December. General Allenby, the Commander of the Egyptian Expeditionary Force, entered the city two days later, closely followed by the 4th Battalion, Royal Sussex Regiment.

The 4th Battalion Royal Sussex Regiment marching into Bethelem, December 1917.
WSRO RSR PH4/56

On 16 June 1918 the battalion was transported by train to Alexandria and the following day boarded HMT *Malwa* bound for Taranto, Italy. From here the men travelled by train, via Genoa and Marseilles, to Etaples in Northern France. Because of closeness to the English Channel and its railway connections across the north of France this small town was of strategic importance to the British Army and it became the principal depot and transit camp for forces landing in France. One soldier wrote:[4]

> We reached the base soon after 12.00 noon disentraining at a small station called Etaples. The Camp was a very large one composed of tents, the dining halls etc. being large, marquees with one or two wooden buildings dotted about which were the YMCA's and such like. There were also one or two large Hospitals adjacent to the Camp and these were composed of several wards, each ward consisting of 3 marquees.

The 1/4th Battalion arrived at Etaples at 11pm on 28 June and by 7pm next evening the men were on a train bound for Proven. Here they camped and took part in training exercises until mid-July when they moved to Chantilly. From here the battalion was bussed and marched to a destination close to the front line at Parcy Tigny. On 23 July their camp was heavily shelled; one officer and fourteen other ranks were killed and several more wounded.

On 28 July the battalion received orders to advance to a destination recorded as approximately the Courdoux-Servenay Road, 'artillery support being called for as required'. At 4.10am the following day, the advance was going well, but in the latter stages the men were held up by several enemy machine guns sheltered in Bois de Beugneux. The war diary records:

> July 29, 6.00am
> It was found impossible to obtain artillery support owing to lack of communication and the line was withdrawn to the road and reorganised. The wood was then successfully rushed with bayonet, a number of the enemy being killed and several machine guns captured.

The final objective was eventually reached but because of further heavy machine-gun and artillery fire they could not hold it and withdrew some considerable distance where they remained for the rest of the day. This fight for a small wood in Picardy exemplifies the futility of many of the larger battles of the Great War. Much of the ground taken during the morning was lost before nightfall with heavy casualties—three officers and forty-two other ranks killed, four officers and 125 other ranks wounded and twenty-six missing. The battalion made a third attempt to take the wood on 1 August and this time it was successfully taken and held, but again there were casualties (ten other ranks killed, 28 wounded, three missing). On 3 August the battalion was rested.

George died of his wounds on 3 August 1918 suggesting that he was wounded on 29 July when there were so many casualties, but it could have been at the beginning of August.

Private George Summersell TF/200811 lies in the Senlis French National Cemetery. The cemetery is on the northwest outskirts of Senlis town on the main road from Compiègne to Paris. The grave reference is II.F.106. George's mother Elizabeth received his back pay and a war gratuity that amounted to £28. 16s. 5d.

Private Summersell was awarded the British War Medal and the Victory Medal. These medals were secured by the author and, in the absence of any known family, they will be retained safely in George's home village.

30

Private William Wadey TF/200499

Royal Sussex Regiment

William Mark Wadey was born on 5 October 1896 in Upperton and was christened at All Hallows' Church Tillington on 29 November of the same year. His parents, Mark and Alice, married on 10 August 1878 at Petworth and their first son, George, was born in 1879. Daughter Mary Jane arrived a year later followed by Felix (1882), Olive (1889), Fanny Rose (1892) and finally William. In 1881 the young couple were living at Gunters Bridge in Petworth, but over the next twenty years they spent some time in Upperton before settling at Little Common.

William Wadey in the uniform of the Royal Sussex Regiment. Courtesy Judith Bartley

William, aged four, was enrolled at Tillington School on 1 October 1900 with admission number 738.[1] At the end of the 1910 summer term before his fourteenth birthday he left school. The following year he was still living at home but employed as an errand boy for a harness maker. As the months went by this job may have become somewhat mundane and the earlier excitement of leaving school and finding employment was perhaps beginning to wane. By 1913 war with Germany was a distinct possibility and many young men were joining the army, but perhaps only on a part-time basis. No doubt William and his friends saw the army as a new and exciting challenge and in September 1914, just before his eighteenth birthday, he made his way to the Armoury in Petworth and enrolled in the Royal Sussex Regiment to become Private William Wadey 2211 of D Company, 4th Territorial Battalion (he would receive a new service number in early 1917 when all TF Regiments changed their numbers and William became TF200499). He reported to the regimental headquarters at Horsham and may have spent some time there before signing the 'Imperial Service Obligation' agreeing to serve overseas. At the beginning of October 1914 he was posted, in a draft with others including Percy Boxall and William Bryder, to the 1/4th Battalion at Newhaven.

Territorial battalions were raised for home defence, early in the war, when the fear of invasion was widespread. Locally there were rumours that the German Army would soon invade the south coast of England and that defending it would be crucial to the safety of the country. Hence key locations along the Sussex shoreline were quickly manned and defences erected. Soldiers from the Royal Garrison Artillery were moved into Newhaven Fort, whilst the 4th Battalion Royal Sussex Regiment collected in Newhaven towards the end of October to guard the swing bridge, harbour and quays. Other units were deployed between Hastings and Newhaven. As the war on the Western Front settled into the stalemate of trench warfare, it became clear that seaborne invasion was unlikely and therefore, in late April 1915 the 4th Battalion was transferred to the 160th Brigade in the 53rd (Welsh) Division and moved to Cambridge for further training. In May the battalion marched the thirty miles from Cambridge to a new training camp in Bedford.

As the service record for William has not survived we know very little of his movements during his period of training, but on 17 July he was not in the battalion when it left Bedford bound for Gallipoli via Devonport on HMT *Ulysses*. He was posted to the 1/5th (Cinque Ports) Battalion Royal Sussex Regiment, presumably some time before mid-July 1915. By this time his new battalion had been in France for nearly six months but the war diary[2] shows no new drafts of men before 22 November, when forty arrived. If he did not join the regiment as part of a reinforcement draft he may have joined earlier as the 1/5th Battalion prepared to go overseas.

The 5th Battalion spent the early part of 1915 on duty at the Tower of London but on 18 February it crossed to France on SS *Pancras* landing at Le Havre. It joined the 2nd Brigade of the 1st Division and first saw action in early March close to Festubert. On 20 August 1915 the battalion became the Pioneer Battalion of the 48th Division, joining them on the Somme at Hébuterne. Pioneer battalions were raised to support infantry both by maintaining roads and railways and acting

The crossed pick and rifle of the Pioneers

as supplementary riflemen. Pioneers wore a brass badge on each collar in the form of a crossed rifle and pick.

Among the Somme battles in which the 5th Battalion fought were Bazentin Ridge, Pozières, Ancre Heights and Ancre. Pioneers variously repaired roads, built light railways, dug new trenches (sometimes only 100 yards from their German counterparts) and held the front line; they were always at risk and often under heavy enemy bombardment and machine-gun fire. The war diary of the 5th Battalion gives an insight into the workload of a Pioneer unit and the range of tasks the men were expected to perform:

> 30 June 1916. During the month very heavy work day and night... often men working 10 to 14 hours a day – wet through and not time to dry – and most of the time under fire. – Night parties nearly every night – Every available man in the Battalion ordered out...very wet & cold month for June and work in this easily soluble soil rendered more difficult that usual.
> 23 November 1916. During the month 18 Amiens [temporary canvas huts] and 10 Nissen huts erected and most of them completed. 150 yards of road cleared and metalled... Stake and Horse standing put up. Ablution trenches made – Canteen built and opened – Tool sheds – Cooker shelters, Soup kitchens and Latrines built.

Men of the Pioneer Corps clearing mud from a road during the Third Battle of Ypres.
Courtesy Royal Pioneer Corps Association

On 24 December the battalion began work on a derelict camp at 'Middle Wood' close to the village of Bazentin. The war diary makes no mention of any Christmas or New Year celebrations, but there are no entries for 25 and

26 December. Work, however, begins again on the 27 December and the diary entry records that the camp is completed by 1 January 1917: 'Our camp to be known as 'Cinque Ports Camp'. All huts numbered and marked'. Unfortunately the battalion only occupied the camp for two weeks for on 16 January: 'Moved by train from Albert to Longpré – Handed over camp to 15th Division, in good condition very clean and sanitary'.

The Pioneers were soon moved again and by late March they were improving roads to the front in the Péronne area. The Germans were experiencing a serious shortage of troops and ammunition on the Western Front and they began to retire towards their major defensive position, the Hindenburg Line. The first signs of this retreat were seen on 14 March and the British and French troops quickly began to move forward. The advance continued until early April when, nearing the Hindenberg Line, the troops met more determined resistance. The 5th Battalion war diary shows that the Pioneers were very much at the forefront of this advance, reconstructing and repairing damage left by the retreating German troops:

> Herbécourt March 17th: All working strength concentrated on roads Herbécourt-Biaches and Flaucourt –Bianches owing to evacuation of Biaches and La Maisonette by the enemy … work to continue on roads West of Somme …. B Coy detailed for light railway from Flaucourt …. C Coy moved to Bussy to take over intermediate roads, the roads allotted to A and D being extended Eastwards as the enemy is driven back.

In early July 1917 the battalion moved into Belgium and after various moves they made their way to West Canal Bank close to Ypres ready for more 'forward work'. They were in fact about to take part in the Battle of Langemarck (16-18 August) at the start of the third battle of Ypres, often known as Passchendaele, where they fought in the front line. The German front lines in this area had suffered continuous bombardment that had turned the battlefields into a quagmire of foul, sticky mud, full of the debris of war; it was here on 16 August that the battalion suffered serious casualties. The August summary in the war diary reads simply: 'Very few reinforcements received during the month and casualties heavy'.

At the beginning of September the men were still close to Ypres where both A and C Companies were occupied repairing local roads and a light railway, whilst C and D Companies moved to a new camp to prepare additional accommodation. However, as soon as the enemy noticed increased activity at the camp they continually bombed the site. There are no relevant entries in the war diary but, sometime in the first two weeks of September, William was severely wounded during one of these raids. We know that he died on 15 September and is buried in Dozinghem Military Cemetery just north of Poperinghe in Belgium. This suggests that following the air raid the wounded

Dozinghem Military Cemetery, Belgium. © Author's collection

Private Wadey was quickly moved to one of the newly constructed Casualty Clearing Stations (CCS) at Dozinghem.

An American wartime surgeon, Major Harvey Cushing wrote a very poignant description of a soldier's burial in the Dozinghem Cemetery on 30 August 1917,[3] just two weeks before William's death:

> We saw him buried in the early morning. A soggy Flanders field beside a little oak grove to the rear of the Dosinghem group - an overcast, windy, autumnal day - the long rows of simple wooden crosses - the new ditches half full of water being dug by Chinese coolies wearing tin helmets - the boy wrapped in an army blanket and covered by a weather-worn Union Jack, carried on their shoulders by four slipping stretcher-bearers.

This soldier was Edward Revere Osler the great-great-grandson of Paul Revere and the son of Sir William Osler, eminent Oxford Professor of Medicine, but it could just as well have been Private William Wadey of the 5th Battalion, Royal Sussex Regiment.

Dozinghem Military Cemetery is located to the northwest of Poperinge, close to Leper (Ypres). The grave reference is VI. D. 18.

Private Wadey was awarded the British War Medal and the Victory Medal.

Private Alfred Wilson G/4072

Royal Sussex Regiment

Alfred George Wilson was born in 1889 in Mill Lane, Gosport to Martha Wilson (status 'married' but no mention of a husband in 1901/11 censuses) who had four other children. The 1901 census records the family was living in Upperton. By 1911 Alfred had left home and was boarding nearby in Tillington with Peter Baker and his wife. Both Peter and Alfred were builders' labourers.

Sometime in October 1914 Alfred travelled to Chichester where he enlisted in the 9th Battalion, Royal Sussex Regiment, becoming G/4072 Private A G Wilson. Alfred was sent to Cooden Mount Camp, close to Cooden Beach Golf Club in Bexhill, for induction and initial training. The camp had only just opened and the first occupants were housed in canvas tents, which were replaced with wooden huts later in the year. In December the battalion moved into billets at Portslade where they continued training. During the month Alfred contracted enteric fever (typhoid) and was quickly moved to the 2nd Eastern Hospital at Brighton. This military hospital occupied the newly opened Brighton Grammar School and several elementary schools. Alfred had a high fever for 18 days and then began to haemorrhage which led to his death on 29 December 1914 at the age of twenty five. His body was brought home and he is buried beneath a Commonwealth War Graves headstone in Tillington Cemetery.

The Headstone for Private Wilson, Tillington Cemetery. © Author's collection

Captain Charles Wilson

Royal Army Medical Corps

In 1881 the Reverend Alfred Wilson and his wife Fanny were living with their two sons, Charles Edgar (born 30 November 1877 in Hammersmith) and Harold, at 2 Woodstock Road in Chiswick where Reverend Alfred was the vicar of the Church of St Michael and All Angels. By 1891 the couple had three more children, Alan (9), Lawrence (6) and Edward (6). Charles had completed his preparatory education at 'Mr Johnson's School' in Ashtead, Surrey and had just become a scholar at Charterhouse, Surrey.[1] He began the 'Long Quarter' spring term in 1891 and joined Daviesites House where he enjoyed the academic challenge and where his musical ability, particularly on the piano, was encouraged. The school magazine *The Carthusian* of February 1893 records: 'C E A Wilson played a pleasing solo pianoforte "Paysage" by Kullak' and again in February 1894 in the Gondoliers 'the pianos were well together and Wilson and Curtis played most steadily throughout'.[2]

Charles left Charterhouse at the end of the 'Cricket Quarter' summer term of 1895 having just been awarded the Science Leaving Exhibition and headed to Christ Church College, Oxford, where he obtained a First Class Honours degree in Physiology. He joined St Thomas's Hospital, London in 1899 and, after a three-year course, graduated with full medical qualifications. As a young medic he held house appointments at Birmingham General Hospital, the Great Ormond Street Hospital for Sick Children, and at Blackheath Cottage Hospital, before finally settling down in general practice at Petworth.

On 23 April 1908, during his time working at Blackheath, Charles married Mary Barnes Mein in Newcastle-upon-Tyne and on 27 February 1909 their only son, Richard Nicholas, was born. They moved to Petworth sometime before April 1911, settling in to The North House, North Street. For some five years Charles tended to the medical needs of the people of Petworth and surrounding villages. He made regular visits to Tillington and was much loved by everyone, particularly the ordinary village folk.

It was perhaps in late summer 1914, on one of his country rounds, that he began to think about the consequences of war and the mounting number of killed and wounded soldiers in France and Belgium fighting for freedom and their country. Perhaps he was torn between the needs of his local patients and those of wounded soldiers on the Western Front. No doubt this inner debate continued for many months, but Charles at last decided and on 15 September 1916 he was gazetted as temporary Captain in the Royal Army Medical Corps.[3] After a very short training period he arrived in France on 27 September 1916 and spent his entire service on front line duty - first with the Northumberland Fusiliers and later with the 9th Battalion, Rifle Brigade, helping the dying and wounded soldiers of his battalion and any others needing such aid.

Captain Charles Wilson. De Ruvigny Roll of Honour

The wounded received medical treatment as quickly and as near the front line as possible. Regimental Aid Posts (RAP) were set up and manned by the battalion medical officer, together with his orderlies and stretcher-bearers. The RAP was situated a matter of yards behind the front line, in a dugout, a communication trench, a ruined house, or a deep shell hole. Some four hundred yards behind the RAP there was an Advanced Dressing Station (ADS) for further treatment. From here seriously wounded soldiers would be dispatched by horse-drawn or motorised ambulances to Casualty Clearing Stations (CCS), some fifteen miles behind the front line and often close to a railway line. Even here surgery was limited and many men were lost before they could be moved. Consequently each CCS unit had a military cemetery close by. Most of these cemeteries survive today under the excellent care of the Commonwealth War Graves Commission.

Those who needed more skilled or extensive surgery were transferred to a General Hospital in safe areas, often near the coast. Great hotels and other large buildings, such as casinos and schools, were requisitioned but other hospitals were set up in huts constructed on open ground. Patients could remain in these large hospitals until fit to be returned to their units or sent on Hospital Ships to the UK for specialist treatment.

Charles's role at the front line, probably in an RAP or ADS, would have continuously put his own life at risk and on 28 March 1918, near St Quentin,

this became a reality. He was seriously wounded in the spine but in spite of the extreme gravity of his wounds he insisted that others should be attended to first. He was, however, soon passed through the RAMC system until he reached the No1 General Hospital at Etretat on the Normandy coast close to Le Havre.

No 1 General Hospital Etretat, Normandy. Unknown copyright

This was 'L'Hotel des Roches Blanches', which in 1914 had been converted to the 1,000 bed No 1 General Hospital; its sixty-five nursing staff received British troops who had been seriously injured anywhere in northern France.

Captain Charles Edgar Andrew Wilson died here of his wounds on 8 April 1918. He was laid to rest in a soldier's grave in the extension to the original churchyard at Etretat.

The Colonel of the Northumberland Fusiliers to which he was originally attached wrote:

> He was loved and admired by us all and I know that, personally, I have lost a great friend, one of the kindest and most sympathetic men I have known.

The Colonel of the Rifle Brigade wrote:

> He is a great loss to us all, the best doctor we ever had; we all loved him.

A medical friend spoke of him as:

> A man of the highest ideals and culture, who strove for the best in everything which he undertook – a delightful companion and staunch friend.[4]

Captain Wilson's headstone. Courtesy André Brochec

Charles was recommended for the Military Cross for conspicuous courage and bravery under heavy fire, but at the time it was not a medal awarded posthumously.

Although he lived and worked in Petworth he must have been very fond of Tillington, because after the war his widow, Mary, financed a memorial to him in All Hallows' Church which reads:

> To the glorious memory of my dear husband Charles Edgar Andrew Wilson B.A. M.B. BCh. Oxon who in 1916 gave up his practice in this neighbourhood to volunteer for active service and as Temp. Capt R.A.M.C. attd 9th Rifle Brigade died on April 8th 1918 from wounds received near St. Quentin on March 28th aged 41. He lies in a soldier's grave at Etretat, France.

The Etretat Churchyard Extension is located just outside the small seaside town of Etretat, some 16 miles north of Le Havre. The grave reference is II. C. 9. Captain Wilson was entitled to the British War Medal and the Victory Medal.

Memorial plaque to Captain Charles Wilson, All Hallows' Church, Tillington. © Author's collection

33

Private Thomas Woolford TF/200531

Royal Sussex Regiment

Thomas Woolford was born in 1893 at Heyshott in Sussex. His parents Thomas and Kate, however, did not marry until the spring of 1894. At the time of the 1901 census the couple were living at West Dean near Chichester but ten years later they had moved to Little Common, Tillington, where father was a labourer, eighteen-year-old Thomas was a carter on a farm and their youngest son Harry, aged fourteen, was a farm labourer.

As for many of his friends and contemporaries, the coming of the Great War promised Thomas adventure and a chance to escape the limitations of village life. He was keen to join the army and, in late September 1914, soon after the outbreak of hostilities, he no doubt walked along the Petworth Road (now the A272) as far as the Armoury, which was the local recruiting office; to enlist in D Company, 4th Battalion Royal Sussex Regiment, Territorial Force to become Private T Woolford 4/2272 (The Territorial Force was re-numbered in 1917 and Thomas's number became TF/200531).

Thomas began his training at the regimental depot in Horsham, but on 24 April 1915 the battalion was posted to the 160th Brigade, 53rd (Welsh) Division in Cambridge. A few weeks later they were on the move again, this time to Bedford where the men completed their training. There was some excitement when, at the beginning of July, orders were received to re-equip for service with the Mediterranean Expeditionary Force and on 16 July the battalion left Bedford aboard two trains bound for Devonport.[1] The next day the men, with several other regiments of the division, embarked on HMT *Ulysses*. After calling at Alexandria and Port Said the ship arrived at the small port of Mudros on the Greek island of Lemnos. From here the *Ulysses* sailed for Suvla Bay on the Gallipoli peninsula arriving off C Beach close to midnight on 8 August. Barges carried the men the last few hundred yards to shore. A letter home from a soldier in the 1/4th Battalion described the landing.

> … landed in water up to our hips in the darkness. But it was a relief to stretch our legs as we had been cramped up under deck in one of the

special boats used for landing called 'beetles'. We then had to climb bit of cliff and after a short march we halted for the night.[2]

At 4.15am the next morning, the battalion moved away from C beach. By 11am the men came under artillery fire for the first time as they made their way into the hills to support troops attacking Scimitar Hill, a strategic position overlooking Suvla Bay. By 2.15pm the 4th Battalion had joined the battle on the hill but the action did not go well. Heavy Turkish artillery from the summit caused mounting casualties and just after midday a scrub fire broke out engulfing the hillside in dense smoke and flames. The Turks were reinforced and the British were forced to retire. Major Hulton of the 4th Royal Sussex wrote:

> ... patrols were sent out to our front to see what was to be seen through the dense smoke and fire that was still burning in the scrub. I remember they came back black in the face and frothing at the mouth with dryness.[3]

Lance Corporal Harold Proctor wrote to his mother in Bognor with his experiences as follows:

> The Turks were ready to receive us, and no sooner than we got within range of their artillery they opened fire, and our warships opened fire on them. You never heard such a terrible noise in all your life. There were shells bursting and killing our chaps by the dozen. Eventually we managed to get on land and we had to

Troops making their way into the hills above Suvla Bay.
Ⓒ Copyright expired

face fire from their machine guns and rifles. I can tell you it is marvellous that everybody was not killed, for the bullets were flying past our heads like rain and anybody else but the British soldiers could never have managed it. Well, we got the order to fix bayonets and charge, and we made a rush. Every one of us went mad. They never waited for us, they are rank cowards when it comes to the bayonets.[4]

The battalion remained in action on the Gallipoli Peninsula until 13 December 1915, when it sailed aboard the SS *Elkahira* to Mudros Bay and on to Alexandria in Egypt. At the end of January 1916 the 4th battalion, Royal Sussex Regiment's roll was 335 men and officers. It took the next five months to restore numbers to 926, the pre- Gallipoli strength.

In late March 1917 after a prolonged period of training in Egypt, the battalion returned to action against Turkish forces in Palestine, initially in the Gaza area taking part in the second and third battles of Gaza. A letter home to Haywards Heath from Private B Cook[5] outlined the 4th Battalion's experiences of their first attack on Turkish positions:

> How we got across that shell-swept plain God only knows, for shrapnel was bursting all around us … The sun was shining down on us pitilessly, and, worst of all, we were short of water, as it was impossible to get transport up, for as soon as the camels … advanced they were cut to pieces. At last we arrived … into a large gully, where we had a breather. Then came the order to fix bayonets and charge. With a mighty shout, over the top we went, into the front line through a perfect hail of bullets and shrapnel, which dealt out death and destruction all about … We put up a brave fight as any Regiment ever did, but we had to retreat at last, for no living thing could hope to get through that inferno of shell-fire … I cannot praise the good old Sussex too highly.

The British forces, however, continued to press the Turkish defenders north towards Jerusalem, which was captured on 9 December 1917. General Allenby, the Commander of the Egyptian Expeditionary Force, entered the city two days later on the 11 December.

On 16 June 1918 the battalion left Egypt aboard HMT *Malwa* bound for Taranto, Italy. From here they travelled by train, via Genoa and Marseilles, to Etaples in Northern France. The men spent the night of 29 June in a local rest camp before continuing on to billets close to Proven in Belgium the next day.

During the summer and autumn of 1918 Thomas fought in the Battle of Soissonais, the capture of Beugneux Ridge and the Fourth Battle of Ypres. Towards the end of the latter battle the battalion was advancing south close to Oostaverne, some five miles from Ypres, when they were ordered to halt. They rested nearby for some time before moving to a bivouac area east of the Ypres-Comines canal. On 7 October the battalion went into the front line which, according to the war diary, remained quiet for the next three days. We know, however, that Thomas died of his wounds on 9 October and therefore he was probably wounded on 25 September during an attack on Spanbroekmolen crater; when the battalion was met with heavy machine-gun fire and sniper bullets. (Spanbroekmolen was a crater left after the British detonated explosives

HMT Malwa. Ⓒ *Copyright expired*

under German positions just before the start of the Battle of Messines in June 1917. Throughout the rest of the war this crater provided cover for advancing and retreating troops of both sides).

The successful attack on the crater took place twelve miles from the village of Lijssenthoek where the British had established a field hospital at a farm called Corfu Farm. It is likely that Thomas was taken there to have his wounds tended and perhaps to undergo surgery. Unfortunately he did not survive and is buried in the peaceful surroundings of Lijssenhoek Military Cemetery.

Lijssenhoek Military Cemetery is located seven miles west of Ypres town centre, on the Ypres to Poperinge road. The grave reference is XXX. B. 1.

Private Thomas Woolford was entitled to the 1914-15 Star, the British War Medal and the Victory Medal.

According to the 'Army Register of Soldiers' Effects 1901-1929' Thomas was owed £30. 4s. 7d back pay and a war gratuity of £23. 10s. 0d. This relatively large sum was sent to his mother in May 1919.

34

Aircraftman Percy Yeatman F/15822

Royal Naval Air Service

Percy was born in Hackney, East London on 23 August 1897 and he was baptised on 21 November in the same year at Christ Church, Jamaica Street in the Borough of Tower Hamlets. The 1901 census shows the family living at 41 Tudor Road, Hackney, when Percy's father, twenty-six-year-old Harry from Gravesend in Kent, was a journeyman carpenter. His mother Selina was twenty-nine years old and from Bath. Sometime after 1901 the family moved from London, probably first to Upperton and then in 1906 to Itchingfield, Sussex where Percy and his sister Selina enrolled at the County Primary School on 5 February. This does not appear to have been a successful move since in August that year they returned to Upperton, where the family moved into No 520, a house owned by the Leconfield Estate and father Harry became a cowman, most probably on an estate dairy farm. Although Percy is recorded as a scholar, there is no record of him having attended Tillington School, but it is likely that at some period between 1906 and 1912 he would have been a pupil there.

On 6 June 1916, when he was nineteen years old, Percy joined the Royal Naval Air Service for the duration of the war. His record shows that at this time he was a 'solicitor's clerk'. He was 5ft 8½in tall, had brown hair and blue eyes, with a fresh complexion and an operation scar on his right side.[1] As Aircraftman 2nd Class F/15822 he joined the training

Aircraftman Percy Yeatman in the uniform of the Royal Naval Air Service. Courtesy of the Yeatman family

ship HMS *President* moored near Tower Bridge in the London Borough of Tower Hamlets. Although based there he was probably training at White City where the huge exhibition spaces had been requisitioned by the Royal Naval Air Service to manufacture aeroplanes. In early 1917 he trained for five months at Eastchurch aerodrome (Isle of Sheppey), which had become the home of the Royal Naval Air Service. He did not train as a pilot and therefore it is likely that he was trained as a gunner, perhaps on the newly built Handley Page Type O/100 bomber.

> The Handley Page Type O/100 was an early biplane bomber and the largest aircraft that had been built in the UK. Early in the war the Royal Navy's Director of the Air Department reportedly requested a 'bloody paralyser' of an aircraft from Handley Page for long-range bombing. They responded with a biplane with a wingspan of 100 feet.[2]
>
> The Handley Page O/100 was far superior, both in size and performance, to anything that the RNAS, had so far flown. Operated by a crew of three - pilot, observer and gunner - it was fitted with two Rolls Royce 250 horsepower engines and carried a normal bomb load of 14 x 112-pound bombs. It was later to carry the first 1650-pound bomb.[3]

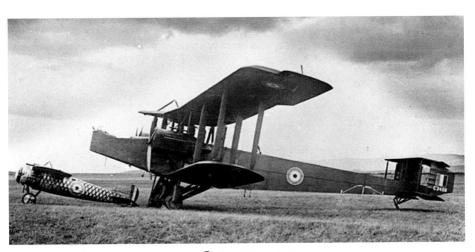

The Handley Page Type O/100 bomber. Ⓒ *Copyright expired*

Further training at Lee-on-Solent (HMS *Daedalus*) and Crystal Palace followed and on 22 July 1917 Percy was posted to No 7 Squadron at Coudekerque Aerodrome in Northern France, the squadron now being equipped with the HP bombers. In early August he was promoted to Aircraftman 1st Class and moved to RNAS Dunkirk. From here he flew bombing missions as the front gunner in HP bomber No. HP3137. This comment by another front gunner illustrates just how vulnerable this position was:

I only once occupied the nose gunlayers's cockpit, on my last raid. Stuck way out in front, I had a marvellous view ahead and made good use of the paired Lewis guns when we strafed the target … At our strafing height - probably only 200ft or so - I could actually see and hear the German ground gunners firing at us from various spots around the aerodrome, and when we got back to Coudekerque I discovered six neat bullet holes in the plywood sides of my cockpit and a seventh through the right sleeve of my outer flying suit … I'd been very lucky that time.[4]

A crew member at the time described how he prepared for the extreme cold and what could happen if even gloves were removed during the flight:

I used to put a silk stocking over my head under my helmet, and Vaseline over my face. Some of the lads used whale oil. We wore sheepskin clothing and I always put a pair of silk gloves under the leather one. One night, however, whilst on a raid, our bombs jammed. So as to free them more easily I took off my gloves, suffering severe frostbite as a result. One arm felt as if it had been in a furnace and was one big blister from wrist to elbow.[5]

German ground defences during 1917 included searchlights, machine guns and rockets. These were relatively ineffective against the low-flying HP bombers which often bombed from as low as 200ft and then returned even lower to give the gunlayers in each machine an opportunity for close strafing of anything resembling a good target. A more dangerous form of opposition, however, appeared in late spring when the bombers began to encounter German night fighters. The prospect of meeting aerial opponents meant that gunlayers, like Percy, now needed to keep a constant lookout on both outward and return flights, and to reserve some ammunition for any such occasion.

By August 1917 No 7 Squadron had escalated its nightly forays, attacking enemy airfields,

Percy dressed for his gunlaying duties. Courtesy of the Yeatman family

railway centres and sidings nearly every night. One night, fourteen Handley Pages took off to raid the Thourout rail centre and a nearby ammunition dump. Direct hits on the railway complex produced several large fires, while the ammunition dump exploded in a series of violent eruptions. Two nights later nine HPs, including HP3137 in which Percy was front gunner, bombed rail targets at Thourout and St Pierre, and the docks at Ghent and Bruges, dropping a total of 120 bombs to good effect. Throughout this very active month German defence opposition remained heavy, yet No 7 Squadron lost only one aeroplane. On the night of 25/26 August seven HPs set off to attack St Denis Westrem aerodrome, dropping eighty bombs, but HP3137, crewed by Flight Sub Lieutenant H H Booth and S A Canning together with Percy as gunlayer, was brought down by flak near Ghent in Belgium.[6] Being in the exposed front gun position, Percy was killed on impact whilst the others survived and were taken prisoner. He was twenty years old.

Percy was originally interred at Balgerhoeke Communal Cemetery fifteen miles east of Bruges. By 1973 this cemetery was no longer maintained and had fallen into disuse. For this reason the Commonwealth War Graves Commission decided that his body should be moved to their own cemetery and he now lies with many others who gave their lives during the Great War in the Cement House Cemetery at Langemark, north of Ypres in Belgium. The grave reference is VIIA. F.10.

Aircraftman Yeatman was awarded the British War Medal and the Victory Medal.

35

The Parish Memorials and Monuments
to the Great War

After the war there must have been very mixed emotions in the Parish. Joy among the families of those who survived the war must have mingled with deep sadness at the loss of so many young men who so recently had been the life and soul of the village. There was, however, a common need - both public and private - to commemorate this appalling loss and to have a village focus for remembrance. Although now a century has passed since the Great War, we have not forgotten and our war memorials are still of timeless interest to visitors and residents. Like all towns and villages we especially remember the sacrifices of our young men at 11am on 11 November each year.

All Hallows' Church is fortunate in having a number of memorials relating to the Great War. In addition to the two brass plaques either side of the chancel arch and the stone Celtic cross on the south side of the church, there are two memorials within the church to two individuals who fought and died in that war.

During the war years the vestry meeting would record the names of the soldiers from the Parish who had fallen during the year. On each occasion Colonel Mitford would move that:

> a message of deep sympathy of the Vestry with the relatives of those brave men from Tillington who had fallen in the war be sent by the Rector to each relative concerned.[1]

All the names are recorded with the exception of those who fell after the Easter vestry meeting of 1918. These soldiers are: Arthur Bridger (October 1918), William Duck (October 1918), John Grice (August 1918), Frederick Scutt (September 1918), George Summersell (August 1918) and Thomas Woolford (October 1918).

At a vestry meeting held on 14 May 1920[2] it was unanimously agreed that an application should be made for a faculty to erect, on each side of the chancel arch, a brass tablet in memory of the men of the Parish who died for England in the Great War 1914–1918. This faculty was granted on 'this thirteenth day of August in the year of our Lord one thousand nine hundred and twenty'.[3]

The brass tablets, bearing thirty names, were dedicated at a special service at 3pm on Sunday 7 November 1920 by Bishop Walter Andrews who, having returned from Japan (where he was Bishop of Hokkaido), was the Parish Vicar of St Peter's Church, St Leonards-on-Sea. The Reverend Goggs and the Vicar of Petworth, Reverend E Powell, assisted. It was the occasion of a most impressive service and the seating accommodation was not nearly sufficient for the congregation.

After Reverend Goggs had read the names of the fallen the Bishop gave an emotional address to the assembled congregation. "Had not those million men suffered and died, there would have been no real life in this country today," he said. "You who belong to this village have a right to be well congratulated in sending so many to defend their country."

Lord Leconfield, Lord Lieutenant of Sussex, then performed the unveiling ceremony by withdrawing the Union Flags from the tablets and Bishop Andrews dedicated them. After the closing hymn, 'O valiant hearts who to your glory came', the Boy Scouts sounded the 'Last Post'. The memorable service was concluded with the singing of the National Anthem.[4]

Discussion in the vestry meetings soon turned to a permanent external memorial to the fallen of the Great War. It was decided that this memorial should take the form of a Celtic cross, technically described as a 'rough hewn Celtic style wheel cross on tapering plinth and two stepped base'.

TILLINGTON WAR MEMORIAL FUND

EXPENDITURE			RECEIPTS		
	£ . s . d.			£ . s . d.	
			Subscriptions.		
Cost of Stone........40 . 0 . 0			Capt. W. Slade Mitford	10 . 0.. 0	
" " Fixing.......10 . 0 . 0			Mr. J. W. Boxall	10 . 0 . 0	
			Tillington W.I.)		
			balance over from)		
			Welcome Home Fund)		
			voted by Members.)	11 .11 .10	
			Mrs. R. Spooner	5 . 0 . 0	
			Miss Murison	10 . 0	
			Sir E. Pooley	10 . 0	
			Mrs. Loader	4 . 6	
			The Rev. Campion	1 . 0 . 0	
				£38 .16 . 4	
			Balance still		
			required	11 . 3 . 8	
	£50 . 0 . 0			£50 . 0 . 0	

ANY PARISHONER DESIROUS OF CONTRIBUTING TOWARDS THE ABOVE DEFICIT, KINDLY HAND THEIR SUBSCRIPTIONS TO EITHER OF THE UNDER NAMED

The Rev. F. R. Campion.   Mr. J. W. Boxall.

Tillington War Memorial Fund accounts. © *Author's collection*

A fund was organised and donations were sought. It is interesting to note that the Tillington Women's Institute contributed the substantial sum of £11. 11s. 10d–the residue from the Welcome Home Fund.[5] Nothing is known of this fund but it is probable, as in many other villages, the money had been raised to provide a welcome home dinner for returning soldiers. The two churchwardens each gave £10 whilst other contributors gave £7. 4s. 6d. The total sum collected was £38. 16s. 4d–somewhat short of the £50 needed to purchase and fix the proposed stone memorial. Since the memorial was completed in July 1925 we can only assume that the shortfall was found in time.

A special service of dedication was held in All Hallows' Church at 7pm on Monday 20 July 1925. After Lord Leconfield conducted the unveiling, the memorial was consecrated by the Archdeacon of Chichester, assisted by Reverend W Goggs.

A local press report[6] of the time records:

> The Church was packed, and the choir augmented by members of Petworth Church Choir, gave a magnificent rendering of the choral part of the service. The first part of the ceremony was conducted in the Church, an address being given by the Archdeacon of Chichester, in which he referred to the proud record of Tillington in the Great War, of whom 30 men had made the supreme sacrifice.
>
> Singing the hymn 'Onward Christian Soldiers' the choir, followed by the congregation, proceeded from the Church to the memorial, a cross which is placed in an eminent position in the churchyard where the unveiling took place.
>
> This was followed by the unaccompanied rendering of 'Supreme Sacrifice' by the choir and congregation. The service ended with the 'Last Post' being sounded and the singing of the National Anthem.

In 1918 the widow of Captain Charles Wilson of Petworth, who before the war was a local doctor, applied to the Rector of All Hallows' Church for permission to install in the church a memorial tablet to her husband who died of his wounds in April 1918, serving with the Royal Army Medical Corps on the Western Front. The optimistic response from Reverend William Goggs appears at first to have caused a little controversy, before all was settled later at a special vestry meeting.[7] The minutes of this meeting are illuminating and are reproduced here in full:

> A special vestry meeting was held in the church on Tuesday July 30th at 11am to discuss the erection of a statuary marble tablet in Tillington Church to the memory of C E Wilson Captain R A M C.
> Present: the Rector in the chair, Colonel W Kenyon Mitford, Mr James Boxall [churchwardens] Mrs Bulmer, Miss Bulmer, Miss Gray, Mrs Nattali, Mr Stringer, Mr Fowles, Mrs Fowles, Mr Edwicker, Mrs Daniels,

198

Mrs Horwick, Mrs Mann, Mrs W Bryder and two others [17 in all].

Mr Goggs briefly told the vestry the object of the meeting. He explained the position viz: Mrs Wilson had applied to him for permission to have the tablet erected in this church. He gave his consent, but at the same time pointed out to Mrs Wilson that the approval of the parishioners, expressed at a properly convened vestry, would have to be obtained before the work could be commenced and also that, even after the vestry had given their consent, a faculty would have to be applied for and granted.

Colonel Mitford, on behalf of the churchwardens then read the following: The churchwardens do not consider that a sufficiently strong expression of opinion has been produced on behalf of the parishioners to warrant them to apply for a faculty for the erection of the proposed memorial in as much as the late Dr Wilson was neither a parishioner of Tillington Parish nor was he, nor his family, regular attendants at Tillington Church.

If this application were granted it might lead in the future to others of a similar nature which it would be difficult to refuse. The matter of the suggested memorial appears to have been taken up with the Rector on his own responsibility without consulting his churchwardens beforehand. The churchwardens consider that they should have been consulted before the matter had been allowed to go so far. They think that without the unanimous wishes of their parishioners, whom they represent, it is undesirable to erect memorials to those unconnected with this parish, either by residence or by attendance at the parish church. The Rector has placed the churchwardens in a very awkward position in not having consulted them when the memorial was first proposed.

The first I [Col Mitford] heard of it from the Rector was on July 28th, 2 days before the vestry meeting. At the same time the churchwardens wish to express their great respect for the late Dr Wilson, as medical officer to the parish and their admiration of his gallantry and desire to convey this feeling to Dr Wilson's family.

Rector's Reply: In reply to this written statement the Rector pointed out:

That this was the largest vestry meeting he had ever presided at in Tillington. That it had been properly convened after six days' notice [one of which was a Sunday] had been posted on the principal church door. The object of the meeting had been explained from the pulpit both at Matins and Evensong on the preceding Sunday:

That though Dr Wilson had not resided in this parish yet he was the Tillington 'Parish Doctor' and was well known and loved by most of the poor people of Tillington who would be more than disappointed if his widow's request were not granted.

That though he (the Rector) was personally against allowing non-parishioners to erect memorials in this church yet this was a <u>Special Case</u> – the case of one who had left his practice and his care of Tillington poor folk in order to go and minister to the wounded and suffering in the shell shocked trenches at the Front somewhere in France and who had been killed 'doing his duty'.

That there was no legal obligation on the part of the Rector to consult the wardens beforehand about a matter which was to be discussed at a vestry meeting.

That the People's warden had been told of the proposed tablet some weeks previous.

That he [Mr Goggs] would certainly have mentioned the subject to his warden when first heard of it had Colonel Mitford not been at the time generally away from home on active service.

That certainly no discourtesy was meant to be shown by the Rector towards his churchwardens.

Result of voting. After some lively discussion the meeting decided by 14 votes to 3 to consent to the erection of the proposed memorial in this church and to apply for a faculty.

W M Goggs [Chairman].

Thankfully the will of the parishioners prevailed and work on the memorial was soon completed. The Parish Service Register[8] records that:

the Wilson tablet was dedicated on 13 October 1918 at 11am Matins by Reverend Goggs.

The tablet lies on the north wall of the church, close to the intersection with the west wall.

The other individual memorial in All Hallows' Church stands on the right-hand side of the chancel arch. It is a magnificent brass lectern of an eagle wing design. It is in remembrance of Victor Annesley Barrington-Kennett and was dedicated by Reverend Goggs at the 6.30pm service on Christmas Eve 1916. The well-rubbed inscription reads:

This lectern
is presented by his brother officers of No 1 Squadron
Royal Flying Corps in affectionate remembrance of
Victor Annesley Barrington-Kennett
Major and Squadron Commander
and as a token of their esteem and sorrow at his loss
He was killed in an aerial fight in France
on March 13th 1916
Aged 28 years

"Be Strong and of Good Courage"'

POSTSCRIPT

In July 1915 Stanley Spencer (1891–1959), the highly regarded twentieth-century artist, enlisted in the Royal Army Medical Corps and initially worked at the Beaufort war hospital on the outskirts of Bristol. In the summer of 1916 he transferred to the Field Ambulance Service and was posted to Macedonia; a year later he became an infantryman in the 7th Battalion Royal Berkshire Regiment and served in the Balkans. On his return home in 1918 he began painting again, but the images of war, particularly the many wounded and dead soldiers, remained with him until in 1923 he planned a major work based on his war experience. A good number of these are on display at the Sandham Memorial Chapel at Burghclere, Hampshire. Spencer told a reporter from the *Birmingham Post* in 1927:

> I had buried so many people and saw so many dead that I felt that death could not be the end of everything.

Have you forgotten yet? …
Look down, and swear by the slain of the War that you'll never forget.

Have you forgotten yet? …
Look up, and swear by the green of the spring that you'll never forget.

Siegfried Sassoon

SELECTED REFERENCES

Church records of baptisms and the Registers of Birth, Marriages and Deaths for England and Wales 1837-2008 have been used for personal details of all soldiers and their families, and the relevant census returns and Kelly's Directories for Sussex have provided information on employment, locations and movements. The use of these reference sources is fully acknowledged but is not repeated in the references for each individual.

INTRODUCTION

1. John Buchan *These for Remembrance – Memoirs of Six Friends Killed in the* Great *War* (Privately printed in 1919. Buchan & Enright, London in 1987).
2. Siegfried Sassoon, *The Weald of Youth*, (Faber and Faber, London 1942).

THE PARISH IN THE YEARS BEFORE THE GREAT WAR

1. www.visionofbritain.org.uk/place/9039. University of Portsmouth, History of Tillington, in Chichester and Sussex.
2. www.visionofbritain.org.uk/unit/10312139/cube/OCC_ORDER1881. University of Portsmouth, TillingtonCP/AP through time.
3. William Cater Swan, *Diary of a Farm Apprentice* (Publisher Alan Sutton 1984).
4. Kelly's Directory of the County of Sussex, 1908. Kelly's Directories Ltd, High Holborn, London.
5. Tillington Women's Institute, The History of the Parish of Tillington Vol 1 page 58. 1965.
6. Ibid, page 106.
7. WSRO PHA 11567
8. Audrey Lucas, *E. V. Lucas: A Portrait* (Methuen & Co. Ltd, London 1939).
9. Kelly's Directory of the County of Sussex, 1911. Kelly's Directories Ltd, High Holborn, London.
10. Tillington Women's Institute, The History of the Parish of Tillington Vol 1 page 22. 1965.
11. WSRO Schools Records (Part 5). Tillington School Log Book 1912. E197/12/1.
12. Ibid
13. WSRO All Hallows' Church, Service Register 1911-1912. PHA 197/3/3.
14. Peter Jerome, *Petworth from 1660 to the Present Day* (Window Press 2006). Pages 199-200.

RECRUITMENT

1. Miles Costello. Petworth Society Magazine No. 106. December 2001.
2. WSRO Petworth House Archives. File Bundle dated 1914 ref PHA 1080.
3. Ibid.
4. Ibid
5. West Sussex County Times. 9 September 1914.

6. Imperial War museum. Catalogue No 33690
7. Reg Pratt's letters home. 23 January 1916. Personal Communication Pratt family.
8. WSRO PHA 11567
9. Ibid, reference 2.
10. The National Archives. Major Basil Herbert Barrington-Kennett. Grenadier Guards. Bundle of papers. WO339/6562.
11. Ibid, reference 2.
12. Melvyn Bridger. Personal communication 2014.

BARRINGTON-KENNETT FAMILY

1. WSRO Annual Vestry Meeting 1911, All Hallows' Church, Tillington. PAR 197/12/3, page 13.
2. Ibid, page 41.
3. Anthony Murphy, *Banks of Green Willow, The Life and Times of George Butterworth* (Cappella Archive 2012). Page 57.
4. Nicholas Duder, Indonesia. Personal Communication. 2013.
5. Ellinor F. Barrington-Kennett, *Four Little Brothers*. (Wells Gardner, Darton & Co Ltd, 1918).

BASIL BARRINGTON-KENNETT

1. The Sandhurst Collection. Basil Barrington-Kennett. Register Entry 1905.
2. Flight, The Official Organ of the Aero Club of the United Kingdom. 19 June 1909, page 368.
3. Ibid, September 1910, No 91, page 776.
4. Ibid, October 1910, No 94, page 840.
5. Ibid, January 1911, No 106, page 11.
6. Ibid, September 1911, No 142, page 805.
7. Jack T C Long, *Three's Company – An Illustrated History of No 3 (Flight) Squadron RAF*. Pen & Sword 2005, page 21.
8. Ibid, pages 21-22.
9. The Bedfordshire Times and Independent, Friday 25 August1 911. Bedfordshire Archives and Records Service, Bedford.
10. Cambridge Community Archive Network. (www.huntingdon.ccan.co.uk)
11. Timothy C Brown, *Flying with the Larks, The Early Aviation Pioneers of Lark Hill*. (The History Press 2013). Pages 107 -108
12. Ibid, page 106.
13. Ibid, 2 February 1912, No 165, page 173.
14. The Flight Logbook for Nieuport No B40. Held by the Empire Test Pilots School, MoD Boscombe Down, Wiltshire.
15. Ibid 2, May 1912, No 177, page 449.
16. Ibid 2, March 1912, No 168, page 238
17. James Byford McCudden V.C. *Flying Fury*. (Aviation Book Club 1918 reprinted1939). Page 18.
18. Ibid 2, May 1912, No 178, page 472.
19. Large Gathering of Aviators, *The Evening Telegraph and Post*, Wednesday 8 January 1913.

20. S. F. Cody killed, Hydroplane Fails. *Evening Post*, 8 August 1913.
21. Maurice Baring, *Flying Corps Headquarters 1914-1918*. (G Bell & Sons 1920).
22. Anne Baker, *From Biplane to Spitfire, The Life of Air Chief Marshall Sir Geoffrey Salmond* (Pen & Sword 2003, UK). Pages 60-61.
23. (www.spartacus-educational.com) - First World War – Soldiers – Oliver Lyttleton.
24. The National Archives. War Diary of the 2nd Battalion Grenadier Guards. WO95/1342.
25. Ibid 22, pages 71-72.
26. Ibid 17, page 18.
27. The National Archives. Major Basil Herbert Barrington-Kennett. Grenadier Guards. Bundle of papers. WO339/6562.
28. Personal Communication. Christopher Gingell.
29. Ibid 2, May 1953, No 2312. Page 620. E.T.P.S. Presentations.

VICTOR BARRINGTON-KENNETT

1. Anthony Murphy, *Banks of Green Willow, The Life and Times of George Butterworth* (Cappella Archive 2012). Page 27
2. The Eton College Chronicle. 30 November 1905. Page 782.
3. Ibid, reference 1.
4. The Sandhurst Collection. Victor Barrington-Kennett. Register Entry 1906.
5. Balliol College Memorial Book. Balliol College Archives. 1924. Page 24.
6. Balliol College Boat Club Records 1902 – 1927. www.flickr.com/photos/balliolarchivist.
7. Ibid.
8. Ibid, reference 1, page 51.
9. Ibid, reference 1, page 79.
10. The National Archives. Captain Victor Annesley Barrington-Kennett. Royal Flying Corps. Bundle of papers WO339/16648.
11. Phillip Jarrett, *Frank McClean: The Godfather of British Naval Aviation* (Seaforth Publishing 2011). Page 81.
12. Flight, The Official Organ of the Aero Club of the United Kingdom. December 1911. No 154, page 1060.
13. Ibid, December 1911. No 155, page 1089.
14. Ibid, January 1912. No 160, page 58.
15. Ibid, March 1912. No 166, page 194.
16. Ibid, March 1912. No 167, page 220.
17. Sara Wheeler, *Too Close to the Sun. The Life and Times of Denys Finch Hatton* (Jonathan Cape Ltd 2006). Page 70.
18. Karen Blixen, *Out of Africa* (Penguin Books 1999).
19. www.airhistory.org.uk/rfc/EF2.html. Royal Flying Corps, Coast Patrols.
20. www.airhistory.org.uk. Royal Flying Corps. Departure of the RFC Expeditionary Force. Coast Patrols.
21. Wayne Smith (Editor) *George Butterworth Memorial Volume* (Caxton Publications 2015). Page39.
22. Anne Baker, *From Biplane to Spitfire, The Life of Air Chief Marshall Sir Geoffrey Salmond* (Pen & Sword 2003), UK. Page 61.

23. Michael Shaw, *Twice Vertical. The History of No 1 Squadron Royal Air Force* (MacDonald & Co Ltd 1971). Page 28.
24. Ibid, reference 16 page 63.
25. Ibid, reference 17, page 30.
26. www.rafjever.org/4squadhistory1.htm. 4 Sqn – History Part 1 – Jever Steam Laundry.
27. Ibid, reference 12, May 1916. No 385, page 402.
28. Aviation History. Magazine published in the USA and www.donhollway.com/immelmann.
29. Don Hollway, *The Eagle of Lille*. November 2013 issue.
30. Ibid, reference 10.
31. Ibid, reference 12, May 1916. No 386, page 419.
32. Ibid, reference 1, page 89.

AUBREY BARRINGTON-KENNETT

1. The Radleian, 23 November 1907 Radley College Archives, Abingdon, Oxford. Page 180.
2. The National Archives. 2nd Lieutenant Aubrey Hampden Barrington-Kennett. Oxfordshire and Buckinghamshire Light Infantry. Bundle of papers WO339/16648.
3. Ibid.
4. Ibid.
5. The National Archives. War Diary of the 2nd Battalion Oxford and Buckinghamshire Light Infantry. Aug – Dec 1914. W095/1384/1.
6. Lt Col A.F. Mockler-Ferryman (Editor), *The Oxfordshire and Buckinghamshire Light Infantry in the Great War, First Year (Aug 1914-July 1915)* Volume 1 (Eyre & Spottiswoode Ltd). Page161.
7. Ibid, page 163.
8. Ibid, page 164.
9. Maurice Baring, *Flying Corps Headquarters 1914 -1918* (G Bell & Sons 1920). Pages 48-49.
10. Tillington Women's Institute. The History of the Parish of Tillington Vol 1, page 37. 1965.

ALBERT H BAILEY

1. The National Archives. War Diary of the 12th Battalion Royal Sussex Regiment, March 1916 – August 1918. WO95/2582/2.
2. ancestry.co.uk. British Army Service Records 1914 – 1920 for George Frederick Balkham.
3. The National Archives. War Diary of the 116th Infantry Brigade Headquarters, May 1917 – April 1919. WO95/2581/4.

AUSTIN BARTLETT

1. findmypast.co.uk. British Army Service Records 1760-1915.
2. www.roll-of-honour/Sussex/Tillington.html. Tillington Roll of Honour.
3. ancestry.co.uk. British Army WW1 Medal Rolls Index Cards 1914-1920 for Austin G. H. Bartlett.

4. The National Archives. War Diary of the 2nd Battalion Royal Sussex Regiment. August 1914 – April 1919. WO95/1269.
5. Ibid.
6. The National Archives. War Diary of the 9th Battalion Royal Sussex Regiment. August 1915 – May1919. WO95/2219/2.
7. Private A Bartlett. De Ruvigny's Roll of Honour 1914 -1919. Volume 2, page 20.

PERCY BOXALL
1. www. findmypast.co.uk. British Army Service Records 1914-1920. Percy Charles Boxall.
2. David Lewis. Personal Communication. 2014.
3. *Sussex Agricultural Express.* Newhaven –Football. Friday 30 October 1914.
4. www.longlongtrail.co.uk/battles/the-campaign-at-gallipoli. The Long Long Trail.
5. http://forgottenwrecks.maritimearchaeologytrust.org/asturias.
6. Ibid, reference 1.
7. *Western Gazette*, Yeovil. Friday 28 December 1917.

ARTHUR BRIDGER
1. ancestry.co.uk. British Army WW1 Medal Rolls Index Cards 1914-1920 for Arthur J Bridger.
2. The National Archives. World War One Medal Rolls. A.J. Bridger. WO329/1395.
3. Percy Fryer, *The Men from the Greenwood, Being the War History of the 11th (Service) Battalion Sherwood Foresters* (Cresswell & Oaksford , 1920). Pages 115-123.
4. Vera Brittain, *Testament of Youth* (First published in 1933. This edition published by Fontana Paperbacks 1979). Pages 436-438.
5. Ibid, reference 3, page 123.
6. The National Archives. War Diary of the 11th Battalion Sherwood Foresters (Nottinghamshire and Derbyshire). September 1918 – February 1919. WO95/2247/5.

THOMAS G BRIDGEWATER
1. Charles Thompson. Personal Communication. 2014.
2. www.westsussex.gov.uk. Arthur Henry Fitt (1890 – 1954) and his War. Peter Cox. 2016. West Sussex County Council and the Great War Project.
3. The National Archives. War Diary of the 13th Battalion Royal Sussex Regiment. March 1916 – August 1918. WO95/2582.

WILLIAM BRYDER
1. www.eastsussexww1.org.uk. The First World War – Defending Sussex Shores.
2. West Sussex Record Office. War Diary of the 4th Battalion Royal Sussex Regiment. 1915 – 1919. RSR MS 4- 64.
3. Mr William Bryder. Personal Communication 2014.
4. The National Archives. War Diary of the 5th Battalion Royal Sussex

Regiment. September 1915 – October 1917. WO95/2751/5.

5. The National Archives. War Diary of the 7th Battalion Royal Sussex Regiment. June 1915 – June 1919. WO95/1856.

6. Sgt Bernard Brookes, *A Signaller's War* (Una Barrie - Author's Daughter 2012). Page 12.

7. Frank Richards, *Old Soldiers Never Die* (Naval and Military Press. 2009). Page 108.

8. Mr William Bryder. Personal Communication 2014.

9. Arthur Conan Doyle, *The British Campaign in France and Flanders. January to July 1918* (Naval and Military Press Ltd 2013). Page 68.

10. Ibid, page 70.

HAROLD BUDD

1. www.findmypast.co.uk. Passenger Lists leaving UK 1890-1960.

2. www.theshipslist.com/passengerlists/petworthimmigrants.

3. Ibid.

4. Library and Archives Canada, Ottawa. Reference RG150. Accession 1992-93/166, Box 1245 – 6. Digitised Service File B1245-S006.

5. Ibid.

6. www.canadaatwar.ca. 75th Canadian Infantry Battalion War Diaries 1916-1918.

7. www.102ndbattalioncef.ca. The Story of the 102nd Canadian Infantry Battalion. From B.C to Baisieux . Chapter 4.

8. Ibid, reference 4.

9. Ibid.

10. Eugene P Ryan (Editor), *Haig's Medical Officer. The Papers of Colonel Eugene 'Micky' Ryan* (Pen & Sword 2013). Page 105.

WILLIAM BUTT

1. The National Archives. War Diary of the 2nd Battalion Royal Sussex Regiment. August 1914 – April 1919. WO95/1269.

2. Ibid.

THOMAS DANIELS

1. WSRO Tillington School Admission Register, 1906. E197/13/1/1.

2. The National Archives. Roll of Individuals entitled to the Victory and/or British War Medal. TP/104, B16. Page 1962.

3. The National Archives. War Diary of the 2nd Battalion Royal Fusiliers. February 1916 –March 1919. WO95/2301.

4. Captain Stair Gillon, *The Story of the 29th Division. A Record of Gallant Deeds* (The Naval and Military Press 2002. First published 1925). Page 122.

5. Ibid, pages 133-134.

6. Ibid, page 141.

7. Supplement to the *London Gazette*, 26 November, 1917. Citation No. 1817 Page 12328.

8. Ibid, reference 4, page 145.

WILLIAM DUCK

1. Max Egremont, *Siegfried Sassoon A Biography* (Picador 2013 edition). Page 63.
2. Ibid, page 65.
3. H. I. Powell-Edwards, *The Sussex Yeomanry and 16th Battalion Royal Sussex Regiment* 1914-1919 (Andrew Melrose Ltd 1921). Page 17.
4. Ibid, pages 18-19.
5. Ibid, page 20.
6. Ibid, reference 1, page 67.
7. Ibid, reference 3, pages 21-22.
8. Ibid, pages 39-41.
9. The National Archives. War Diary of the 16th Battalion Royal Sussex Regiment. January 1917 – April 1918. WO95/4678.
10. Ibid, reference 3, page 222.
11. Ibid, pages 226-227.

JOSEPH DUMMER

1. www.findmypast.co.uk. Military. Joseph Dummer. British Army Records Captain P.F. Stewart, *The History of the XII Royal Lancers* (Oxford University Press 1950). Page 185.
2. Ibid, pages 192-195.
3. Sir John Frederick, *History of the War in South Africa 1899-1902* (Hurst and Blackett Ltd 1906). Chapter VI Pursuit of Cronje (continued). Page 103.
4. Ibid, reference 2, page 206.
5. www.findmypast.co.uk. 1911 Census for England & Wales. Overseas Military and Overseas Establishments. RG14 Potschefstroom. South Africa.
6. Ibid, reference 1.

CHARLES EDWICKER

1. The National Archives. War Diary of the 8th East Surrey Battalion. July 1915 –.May 1919. WO95/2050

WILFRED EVERLEY

1. Hampshire Archives. National School Admissions Registers & Log Books 1870-1914.142M87/A1. 1902.
2. Ibid, 241M86/A1. 1904.
3. Ibid, 226M86/A2. 1905.
4. Surrey Recruitment Registers 1908-1933. 2496/38. Surrey History Centre, Woking, UK.
5. The National Archives. War Diary of the 32nd Brigade Royal Field Artillery October 1914 –March1919. WO95/1467/1.
6. WSRO. All Hallows' Church Minutes Book for Vestry Meetings PAR 197/12/3 page 81.

GEORGE HILLS

1. www.findmypast.co.uk. Soldiers Died in the Great War 1914 – 1919. George Hills.
2. ancestry.co.uk. British Army WW1 Medal Rolls Index Cards, 1914-1920 for

George Hills.

3. The National Archives. War Diary of the 1st Life Guards August 1914 – March 1918. WO95/1155/1.
4. Private notebooks of Trooper Frederick Eames 2nd Life Guards. Lost Reference.

CHARLES JUDGE
1. The National Archives. War Diary of the 2nd Battalion Royal Sussex Regiment August 1914 –April 1919. WO95/1269.
2. www.ancestry.co.uk. UK Army Register of Soldiers' Effects, 1901-1929.

GEORGE PEACOCK
1. www. circlecity.co.uk. Alan Greveson's World War 1 Forum/george peacock.
2. 1911 Census. overseas Military Ships and Overseas Establishments.
3. Colonel H.C. Wylly, *The Loyal North Lancashire Regiment 1914-1919* (Naval & Military Press Ltd 2007). Page 2.
4. The National Archives. Diary of a Second Lieutenant. 1st Battalion The Loyal Regiment. 5 August 1914 – 15 November 1914. WO95/1270/1.
5. Ibid.
6. The National Archives. Original War Diary of the 1st Battalion Loyal North Lancashire Regiment. WO/95/1270/1. Page 84.
7. Ibid, reference 3, page 14.
8. www.grandeguerre.icrc.org. International Committee of the Red Cross. ICRC 1914-1918 Prisoners of the First World War. ICRC Historical Archives.
9. www.iwm.org.uk. Podcast 42, Prisoners of War and Painting Thomas Henry (IMW Interview), Catalogue No. 212, 1974. Transcription.

WILLIAM PELLETT
1. www.findmypast. 1911 Census for England & Wales. Shoeburyness Garrison, Essex.
2. Tony Hill, *Guns and Gunners at Shoeburyness* (Baron Birch. USA). 1999.
3. The National Archives. War Diary of the 47th Siege Battery, Royal Garrison Artillery December 1915 – January 1918. WO95/465.

EDGAR PRATT
1. Reg Pratt's letters home. 23 January 1916. Personal Communication Pratt family.
2. Ibid, 5 February 1916.
3. www.getjackback.wordpress.com. The First World War Story of Jack Wilson.
4. Ibid, reference 1, 16 April 1916.
5. Ibid, 10 June 1916.
6. Ibid, 13 June 1916.
7. The National Archives. War Diary of the 123rd Machine Gun Company. WO/95/2639.
8. Ibid, reference 1. 9 September 1916.

9. Ibid, 4 November 1916.
10. Ibid, 14 December 1916.
11. The National Archives. War Diary of the1st Canadian Tunnelling Company. WO/95/245.

FREDERICK SCUTT
1. The National Archives. WO/329/1251 Royal Sussex Regiment other ranks : medal rolls page 1533.
2. The National Archives. War Diary of the 13th Battalion, Royal Sussex Regiment Company. WO/95/2582.
3. The National Archives. War Diary of the 7th Battalion, Royal Sussex Regiment Company. WO/95/1856.

CHARLES STONER
1. www. 1914-1918.net/sussex. The Long Long Trail.
2. The National Archives. War Diary of the 2nd Battalion, Royal Sussex Regiment Company. WO/95/1269.
3. ancestry.co.uk. UK Army Register of Soldiers' Effects 1901 – 1929.

WILLIAM STONER
1. ancestry.co.uk. British Army WW1 Medal Rolls Index Cards, 1914-1920 for William G Stoner.
2. The National Archives. War Diary of the 1st Battalion, Coldstream Guards. WO/95/1263.
3. The National Archives. War Diary of the 1st Battalion, Coldstream Guards. WO/95/1219.
4. Philip Warner, *The Battle of Loos* (William Kimber & Co. Ltd 1976). Page 30.

GEORGE SUMMERSELL
1. www.findmypast.co.uk. British Army Records 1914-1920.
2. www.findmypast.co.uk. British Royal Air Force Airmen's Service Records 1912-1939.
3. West Sussex Record Office. War Diary of the 4th Battalion, Royal Sussex Regiment. RSR MS 4/64.
4. www.culpitt-war-diary.org.uk. The War diary of George Culpitt, Royal Welch Fusiliers. Chapter 2 Etaples Camp.

WILLIAM WADEY
1. WSRO. Tillington School Admission Register dated August 1906. E197/13/1/1.
2. The National Archives. War Diary of the 5th Battalion, Royal Sussex Regiment. WO/95/1269.
3. Harvey Cushing, *The Life of Sir William Osler, Volume 2*. (Oxford University Press 1925).

CHARLES WILSON
1. Charterhouse Register 1872 – 1900. Page 189.

2. The Carthusian, February 1893, page 55 and February 1894, page 201.
3. De Ruvigny's Roll of Honour, 1914 – 1919. Volume 3, page 288.
4. Christ Church College, Oxford. Roll of Honour: Lives Lost in World War 1.

THOMAS WOOLFORD
1. West Sussex Record Office. War Diary of the 4th Battalion Royal Sussex Regiment. 1915 – 1919. RSR MS 4- 64.
2. Littlehampton Observer 29 September 1915 page 8.
3. Steven Chambers, *Gallipoli: Sulva August Offensive*. (Pen & Sword 2011). Page 94.
4. Bognor Observer, 1 September 1915, page 5.
5. Mid-Sussex Times, 14 September 1915, page 7.

PERCY YEATMAN
1. www.ancestry.co.uk Royal Navy Registers of Seaman's Services 1853-1928. Percy Maurice Yeatman.
2. www.ww1aviation.com/bombers WW1 Allied Bombers: Britain- WW1 Aviation.
3. www.207squadron.rafinfo.org.uk 207 Squadron RAF History – WW1 -7 Squadron RNAS in Europe. 1917 HP 0/100.
4. www207squadron.rafinfo.org.uk 207 Squadron RAF History – Personal Accounts – Harold Peterson. 1917 HP0/100.
5. Ibid, William Wardrop.
6. Ibid, reference 3.

THE PARISH MEMORIALS AND MONUMENTS TO THE GREAT WAR
1. WSRO All Hallows' Church, Tillington. Annual Vestry Meeting 1916. PAR 197/12/3 page 69.
2. WSRO Application for a Faculty. PAR 197/4/3.
3. WSRO Grant of Faculty. PAR 197/4/3.
4. Sussex Daily News. November 1920.
5. WSRO Tillington war Memorial Fund. PAR 197/4/3.
6. PRESS REPORT
7. WSRO All Hallows' Church, Tillington. Annual Vestry Meeting 1918. PAR 197/12/3 page 93-103.
8. West Sussex Record Office. Tillington Church Service Register 1906-1929 – 1918. PAR/197/3/2.

SELECTED BIBLIOGRAPHY

Airfields & Airmen Somme, Mike O'Conner, Pen & Sword Books, Barnsley. 2013.

Airfields & Airmen Arras, Mike O'Conner, Pen & Sword Books, Barnsley. 2004.

A Record of H.M. 52nd Light Infantry in 1914. Lt.-Col. R.B. Crosse D.S.O. Spennell Press Ltd, Warwick. 1956.

A Signaller's War. Sergeant Bernard Brooks, Published by Una Barrie, England. 2012.

A Shropshire Lad. A. E. Housman. George G Harrap & Co Ltd, London. 1942.

Banks of Green Willow. Anthony Murphy, Cappella Archive, Great Malvern, England. 2012.

British Campaign Medals 1914 – 2005. Peter Duckers. Shire Publications Ltd England. 2007.

Departed Warriors – The Story of a Family in War. Jerry Murland. Matador, Leicester. 2008.

E.V. Lucas - A Portrait. Audrey Lucas. Methuen & Co Ltd. 1939.

Flying Corps Headquarters 1914 – 1918. Maurice Baring. William Blackwood & Sons Ltd, London. 1968.

Flying Fury, James B McCudden, V.C. The Aviation Book Club, London. First published 1918.

Flying with the Larks. Timothy C Brown. Spellmount in association with National Trust, Stroud. 2013.

Four Little Brothers. Ellinor F Barrington-Kennett. Wells Gardner, Darton & Co Ltd, London. 1918.

From Biplane to Spitfire. Anne Baker. Pen & Sword Books, Barnsley. 2003.

Gallipoli: Helles Landing. Huw & Jill Rodge. Pen & Sword Books, Barnsley. 2003.

Gallipoli: Suvla August Offensive. Stephen Chambers, Pen & Sword Books, Barnsley. 2011.

George Butterworth Memorial Volume, Centenary Edition. Edited by Wayne Smith. YouCaxton Publications, Oxford. 2015.

Great War Britain – West Sussex Remembering 1914-1918. Edited by Martin Hayes and Emma White. West Sussex County Council. 2014.

Haig's Medical Officer. Edited by Eugene P Ryan, Pen & Sword Books, Barnsley. 2013.

History of the 53rd (Welsh) Division (TF) 1914-1918. Major C. H. Dudley Ward. The Naval & Military Press, Uckfield. First published 1927.

Number one in War and Peace - The History of No. 1 Squadron 1912 – 2000. Norman Franks and Mike O'Conner. Grub Street, London. 2000.

Old Soldiers Never Die. Private Frank Richards. Naval & Military Press, Uckfield. 1996.

Petworth From 1660 to the present day. Peter Jerome. The Window Press. 2006.

Poems of the Great War 1914 - 1918. Penguin Books, London. 1998.

Stanley Spencer. Kitty Hauser. Tate Publishing, London. 2001.

Sussex in the First World War Edited. Keith Grieves. Sussex Record Society, Volume 84. 2004.

Testament of Youth. Vera Brittain. Fontana Paperbacks. 1979.

The 18th Division in the Great War by Captain G H F Nichols. The Naval & Military Press, Uckfield. 1922.

The Battle of Loos by Philip Warner. William Kimber & Co. Ltd, London. 1976.

The British Campaign in France and Flanders − January to July 1918. Arthur Conan Doyle. The Naval & Military Press, Uckfield. 2003.

The Countryside at war 1914 − 1918. Caroline Dakers. Constable and Company Limited, London. 1987.

The History of British Aviation 1908 - 1914, Vol I & II. R Dallas Brett. Aviation Book Club, London. 1933.

The History of the Seventh (Service) Battalion - The Royal Sussex Regiment 1914 - 1919. Edited by Owen Rutter. The Naval & Military Press, Uckfield. 2003.

The History of the XII Royal Lancers. Captain P.F. Stewart, M.C. Oxford University Press 1950.

The Loyal North Lancashire Regiment 1914 − 1918. Colonel H. C. Wylly. The Naval & Military Press, Uckfield. 2007.

The Penguin Book of First World War Poetry. Edited by George Walter. Penguin Books, London. 2004.

The Story of the 29th Division - A Record of Gallant Deeds. Captain Stair Gillon. The Naval & Military Press, Uckfield. 1925.

These for Remembrance. John Buchan. Buchan & Enright Ltd. Privately printed 1919.

The Sussex Yeomanry and 16th (Sussex Yeomanry) Battalion Royal Sussex Regiment 1914 - 1919. H I Powell Edwards. Andrew Melrose Ltd, London. 1921.

Three's Company - An Illustrated History of No. 3 (Fighter) Squadron RAF. Jack T.C. Long. Pen & Sword Books, Barnsley. 2005.

The Weald of Youth. Siegfried Sassoon. Faber and Faber Limited, London. 1942.

Too Close To The Sun − The Life and Times of Denys Finch Hatton. Sara Wheeler. Jonathan Cape, London. 2006.

Tracing British Battalions on the Somme. Ray Westlake. Pen & Sword Books. 2011.

Twice Vertical - The History of No1 Squadron Royal Air Force. Michael Shaw. MacDonald & Co. (Publishers) Ltd, London. 1971.

We Wunt Be Druv - The Royal Sussex Regiment on the Western Front 1914-18. Hugh Miller. Reveille Press, England. 2012

Royal Naval Air Service Pilot 1914 − 1918. Mark Barber. Osprey Publishing, Botley Oxford. 2010.

With a Machine Gun to Cambrai. George Coppard. Macmillan Publishers Ltd, London. 1986.

World War One − A Chronological Narrative. Philip Warner. Arms and Armour Press, London. 1998.

TRICORN
BOOKS